D0745542

GLACIERS, BEARS AND TOTEMS

GLACIERS, BEARS AND TOTEMS

Sailing in Search of the Real Southeast Alaska

Elsie Hulsizer

HARBOUR PUBLISHING

Harbour Publishing Co. Ltd.
P.O. Box 219, Madeira Park, BC, V0N 2H0
www.harbourpublishing.com

Edited by Carol Pope and Cliff Rowlands
Maps by Roger Handling
Printed and bound in Canada

Caution: Every effort has been made to ensure the reader's awareness of the hazards and level of expertise involved in the activities in this book , but your own safety is ultimately up to you. The author and publisher take no responsibility for loss or injury incurred by anyone using this book.

Harbour Publishing acknowledges financial support from the Government of Canada through the Canada Book Fund and the Canada Council for the Arts, and from the Province of British Columbia through the BC Arts Council and the Book Publishing Tax Credit.

Library and Archives Canada Cataloguing in Publication

Hulsizer, Elsie, 1946–
        Glaciers, bears and totems : sailing in search of the real southeast Alaska / Elsie Hulsizer.

Includes index.
ISBN 978-1-55017-516-5

        1. Hulsizer, Elsie, 1946– —Travel—Alaska, Southeast. 2. Sailing—Alaska, Southeast. 3. Alaska, Southeast—Description and travel. I. Title.

GV815.H83 2010   910.9164'34   C2010-904450-9

ACKNOWLEDGMENTS

In the teamwork of writing this book, my husband Steve ranks first. He likes to say, "I just drive the boat," but he does far more. His engineering, mechanical and navigational skills made our three sailing trips to Southeast Alaska possible. His willingness to take *Osprey* beyond the guide books and his ability to engage strangers in conversation enhanced our adventures.

Back in Seattle members of my writers group acted as cheerleaders, taskmasters and critics. Debra Daniels-Zeller, Kathy Gehrt, Wendy Hinman, Sheila Kelly, Sharon Morris and Janice Schwert all participated. Roberta Cruger's writing retreats were yearly inspirations.

At Harbour Publishing the publisher encouraged me to pursue the dream of an Alaska book. Anna Comfort orchestrated the details of its production. My editors, Carol Pope and her husband, saved me from redundancy and smoothed my prose. Roger Handling produced the excellent maps and Mary White did the layout.

Finally, I want to thank the many wonderful people of Southeast Alaska and coastal British Columbia who gave us assistance, advice and friendship along the way. Their generosity guaranteed we will return.

CONTENTS

Tlingit totem pole in Seattle's Pioneer Square.

INTRODUCTION

I saw my first Alaskan totem pole, in miniature, in Ye Old Curiosity Shop on Seattle's waterfront when I was a child of six or seven. Along with the shop's famous shrunken heads and Sylvester the mummified corpse, the totem poles fascinated me. I knew that the strange brightly painted carvings of eagles, ravens and bears were from an exotic place.

Mementos of Alaska abound in my hometown: relics of the time when Seattle's boosterism turned the city into *the* place to outfit for the Klondike Gold Rush. To this day, a street named Alaskan Way runs along Seattle's waterfront. It was there, in 1897, that hordes of stampeders fought to board ships bound north, spurred on by headlines in the *Seattle Post-Intelligencer* of "Gold! Gold! Gold! Gold!" The tall Tlingit totem pole that graces Seattle's Pioneer Square was stolen from Tongass Island, Alaska, in 1899 by some of Seattle's leading citizens. And on the University of Washington campus, the Drumheller Fountain is a remnant of the boosterish Alaska Yukon and Pacific Exposition of 1909.

The boosterism of that time was more to promote Seattle than Alaska, but still it affected me deeply. Inspired by stories in Seattle's museums, I saw Alaska as "the last frontier," a destination of terrifying beauty where hardy and independent people conquered the wilderness.

Despite Seattle's ubiquitous reminders of Alaska, or because of them, I didn't consider Alaska a place where just ordinary people went. I grew up, attended college and moved back east without ever visiting our most northern state. It was my husband, Steve—who had grown up in Boston and Illinois—who first suggested sailing to Alaska. In 1979 we were sailing our 32-foot sloop, *Velella,* from Boston to Seattle, via the Panama Canal and Hawaii. When plotting our final ocean leg, from Oahu to Cape Flattery, Steve pointed out how close Alaska was to our route. A slight shift in the wind could take us there by accident.

In the end, the wind held steady and we arrived in Seattle without a detour. Once there, we focused on our careers: Steve's in shipbuilding, mine in environmental regulation. A 700-mile sail to Alaska was far from our thoughts. Instead, we spent our summer vacations sailing the west coast of Vancouver Island, a two-day sail from Seattle, for the first few years in *Velella*, then in *Osprey*, an Annapolis 44 sloop. In those rocky, fogbound waters, we honed our navigation and sailing skills. Steve reveled in the challenge of braving the elements and hearing the gurgle of a sailboat's wake as we tacked in a smart breeze. I enjoyed gliding into an anchorage as the evening sun lit up the trees, poking among stores in small towns, and visiting with locals. Most of all, I liked taking the time to get to know a place: its history, people and moods.

Returning from a sail to Haida Gwaii (Queen Charlotte Islands) in 1999, Steve declared, "We should go cruising." He had in mind an extended voyage to the South Pacific or Europe. "We've got the boat for it. And our investments are doing well. We can do it."

I resisted. I yearned for longer vacations, but didn't want to give up our life in Seattle. I was in the midst of a six-year certificate course in fine-arts photography, writing a book on the west coast of Vancouver Island and had a challenging career. We also owned a pleasant older house in Seattle's Ballard neighborhood. I knew what cruising by sailboat meant: doing laundry in a bucket, bouncing around in the middle of the ocean for weeks at a time and never having time or a place to just be by myself. And although I was writing a book about sailing to windward, I really didn't like ocean sailing. To me, the best parts of cruising on the west coast of Vancouver Island were the quiet anchorages every night and coming back to our home in Seattle after every trip.

The dot-com stock-market crash of 2000 diminished our savings and ended the discussion of cruising for a few years, but an idea for a compromise was growing: sailing to Southeast Alaska—a place where we could find navigational challenges for Steve and quiet anchorages for me. We could take repeated trips over several summers, enough to get to know this land and write about it. Alaska's Southeast offered us tidewater glaciers, wildlife including whales and bears, a Native population with a rich artistic culture, and a recent history that included the rambunctious Klondike Gold Rush. As Steve put it, "glaciers, bears, totems and gold."

But still I dragged my feet. I had grown up in the age of women's liberation, when a woman had to struggle to have a professional career. Giving up my job wasn't going to be easy. At work I was a manager. On the boat, I'm crew. I wasn't sure I was ready for that demotion full-time.

Then something happened to change my mind. In the winter of 2004, Steve started complaining about cold hands. He was losing the feeling in his fingers—he would reach for a screw when working on *Osprey* and couldn't tell if it was in his hands or not. Soon Steve needed a cane to walk. A slow tedious journey of medical appointments and tests led to a diagnosis of cervical stenosis; his backbone was squeezing his nerves.

"This looks permanent," said his surgeon. The deterioration could be stopped but Steve might not improve.

I agonized over the fact that I had resisted Steve's request to go cruising. Now it might be too late.

Steve was one of the lucky ones who benefited from surgery. As he woke after the operation, he discovered he could feel a difference between the blanket and the sheet. In a few days he was walking without a cane. By the end of the summer, he was sailing again.

It was time to head to Alaska.

Our Annapolis 44 sloop, *Osprey*, was already well equipped for a trip to Alaska. We had the works—radar, GPS, depth sounder, VHF radio and satellite email. For Alaska we added an electronic chart plotter with Automatic Identification System capability (to identify large ships). We packed our chart locker to the top with paper charts—and then filled half the quarter berth with the overflow. On deck we carried a four-person life raft and behind us we towed an inflatable dinghy. A hydraulic anchor windlass on the foredeck provided power to raise our 60-pound plow anchor with 275 feet of chain—we would need it all in Alaska's deep anchorages. In the cockpit, a canvas dodger gave us space to duck out of the rain, although not the enclosed steering space that many sailors to Alaska claim is essential. We would have to make do with foul-weather gear.

Below deck, a diesel engine and a tank holding 70 gallons of fuel promised to get us through calm winds. Another two tanks held 70 gallons of water. The galley provided a gas stove with oven, a refrigerator (but not a freezer) and ample storage. The main cabin had a diesel heater and later we added a Red Dot heater, which blows waste heat from the engine cooling system into the cabin when underway. Kerosene lanterns added to the warmth. Our long-haired black cat, Jigger, had his own snug bunk in the quarter berth above the heater and a litter box aft.

We knew we would be journeying to remote and wild locations and be dependent on our own resources. I filled lockers with cans of beans and soups, bottles of olive and canola oil, sacks of rice and flour, boxes of cereals, jars of jam, spices and condiments, and bags of kibble for Jigger. Fresh fruits, vegetables and other perishables we would buy along the way. Steve wedged jugs of engine oil into lockers under the V-berth, crammed spare filters, water pumps, gaskets, belts and every other spare part imaginable into storage boxes, and stuffed lockers with extra anchors, lines and more spare parts. Cruising guides, tide and current tables, coast pilots and paperback novels filled every inch of *Osprey*'s ample bookcases. My cameras and computer filled the remaining spaces.

We left for the first of three sailing trips to Southeast Alaska on May 14, 2006, when the trees on the hillside above the Shilshole Marina still showed new yellow-green leaves. For someone used to departing in July it seemed too early and too cold, but we had almost 1,000 miles to travel. Our goal was to experience as much of Southeast Alaska as we could, to get to know its lands, its waters, its people and its history: to savor its magnificent scenery and wildlife.

Our route took us north through the Inside Passage. Determined to spend as much time as possible in Southeast Alaska, we pushed hard at the beginning of the trip, making good time in the 600 miles of protected waters in British Columbia's channels and inlets.

Once we crossed the border between British Columbia and Alaska, we traveled another 300 miles to the top of Alaska's panhandle, and another 1,000 following our whimsies up inlets and around remote islands of Southeast Alaska's Alexander Archipelago.

On our first trip, we wore ourselves out trying to see everything. We hunted for abandoned totem poles in Kasaan Bay on Prince of Wales Island; sailed east and north through Zimovia Strait and Wrangell Narrows to the towns of Wrangell and Petersburg; ventured through ice to glaciers in Tracy Arm; toured Juneau and Skagway, then headed west for Glacier Bay National Park. From Glacier Bay we sailed east to Chatham Strait, then back west through Peril Strait to Sitka and the west coast of Baranof Island, ending our Alaskan explorations on the west side of Prince of Wales Island where we joined a celebration of Haida culture at the town of Hydaburg.

On our second trip, we filled in some of the holes in our first year's itinerary, visiting places we had skipped the year before and revisiting some of our favorites. From Ketchikan, we looped south to explore Misty Fiords National Monument before repeating the previous year's journey to Juneau with side excursions to new anchorages. After visiting Glacier Bay for the second year in a row, we sailed west through Icy Strait to the fishing villages of Elfin Cove and Pelican, then south down the outside of Chichagof Island to Sitka. From Sitka we went east through Peril Strait to Chatham Strait, working our way south to the small town of Port Alexander. From Port Alexander, we turned back north to the Tlingit village of Kake, then south again through the narrow rocky channels of Keku Strait to Wooden Wheel Cove. From there we sailed east and south through Sumner Strait and Clarence Strait, ending our second trip to Alaska at the celebration of the 120th anniversary of the Tsimshian town of Metlakatla.

By our third trip we felt we were spending too much time getting to places and not enough time enjoying them. We skipped Glacier Bay, Sitka, and the outer coasts of Baranof and Chichagof Islands to spend more time in the Icy Strait region and the west coast of Prince of Wales Island where we explored El Capitan Passage, Sea Otter Sound, and Davidson Inlet before visiting the towns of Klawock and Craig. From the south tip of Prince of Wales Island we headed east in Dixon Entrance, spending our last night in Alaska anchored off Kanaguni Island, next door to the island of Tongass where Seattle's leading citizens had chopped down the Pioneer Square totem pole many years before.

In our three summers in Southeast Alaska, we drifted in front of calving glaciers, watched bears feeding in green marshes, smelled the fresh cedar of newly carved totem poles and followed the path of gold prospectors on the White Pass and Yukon Route Railroad. In a land where giant cruise ships make glaciers look small and Alaskan store-keepers mine gold from the pockets of tourists, we sometimes found it hard to discern the real Alaska from its façade. The land of "glaciers, bears, totems and gold" had become the land of "glaciers, bears, totems and tourists." Were we victims of the same boosterism that the city of Seattle had used to lure the gold-rush stampeders many years ago? Or was the real Alaska, the "last frontier" with its hardy, independent characters and rich Native culture, still around the next corner, waiting to be found? This book represents our search for the real Southeast Alaska. We found it in many places—and sometimes even where the tourists go.

Note on Measurements

Throughout *Glaciers, Bears and Totems* when I use the term "miles," I am referring to nautical miles, not the statute or English-system miles commonly used on road signs in the United States. A nautical mile is a unit of length corresponding to approximately 1 minute of arc of latitude along any meridian. By international agreement it is exactly 1,852 meters (approximately 6,076 feet or 1.15 statute miles). Boat speed and wind speed are given in knots. A knot of speed is 1 nautical mile per hour.

Alaskan charts give water depth in fathoms and feet, which is how I reported them. One fathom equals 6 feet or 1.8288 meters and 1 foot equals 30.48 centimeters.

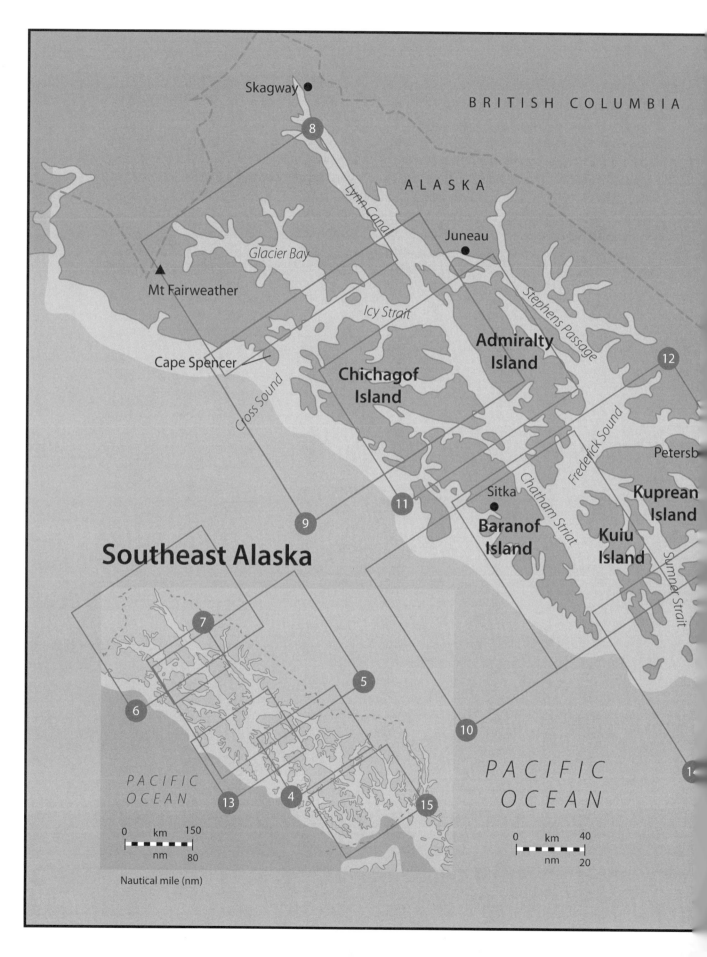

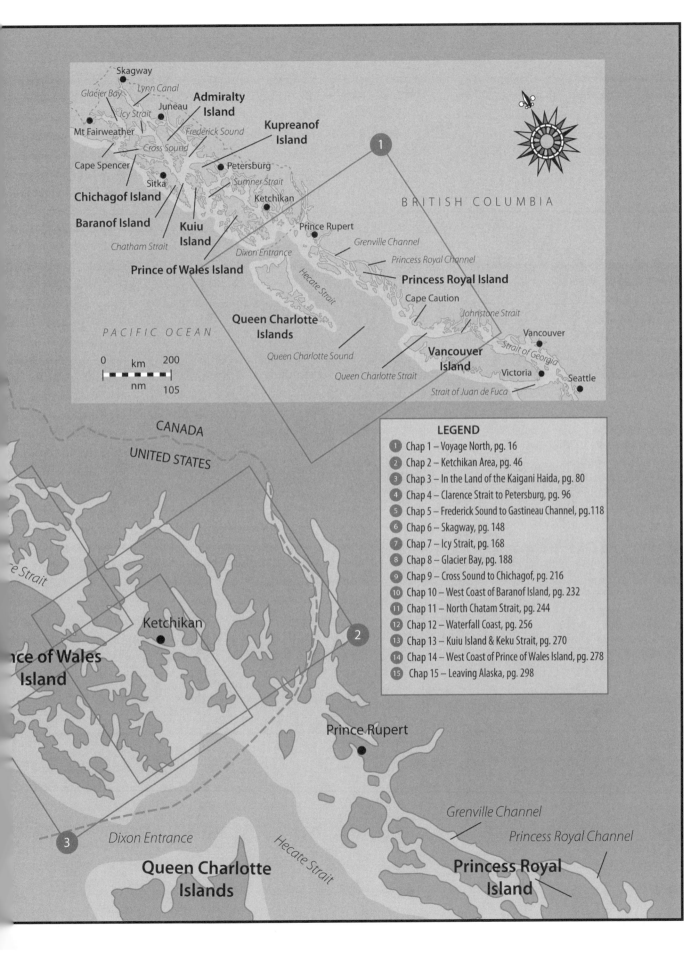

Skagway

Glacier Bay
Lynn Canal

**Admiralty
Island**

Juneau

Icy Strait

Mt Fairweather

Frederick Sound

**Kupreanof
Island**

Cape Spencer

Cross Sound

Petersburg

Sitka

Sumner Strait

Chichagof Island

Ketchikan

B R I T I S H   C O L U M B I A

Baranof Island

**Kuiu
Island**

Prince Rupert

Chatham Strait

Grenville Channel

Dixon Entrance

Princess Royal Channel

Prince of Wales Island

Hecate Strait

Princess Royal Island

Cape Caution

**Queen Charlotte
Islands**

Johnstone Strait

Vancouver

PACIFIC OCEAN

Strait of Georgia

0   km   200

Queen Charlotte Sound

**Vancouver
Island**

Victoria

Seattle

nm   105

Queen Charlotte Strait

Strait of Juan de Fuca

CANADA

UNITED STATES

e Strait

Ketchikan

**ce of Wales
Island**

2

Prince Rupert

3

Dixon Entrance

Hecate Strait

Grenville Channel

Princess Royal Channel

**Queen Charlotte
Islands**

**Princess Royal
Island**

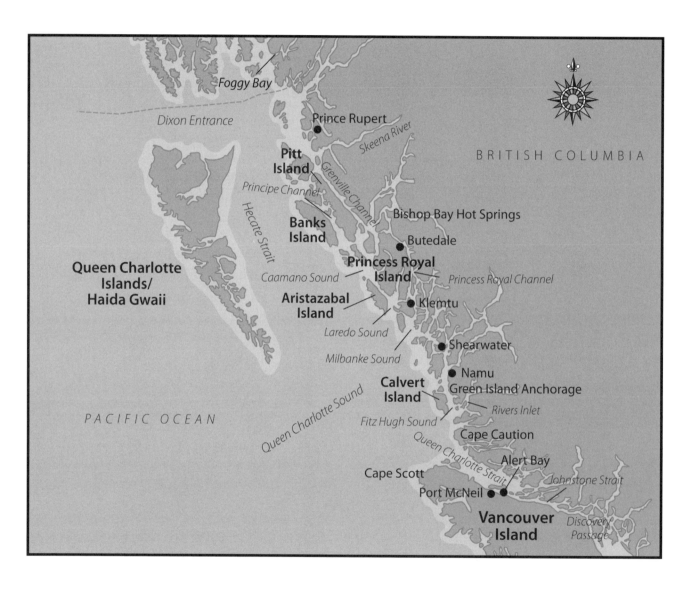

CHAPTER 1

THE VOYAGE NORTH

1.1 DISCOVERY PASSAGE TO ALERT BAY
Sailing in Place

Osprey surged through the waters of Discovery Passage with sails flying wing-and-wing, spray splashing the bow and a stern wave building behind. Sunlight bounced off white sails, blue water sparkled like diamonds—a perfect day for sailing. It was May 2007 and we were five days into our second sailing trip from Seattle to Southeast Alaska.

I glanced down at the knot meter that measured our speed through the water and confirmed what our motion already told me: we were making a brisk 7 knots.

But something was wrong. Cursing under his breath, Steve was fiddling with the chart plotter, the vital instrument that tells us our location.

"The heading indicator must be off."

On the chart-plotter screen, located on *Osprey*'s cabin roof under the canvas dodger, the little electronic bug that represents our boat was thrashing about like a fly in its last throes of death—pointing one way, then another. I glanced to starboard where I expected to see the shore of nearby Quadra Island flying by. It was standing still. Then I looked at the corner of the chart-plotter display showing our speed over land—0.7 knots. With 25 knots of wind behind us and 7 knots of current against us, we were sailing in place.

We'd just had a lesson in the currents of Discovery Passage. In this region Vancouver Island bulges to the east, while the coast of British Columbia's mainland and its associated islands turn west to meet it, squeezing tidal currents into ever narrower passages—which makes for faster and faster currents. Discovery Passage leads to the infamous Seymour Narrows, where currents can race through at 16 knots, creating overfalls, upwellings and whirlpools that can swallow small boats in one gulp. The *BC Sailing Directions* advise mariners to "navigate Seymour Narrows only at or near slack water if their vessel is of low power . . . or is . . . under 20m [66 feet] long." Dangerously fast currents were not something we were used to when sailing in Puget Sound and along the west coast of Vancouver Island so we had taken this advice seriously, checking and rechecking the current tables to make sure we had the right time for slack water. But we'd been so fixated on the narrows that we hadn't checked the currents through Discovery Passage leading up to them. The ebb tide in both the narrows and the passage runs north so aiming for the slack-before-the ebb in the Narrows put us against the flood in the passage.

Realizing that our plans to transit the narrows that evening were over, Steve turned on the engine to boost our speed, then steered toward shore where the current was weakest. *Osprey* crawled past the land, engine and sails straining. Finally, we reached the quiet waters of Gowlland Cove where we anchored for the night. We'd try again the next morning.

We'd just had a reminder that sailing *to* Alaska is as much a challenge as sailing *in* Alaska.

While the tidal currents kept us sailing in place in 2007, other less-visible forces worked against our passage north in 2008.

That year Steve had been in a rush to get north. "We've got to get out of here," he had reminded me insistently the week before we left, his voice becoming more strident as each day ticked by and the to-do list grew only incrementally shorter.

The best months for cruising in Alaska are May and June, so the sooner we left Seattle the better. During the winter I had filled my time with writing and volunteer work while Steve had labored to get *Osprey* ready to leave. He had replaced the marine sanitation system, the refrigerator heat pump, the steering cables, the hydraulic cylinder for the autopilot and the pressure switch for the fresh-water pump. Now I was reluctant to leave while Steve was impatient to put the winter of work behind him. I pleaded for one more week, then another, to attend meetings others considered important. Meanwhile Steve continued working on *Osprey*. Just when he thought everything was ready, the exhaust system sprang a leak. He removed it for repairs—twice. Most of that equipment resided in very cramped quarters, requiring him to curl up like a contortionist to reach it.

"I feel like I spent the whole winter in the port seat locker," he complained.

Finally we were on our way north. All my critical meetings were over and Steve had made the necessary repairs. In fact, we felt that so many things had been fixed, there surely would be nothing more to break. We departed Seattle on the afternoon of Monday, May 14, motoring against the wind to make up for a late departure, then sailing through rain in the San Juan Islands when we would have preferred to wait for better weather. In Nanaimo we rushed to stock up on fresh food and liquor in one day instead of our usual two. Several days into the trip, I still felt torn by the rush to leave Seattle and the struggle to adjust to the cruising life. *Osprey*'s cabin felt crowded as Steve and I stepped around each other in the narrow galley and navigation area, then tripped over Jigger who always seemed to be in the way. Two people and a cat seemed one person and a cat too many.

We were riding the ebb through Johnstone Strait north of Seymour Narrows when I heard a strange whining noise coming from the engine compartment. Steve went below to inspect. He poked and prodded the engine but couldn't find anything wrong. He slowed the engine, sped it up again, and the whining subsided. We continued on our way. A while later we noticed a faint burning smell coming from the engine, but when Steve checked again, it quickly dissipated.

We kept motoring but I felt uneasy. The engine didn't sound quite right, yet I could not pinpoint the difference, and Steve, who is hard of hearing, was unable to discern what the problem might be.

At dusk we looked for an anchorage. Helmcken Island was close. As we rounded the point into Billygoat Cove, I looked back to see a large cruise ship, the MS *Veendam*, heading south in Johnstone Strait, its windows ablaze with lights.

As I let the anchor go in the quiet water, I thought about the MS *Veendam*. As it was heading south, I knew it was returning from Alaska, having left Seattle or Vancouver only two days before we did. While we had sailed a mere 200 miles north, the MS *Veendam* had gone all the way to Alaska and back. On board, the passengers would be sitting down to elegant meals cooked by chefs and served by waiters while I hadn't even started our simple dinner yet. Brochures from the cruise-ship lines promised "one of life's great adventures . . . spectacular scenery, majestic mountains, fascinating wildlife, stunning glaciers." That's what we sought too, only we would spend the whole summer seeking it while, according to the brochures, the cruise-ship passengers would find it within one week. Were we crazy?

I went below to make dinner and was just taking the rice off the stove when I looked out and saw the moon rising over the trees. I went out on deck to get a better view. A damp smell of evergreens drifted off the nearby shore. It was a beautiful sight to see the trees silhouetted against the evening sky, one that few cruise-ship passengers would distinguish from their brightly lit ship.

Jigger, sitting on top of the dodger, let out a plaintive meow and I reached out my hand to pet him. You couldn't take a cat on a cruise ship, I reminded myself.

The next morning we left in a flat calm under blue skies. We were motoring toward Robson Bight when we heard a loud clanking sound like metal grating on metal coming from the engine.

"Take the wheel," Steve yelled to me as he rushed down the companionway. As he opened the engine compartment, noxious-smelling smoke poured out.

"Turn it off!" he shouted.

I shut down the engine and we drifted. The long narrow passageway of Johnstone Strait stretched out ahead, lined by miles of forested coastline below snow-topped mountains. We were a long way from the next town and help. No other boats were to be seen.

"It's the clutch to the hydraulic pump," Steve announced a few minutes later.

At least the engine was okay. The hydraulic pump operated the anchor windlass. We wouldn't be able to anchor, but Steve could disconnect the pump, allowing us to motor to a dock, tie up, and see what we could do for repairs.

That night we tied up between two big fishing boats in the marina at Alert Bay on Cormorant Island. It was the Saturday of a three-day weekend. If we needed help, we were going to have to wait.

Sunday morning Steve dismantled the hydraulic clutch and discovered that he would need new bearings to repair it. We were unlikely to find them in the small towns nearby—they would have to be flown up from Seattle.

Needing a phone number for a Seattle airline, we set off in search of a phone book, walking along the beach until we came to an old brick building that used to be a residential school but now serves as the community center. A sign advertised carvings for sale. The rest of the building was closed, so we followed the sign to a basement door. Down a short flight of stairs we found three men, each sitting in front of a carving and surrounded by cedar shavings, cigarette butts and carving tools. Elegant wooden masks of eagles, ravens and a face surrounded by rays of the sun hung on the walls. The men looked up from their work to greet us but kept carving. Steve started telling them our story of the broken hydraulic clutch.

One of them interrupted to say quietly, "That's the creator telling you to slow down." Another man nodded. "Everything happens for a reason."

Obligingly, one of them dredged up a phone book from under a pile of magazines.

Back at the boat, Steve called the airline and learned the next flight from Seattle to Port McNeil (the nearest landing spot, five miles to the northwest) was Thursday, five days away. Whether we liked it or not, we'd have to take the advice of the carvers and slow down.

We spent the next day and a half getting to know Alert Bay, a town with a mixed population of Native and European descent. Strolling along the crescent-shaped bay, we passed brightly painted houses, a white Victorian-era church and a burial ground marked by carved memorial poles. Near the center of town we found a waterfront promenade and marveled that a population of less than 600 could afford such elaborate light fixtures, benches and planters.

On our second day in the town, we visited the U'Mista Cultural Centre with its displays of ceremonial masks and other Kwakwaka'wakw artifacts. The Canadian government had seized the masks in a 1921 raid of an illegal potlatch. They were finally returned to the community in the 1970s and '80s.

I sat in front of a display of raven masks and contemplated the different ways one bird could be depicted. Soft light illuminated the art and the room had a hushed church-like atmosphere designed to encourage viewers to slow down.

Walking around town we saw announcements of the visit of representatives of the Haida Nation to dedicate a mortuary pole. We didn't understand why Haida from the Haida Gwaii (Queen Charlotte Islands) were dedicating a pole here, but nevertheless thought it would be interesting to see the ceremony.

At 5:00 p.m., we joined a stream of people walking to the Big House, a large one-storey building with a peaked roof and the world's tallest totem pole marking the entrance. Inside we found a crowd sitting on bleachers, while on the floor below, men fed a roaring fire. Massive carved wooden arches dominated both ends of the building. Nothing much seemed to be happening and the time dragged on, with people coming and going and men continuing to stack logs on the fire.

I was getting hungry and wished we had eaten beforehand, when I saw men carrying tables onto the floor and women arranging bowls of food. People started getting up to help themselves, and we were just about to do the same when a woman brought me a plate of food. "This is for you. You're a guest here." The plate contained salmon, potato salad, and hunks of something white with black speckles. I ate the salad and

This mortuary pole was erected at Alert Bay by Natives from Haida Gwaii to bring closure to the tragic loss of their ancestors from smallpox at a nearby island in the 1800s.

the salmon, which tasted smoky and delicious, and bit into the white hunks. The speckles were crunchy and fishy tasting. The woman sitting next to me told me they were herring eggs—a delicacy.

When everyone had eaten and the tables had been put away, a Haida chief addressed the crowd. He explained that they had come to bring closure to the sad event of the smallpox outbreak in the 1800s. When the epidemic struck, Natives from many nations had been gathered in Victoria. Authorities ordered them to leave, causing the spread of the disease up and down the coast. Many perished on their way home. The Chief explained that

Native dancers visiting from Haida Gwaii perform at Alert Bay's Big House.

some of their people had died near Alert Bay, which was why they were dedicating a mortuary pole here. For many years this tribe had been left in the dark about why their ancestors had not returned home.

We sat transfixed as a woman accompanied by a drummer sang a plaintive and beautiful song in the Haida language. A dancer clothed in a brown and tan woven blanket and wearing a gigantic wooden mask of a human face undulated across the room lit only by the flickering light of the fire. Thinking about what it must have been like for a community to lose 90 percent of its population and not even know where many had died, I was deeply humbled. And reflecting about smallpox victims who had perished on the Inside Passage reminded me that although we use the passage for recreation today, for centuries it served as a route for trade, cultural exchange, battle and in this case for disease to travel to the unprotected.

A Haida dancer performs in a raven mask at Alert Bay's Big House.

As the evening wore on, the dancing became increasingly cheerful until finally Alert Bay residents joined the Haida on the floor in a rousing stomp of a dance. We left as more speechmaking and gift giving was getting underway. As we walked back to the boat, I remembered the MS *Veendam* and its promise of adventure. Adventure wasn't all we were after. We also wanted to experience new cultures and acquire a better understanding of our world. To do that we had to slow down. If the hydraulics failed for a reason, it must have been so we could see this wonderful event and put our own problems in proper perspective.

1.2 CROSSING QUEEN CHARLOTTE STRAIT
On the Tail of a Gale

From Alert Bay we motored to Port McNeil, which we left five days later on the tail of a dwindling gale. We had waited four days for parts for the hydraulic system to arrive by seaplane from Seattle. At first, as the rain came down in sheets and the wind howled, I was glad the wait gave us an excuse to stay ashore. From Port McNeil we would be crossing Queen Charlotte Strait and rounding Cape Caution in Queen Charlotte Sound, a passage that could be the roughest part of our trip and, although Steve will venture out in almost any weather, I prefer to at least avoid the storms.

Port McNeil is a lumber town about three quarters of the way up the east coast of Vancouver Island. Its well-protected marina has antique logging equipment on display on the lawn and two restaurants across the street. A flock of bald eagles stand guard on the mud flats next door. The marina is the most pleasant spot in a town of unexceptional buildings surrounded by acres of empty parking. After spending four days there, reluctant sailor though I might be, I was eager to move on.

By the time the parts had arrived and Steve installed them, the weather in Queen Charlotte Strait had moderated from gales to strong winds.

We were getting *Osprey* ready for departure the morning of the fifth day when our neighbor from the powerboat across the dock came over to talk to us.

"The weather forecast still says gales in Queen Charlotte Sound. We're going to wait a day."

Steve pointed to *Osprey*'s mast. "This is a sailboat. We like wind."

"But not too much wind," I said silently to myself as I stuffed the water hose into the seat locker. Still, despite the weather report, I was optimistic. The sun was out and the wind in the harbor was quiet. The route we had chosen would keep us in Queen Charlotte Strait the first day, where the winds were only strong. By the time we got to Queen Charlotte Sound the next day, we hoped the gales would be over.

An hour after leaving Port McNeil, we were riding a washboard of short glassy swells. By noon the air had warmed and I took off a layer of clothes and made salad for lunch. As we

Port McNeil marina has antique logging equipment on display.

passed a small herd of sea lions sunning on a rock in Ripple Passage, I decided we'd been right to leave.

We'd just passed the Walker Group of islets and were coming up on Ragged Rock when we looked ahead and saw the Australian sailboat *Volo,* which had left Port McNeil just ahead of us, heeled over in a freshening breeze. A minute later, wind sent *Osprey*'s halyards tapping against the mast.

"Let's get the sails up!" said Steve.

Steve went forward to raise the mainsail while I took the wheel to hold the boat into the wind. The sail was about halfway up when I heard a loud clatter and saw it crash back down to the boom.

"The halyard's gone," Steve yelled over the sound of loose sail flapping in the wind. I looked at the sail and could see the mainsail shackle, bare of its line, still attached to the headboard. The halyard was nowhere to be seen.

"Son of a bitch!" cried Steve. He tied up the sail and returned to the cockpit. "That damned halyard! It must be caught on the radar cable inside the mast." *Osprey* has internal rope halyards that run over sheaves at the top of the mast, then back down inside, before exiting through slots near the bottom. Now the end was firmly wedged inside, somewhere around the spreaders. Unless we could retrieve it, there would be no way to raise the mainsail.

"We'll never get that halyard out without breaking the radar cable." Steve scowled in frustration. "Not without taking the mast off."

"Port Hardy's only 12 miles away," I said, referring to the northernmost town on Vancouver Island. "Should we go there?"

"What good would that do? They won't be able to fix it."

"They might have a crane to take the mast off."

"That damned halyard wouldn't come out even with the mast down."

"Maybe we should just turn around, go back to Seattle, and forget about Alaska this year." I was frustrated. We'd already lost five days to the hydraulic system. I saw the best months for cruising in Alaska—May and June—slipping away.

"No. Let's go on to Skull Cove. We're almost there anyway."

I agreed and we both remained quiet as we motored the rest of the way to Skull Cove. We threaded through the narrow entrance past smooth white cliffs into a pretty little cove sprinkled with small rocky islets.

Steve's mood had improved as he pondered what to do with the halyard.

"I don't think it's caught on the radar cable. It's probably hung up where the

Surf pounding on rocks in Queen Charlotte Strait is a reminder of how rough this coast can be.

Skull Cove provides quiet waters to prepare for the rounding of Cape Caution.

The ability to do repairs en route can be critical. Steve retrieves a broken halyard from inside *Osprey*'s mast.

spreaders and lower shrouds attach to the mast." As he talked, he wound the halyard around a winch on the mast and cranked. The halyard grew taut but wouldn't budge.

"There's only one way to get it down," he announced. "I'll have to go up the mast and remove some of the fittings. That should loosen it up."

We were discussing the next steps when the crew of *Volo* motored over in their dinghy to offer help. While it was nice to know we were not alone, there was nothing they could do and no tools needed that we didn't already have.

I got out the boson's chair and set it up while Steve loosened the forward lower shrouds at the deck. Then, using the jib halyard and the hydraulic windlass that Steve had repaired just the day before, I hoisted him up the mast to the spreaders—along with a bucket containing a heavy mallet, a collection of wrenches and six four-foot lengths of seine twine. Steve unbolted the shrouds, tying everything he could to the spreaders. He wanted to make sure that if he dropped anything, it wouldn't fall into the water. By the time he finished, the spreaders looked like a knitting project.

While we worked, a red-throated loon cried a warning while a whistle buoy moaned out on the ocean and surf pounded against the rocks just outside the cove. Even with *Volo* nearby, Skull Cove felt isolated and lonely.

Finally, Steve yelled down, "Pull on the halyard." I grabbed the stiff Dacron halyard at the mast and pulled as hard as I could. Nothing happened.

Steve worked some more, then hollered, "Try again." I held my breath and yanked. This time I felt the halyard come free. A few seconds later, I was holding the end in my hand and looking at the loose threads where the splice had failed. We were going to get to Alaska after all.

1.3 ROUNDING CAPE CAUTION
The Toughest Part Behind Us

I stood on *Osprey*'s deck watching the morning sun bounce off the water and light up the rocks and islets of Skull Cove. Across the cove, *Volo*'s crew was raising the mainsail. The boat's red hull and white sail reflected perfectly in the water below. I thought about our plans for the day: a 30-mile trip north up the coast, through Queen Charlotte Sound, past Cape Caution and into Fitz Hugh Sound. I wasn't looking forward to the passage, but was grateful for sunshine.

The word "Sound" in Queen Charlotte Sound is misleading. Unlike Puget Sound with its protected waters, Queen Charlotte Sound is open on the west to the Pacific Ocean. With a reputation for rough seas, strong winds and adverse currents, Queen Charlotte Sound can put dread into a sailor's heart. Timid boaters have been known to fly to Alaska and join the rest of their boat's crew there just to avoid this stretch of open water. And Captain George Vancouver, who nearly lost a ship on a rock just a few miles from Skull Cove, knew what he was doing when he named Cape Caution.

The surf no longer beat on the rocks outside the cove and the cries of the loons sounded less forlorn than the day before. From the VHF radio in the cockpit I heard, "West Sea Otter Buoy, combined seas 1.4 meters." Boaters use the height of the seas at West Sea Otter Buoy, an automatic weather buoy 25 miles out in Queen Charlotte Sound, to decide when to cross the Sound and round Cape Caution. Combined seas of less than 1 meter are ideal. From 1.4 meters we could expect some swells, but they would be tolerable. Wind speed was also good; only moderate southerlies were predicted.

We followed *Volo* out of the cove, winding our way through the rocks to the ocean. *Osprey* pitched and rolled in seas that went every which way. But once we reached deep water, the seas subsided to uniform swells.

With only a light breeze, sailing was out of the question and we motored along the coast, admiring green forests against blue sky. Cape Caution, when we passed it, struck me as an anticlimax: a low wooded point with a small white latticework tower as a beacon.

Good weather and reduced seas had brought out the boats whose crews had been waiting for better weather in harbors all along Queen Charlotte Strait. A parade of powerboats sped by us on their way north. Farther out to sea a large white cruise ship steamed south. To the north we could see one of the State of Alaska's blue and white ferries approaching Cape Calvert.

As we passed Egg Island at the entrance to Fitz Hugh Sound, we raised sail in a freshening breeze. We were moving along briskly when suddenly Steve cursed and pointed at the mast. It was moving back and forth erratically. "Just what I need," he griped, "another evening doing boat projects!" *Osprey*'s mast fits through a hole in the cabin roof, and is well padded with foam to keep it from wobbling back and forth. The padding had come loose—fortunately, replacing it was something we had done before and, as long as the seas weren't too rough, we didn't need to stop sailing.

The wind rose to 25 knots, and we

The entrance to Green Island Anchorage is through a series of islands and rocks.

heeled hard as we tacked up the channel in smooth seas. As we approached our planned anchorage, a blast of hot dry air came streaming off the land to meet us. I went forward and stood at the mast, enjoying the rare sensation of warm air on bare arms—something I might not experience again for months. A few minutes later, we sailed out of the wind into the lee of the land. I dropped the sail and we motored through a narrow channel between two islands and into the Green Island Anchorage. *Volo* and four big powerboats were ahead of us. A rough wooden sign nailed to a tree named the anchorage. One of many similar signs on the British Columbia coast, it seemed very Canadian in its politeness, as if someone wanted to be sure we knew where we were.

We dropped the anchor and prepared to work. Steve took off the mast boot, the fabric that covers the base of the mast, and tried to stuff the foam padding back in with a tack hammer. But the mast wasn't centered in the hole, so the padding was too loose on one side and too tight on the other. We tied lines around the base of the mast and used the sheet winches to center it. Once properly positioned, it was possible to push the padding into the space around it with the hammer.

Our project successfully behind us, we had time to relax and enjoy the sunshine. With relief, I realized that the toughest part of the coast was behind us. If every rounding of Cape Caution could be like the one we'd had that day, the north coast of British Columbia and Southeast Alaska would be crowded with boats.

From his spot on top of the dodger, Jigger meowed his pleasure. He had adjusted to life on board and so had I. I was looking forward to the trip through British Columbia's sheltered waters.

1.4 FITZ HUGH SOUND TO SHEARWATER
Entering the Great Bear Rainforest

We motored north up Fitz Hugh Sound as morning light reflected off the still sea.

Steve sighed as he looked at the flat water. "I was hoping for some wind so we could sail." But it remained quiet through the morning.

Green wooded mountains, their peaks still white from the past winter, stretched ahead on both sides of the channel. I gazed at the uninterrupted forest in wonder; it was so different from the clear-cuts I was used to seeing on the west coast of Vancouver Island. This part of the coast is variously called the BC Central Coast, the Discovery Coast and, more recently, the Great Bear Rainforest—a magnificent name adopted by environmental groups in the 1990s for the broad swath of islands, inlets and rivers stretching from North Vancouver Island to the south to the Alaskan border on the north. The Great Bear Rainforest includes some of the largest remaining tracts of unlogged temperate rainforest in the world. Thanks to a 2006 agreement between the BC provincial government and a coalition of conservationists, loggers, hunters and First Nations, much of it will remain untouched, while the minimal logging scheduled to take place will be regulated by a management plan designed to ensure sustainable harvesting.

Although this coast escaped industrial logging, a commercial fishing industry once thrived here. Mid-morning we passed the site of Namu, a former fishing cannery and now a ghost town. I looked through binoculars to see moss-covered roofs, crumpled walls, and a tangle of rusted pipes and machinery.

Namu was established as a cannery and sawmill in 1905. Over the years Namu grew and evolved into a company town with ice plants, salmon and herring packing lines, fuel docks, stores, repair shops, bunkhouses, hotels, a restaurant and gymnasium. Trends in commercial fishing—ice holds, refrigerators and faster boats—all encouraged the consolidation of plants into fewer and larger sites. Because of its central location, midway between Queen Charlotte and Millbank Sounds, Namu benefited from those trends as smaller, more-distant plants closed. But even a large facility like Namu couldn't buck the three punches of declining fish stocks, increasing transportation costs and decreasing fish prices. Namu was shut down in the 1980s.

We first visited Namu in 1999 on our way to Haida Gwaii (Queen Charlotte Islands). From the harbor entrance, we saw what looked like a booming complex. As we approached, however, we could see tumbledown buildings with peeling paint, boarded windows and sagging roofs.

We tied up at a dilapidated float and wandered deserted streets. Peering into windows, we saw fan belts hanging from hooks, ready for machines now silent. At the abandoned diner, a blackboard announced a long-ago breakfast menu. From the cannery we followed a boardwalk along the shore, past vacant bunkhouses, offices, and a hotel

The former cannery town of Namu is intriguing to explore, but there is less to see every year.

labeled Namu Hilton (was it a joke?). From the shore, the boardwalk turned uphill through the forest to Namu Lake, where we went for a swim. From other boaters on the dock we learned of plans to restore the town and turn it into a fishing resort. There was a sense that great things were about to happen.

Seven years later, in 2006, we returned. We tied *Osprey* to a float alongside a small fleet of gillnetters, powerboats, and sport-fishing boats. Across the dock was a floating community of small houses, workshops, and a fish-cleaning station. As before, we wandered Namu's deserted streets and peered through windows. The processing and machinery buildings, constructed of cement blocks and metal siding, still looked solid. New T-shirts hung in the windows of one of the shops, and cheerful red flowers grew in containers scattered among the buildings. The fuel dock pumped diesel and gasoline. But on the boardwalk a crude hand-lettered sign warned, "Danger. Do Not Enter. Rotten Wood." Buildings that looked serviceable just seven years before now sagged, their roofs worn and moss-covered. The trail to the lake was impassable. The forest was winning.

That evening we joined others for a potluck dinner of crab, clams and fish served in a floating communal kitchen and eating area. One wall displayed a large photograph of Rene and Pete, Namu's caretakers, dressed in plaid shirts and suspenders, holding chainsaws. A caption under the photograph asked "What size is your boat? We'll fit it in." The world of Namu had shrunk to the area of the dock and the small group of buildings that surrounded it. The air of decay depressed us. Now, in 2008, we motored by.

Several hours later we rounded Cypress Island and entered Kiksoatli Harbour to see Shearwater Marine with its complex of docks and service buildings. The facility also has a restaurant and hotel. While Namu struggles, Shearwater Marine thrives. First established as an antisubmarine bomber reconnaissance unit in 1941, Shearwater was abandoned in 1944 and subsequently purchased for conversion to a resort. Boats under repair now occupy the former hangar. The Native community of Bella Bella, just three miles away, provides a ready source of labor.

I saw that the powerboat whose owner had planned to wait another day to leave Port McNeil was there ahead of us. We joined a small group of boaters gathered in the sunshine and talking about the passage around Cape Caution. "It was terrible," a woman was lamenting. "The boat rolled and pitched and I felt so seasick." Most of the group consisted of powerboaters who had left Port McNeil the same day we did, but stayed on the west side, going to Port Hardy that night and crossing Queen Charlotte Sound from there as we were rounding Cape Caution from Skull Cove. Their route would have put them farther out in Queen Charlotte Sound.

Later that evening over baked-salmon dinners at the restaurant, I commented to Steve. "It looks like we made the right decision to go to Skull Cove. We had an easier crossing than the others."

He smiled. "Maybe. Or perhaps it's just that they're powerboaters and can't take a few waves!"

1.5   SEAFORTH CHANNEL TO KLEMTU
A Road for Tourists

"I don't care if the wind is against us," insisted Steve. "I want to sail." We had left Shearwater about 11 o'clock that morning and were motoring out of Seaforth Channel when the wind came up.

Steve raised the sails, and I reached to turn off the engine. But before I could pull the handle, I heard the engine change from a steady thrum to a cough, then die. "Doesn't anything go right?" Steve grumbled as he tried to restart it. "Check the fuel pressure gauge," he told me when the engine coughed and died again. I leaned through the cabin door and looked at the gauge inside: zero!

Steve rushed past me to get below, leaving me to sail the boat. "Let me know when we need to tack." Half an hour later, we were approaching the shore. I could see a string of rocks stretching out from the beach. I peered below and saw tools spread over the cabin floor.

"We'll need to tack soon."

"I'm almost done," he reassured me. "It's just a broken electrical connection." I stayed on course, but we were moving closer and closer to the rocks. How much longer could I wait without putting *Osprey* in danger? If I tacked, all the loose tools would roll across the cabin floor. I held course, alternately checking the rocks ahead and our position on the chart plotter. As we approached the shore, the wind speed dropped and the boat correspondingly slowed down. Just as I had determined to tack on my own, Steve finished the repairs, put away the tools and came up on deck to take the sheets.

"Let's hope that's our only problem for the day," I told him. I was almost used to having to do repairs daily. And while Steve can't help but get frustrated when something goes wrong, he always manages to fix it.

We tacked out of Seaforth Channel, past Ivory Island with its red and white light-house, and around the island's off-lying rocks before turning to head north up Milbanke Sound. The wind followed us up channel, only to change direction and come up from the north. We tacked back and forth against wind and current until Steve observed: "It's taken two hours to go the distance we'd normally go in an hour. We're going to have to motor if we want to get anywhere today."

Klemtu

Ahead we could see coned-shape Bell Peak marking the channel to the Native village of Klemtu. I had good memories of several visits there and wished we could stop this time, but we wanted to put more distance behind us before we quit for the day.

The first time we visited Klemtu was in 1999, on our way to Haida Gwaii (Queen Charlotte Islands). Ignoring the advice of our guidebook to anchor in Clothes Bay away from the village we dropped anchor in Trout Bay in front of the village itself. Taking the

Trout Bay, Klemtu's harbor, is a safe and interesting anchorage.

dinghy ashore, we discovered a boardwalk running along the bay all the way from the fish-processing plant in the north to a residential area in the south.

It was a sunny afternoon and the residents were out in full force. Toddlers rode tricycles, mothers carried babies, and old folks relaxed on benches in nooks at the water's edge. Everyone we met smiled and said hello in the lilting voice of the Natives.

At the head of the bay we stopped to look at a newly carved totem pole. Several elderly men sat on benches at its base, and I asked them if they could tell me about the pole.

"The carvings are our clan crests," one of them told us. "The top is the eagle. Then there's raven, wolf and blackfish. [By blackfish he meant orca or killer whale.] It's the first new totem pole we've had in the village for over 100 years."

Another man spoke up. "We don't know any stories. We're old but we don't know our history. The missionaries came and sent us to school. Our elders told us the Christians wouldn't allow them to tell the stories."

When we went back to *Osprey* that night, I felt sad for the loss of the village's history, but was uplifted by the friendliness of its residents and the way the boardwalk seemed to draw out the community.

The next morning, as we lay sleeping at anchor in the town harbor, a large crash awoke us. We looked out *Osprey*'s windows, horrified to see a bulldozer taking bites out of the boardwalk. We went ashore and learned that the village was demolishing it to make way for a road. The friendly people we'd met had been enjoying the boardwalk's last day. I wondered why a small community with no road access to the outside world needed a road.

Designs on the door of Klemtu's Big House represent the four clans of the village: raven, blackfish, wolf and eagle.

We visited Klemtu for the second time in 2006. I was curious to see how the loss of the boardwalk had affected the community and wanted to learn more about the village. As we entered the harbor, our attention was drawn to a brand-new Big House on the point. With black and red drawings on the walls and a dugout canoe on the beach in front, it looked like something on a movie set.

We anchored in the bay, surrounded by a flock of small gulls flying so close we could hear wings beating the air. A light rain started to fall, but we didn't let it discourage us from going ashore where we discovered that a neatly paved road had replaced the boardwalk. I was pleased to see that the road included nooks with benches at the water's edge, just like the boardwalk before it. Despite the rainfall, three elderly men were seated on one of the benches. We stopped to talk to them, and Steve told them about being there the very last day of the boardwalk.

"We were in the *Guinness Book of World Records* for that boardwalk," one of them told us, "the longest one in the world. Now we just have the rain."

"And a new longhouse," I reminded him.

"Yes, that's right. People from all over the world come here now. Chinese, Japanese. A spirit bear came right up to the Big House, soon after it was built. The elders said, 'No big deal, he's just coming to see his relatives.'" The spirit bear he was referring to is a rare white-furred genetic subspecies of the black bear. Also called a kermode bear, it is found exclusively in this region.

"Would you like to see the Big House?" the man asked us. "I can show it to you." I had been hoping to see it so we jumped at the chance.

Our guide introduced himself as Francis Robertson. He had graying black hair and wore a red plaid shirt and jeans. He gestured toward the road, and Steve and I started walking briskly toward the Big House.

"I can tell you're from a big city," Francis told us. "You walk fast. In Klemtu we walk slower but we get there just the same." We slowed our pace.

We strolled along the road, passing the totem pole we had seen on our last trip, as well as a row of houses. Derelict cars sat in front of some of the houses: a side effect, I assumed, of the new road. At the Big House, Francis led us to the front door facing the water. A carved figure holding two wooden "coppers" (shield-shaped symbols of wealth), each painted with a face, confronted us. Francis explained that the carving was actually a welcoming figure and that the faces represented the two bands of Klemtu—the Kitasoo and the Xai'xais. He pointed to a wall design of a blackfish with two dorsal fins. "My grandfather actually saw a blackfish with two fins."

Francis opened the door and we walked into a cathedral-sized room dimly lit by daylight streaming through a fire hole in the roof. The sound of drums came from the other end. "You're in luck. They're practising for a potlatch." Two huge beams ran the length of the building and at each end was a massive sculpted wooden arch. A carved frog topped one of the arches while the other was adorned with an impressive grizzly bear. Magnificent eagles, blackfish, ravens and wolves, representing the village's four clans, supported the arches.

We sat on a bench while Francis relayed stories to the accompaniment of the drummers. He pointed to a carved raven and told us the raven was his people's creator. At the moment of creation two raven feathers drifted down—one became a man, the other a woman. I remembered the men telling us seven years before that they didn't know any stories and marveled at the change.

As we left the Big House, Francis pointed to a dugout canoe on the beach. "We have a saying, 'when a canoe comes bow first, it comes for war; when it comes stern first, it comes for peace.' I

Ravens are everywhere in Klemtu, screeching, clonking and croaking.

told that to a cruise-ship skipper and the next time his ship came here, he came in stern first."

On the way back, Francis told us about himself. He was a member of the blackfish clan and so was his wife—a situation that would have been taboo in earlier years when their culture forbade marriage between a man and a woman in the same clan. His grandchildren, he told us, were "spaghetti Indians," meaning they ate western food.

When we woke the next morning after our tour, we saw that a small cruise ship had tied up in front of the fish-processing plant. A long string of people, all carrying umbrellas, walked toward the Big House.

"So that's why they needed the road," I said to Steve, "It's not just for the town; it's for the cruise-ship passengers."

The Klemtu Big House had generated a renewal in the culture of the Klemtu bands. It had also brought tourists. At what price? It was a question I would ask many times in the months to come.

1.6   THE NORTHERN CHANNELS
A Decision to Make

Upon leaving Klemtu we had a decision to make. We could continue north up Finlayson Channel and from there travel through the straight and narrow channels of Princess Royal and Grenville (called "the ditch"), or we could loop south and west through Meyers Passage toward the coast and then north through a second series of outer channels.

When people speak of the "Inside Passage" to Alaska, they are usually referring to Princess Royal and Grenville Channels, the route cruise ships and ferries take. Both routes are in protected inside waters and get you to Prince Rupert in about the same distance and time.

Iain Lawrence, author of *Far-Away Places: 50 Anchorages on the Northwest Coast*, sailed both routes many times in his small gaff-rigged sloop, and describes the Inside Passage as a marine highway—a route for boaters who like to travel with other boaters and anchor in crowds. In contrast, the outer passages appeal to those who like to find their own way, those who don't like ruler-straight lines on their charts. The winds blow stronger in the outer passages, the channels are wider, and islands and anchorages are more numerous and diverse.

"The Inside is boring," said Steve. "There's no wind and everything looks the same for miles. If we take the outside channels, we might be able to sail."

I thought both Steve and Lawrence were giving the inner channels short shrift. Monotonous is a more accurate description, and in my opinion a good monotonous: miles and miles of green forested mountains stretch ahead on either side of the boat as it moves north. The inner channels run along the edge of the continent and its bays and coves offer spots of exceptional beauty not found on the outer route: waterfalls tumbling down steep slopes, snow-capped mountains, solid-rock cliffs and ancient cirques left by long-ago glaciers. And although Lawrence may call the inner route "crowded," when compared to Puget Sound and other southern waters, it's almost deserted, plus it has more wildlife and a richer history.

The Inner Channels

We had our first experience with the Inside Passage in 2006. Gales and rain in the outside channels sent us inland looking for calmer weather. We motored north in the rain, through quiet waters until about halfway up Princess Royal Channel where we turned into Khutze Inlet for the night. As we entered the inlet, the sun broke through the clouds, lighting a steep glimmering green hillside sliced by an impressive waterfall, a broad alluvial marsh and snow-capped mountains in the distance.

We anchored off the waterfall and took our dinghy into the marsh. As the evening sun sent slanting rays through the tall grass, we wove our way through narrow channels. Coming around a bend, we surprised a wolf out for an evening stroll. Then, as sunset faded to dusk, we glimpsed a large light-colored bear feeding among the sedge grass. The bear took one look at us and fled. As it disappeared into the tall grass, I thought I saw a hump above its shoulders—an identifying characteristic of a grizzly bear. "No, it couldn't have been a grizzly," insisted Steve. "It was too light and I didn't see a hump. It must have been a spirit bear." We were in the spirit bear's territory, but grizzlies live there too. Three years later we still argue about what kind of a bear it was.

In 2007, on our second trip up the Inside Passage, we got to Princess Royal Channel too late in the afternoon to go all the way to Khutze Inlet, so we headed instead to Horsefly Cove at the mouth of Green Inlet. But when we rounded the point into the cove, a solid mass of floating logs confronted us: a storage boom from a logging operation. There was no way into the cove.

We chugged up the channel as dusk fell. Dark trees pressed from both shores and the mountains cast deep shadows. A straight body of water stretched ahead. As the last light faded from the sky we reached Swanson Bay where we anchored off the mouth of a creek.

Khutze Inlet with its steep-sided hills and waterfall is one of the most impressive anchorages on the Inside Passage.

In the morning, we looked ashore to see rows of old pilings ringing the beach. An eagle was perched in a tall spruce tree, and just beyond it, a towering brick chimney rose among the trees.

Swanson Bay once boasted a pulp mill, a post office, sawmills, wharves, stores and many homes. In 1918, 500 people worked here to provide pulp to the Japanese market, but a market collapse forced the mill to close in 1923. The sawmill closed shortly

When Swanson Bay's mills were operating, the town's residents enjoyed this view of mountains and waterfalls.

The forest has grown around the former town of Swanson Bay. An old building is just visible among the trees.

A helicopter carries a tree from the forest, dropping it into the water in Finlayson Channel in an effort to use sustainable logging practices.

Only one person now lives at the former cannery town of Butedale, selling moorage and ice cream to passing boaters.

after. By 1937, when author Betty Carey visited Swanson Bay on a journey from Anacortes to Ketchikan in her dugout canoe, *Bijaboji*, Swanson Bay was a ghost town with only a lone watchman to patrol the dilapidated site.

As we motored out of Swanson Bay, I looked across the channel at a waterfall slicing through a steep green forest beneath white-capped mountains. The people who had worked and lived here so briefly must have regretted leaving such beauty behind.

More than just the community of Swanson Bay has disappeared from these channels. When Betty Carey made her trip, she found trappers' cabins, small fish canneries and lumber camps tucked in the bays and inlets. She spent many comfortable nights in their facilities, visiting with residents, eating home-cooked meals and sleeping in borrowed beds along the way. Faster, more-efficient boats and the decline and industrialization of the fishing and logging industries eliminated the need for these far-off businesses. Most of the structures they occupied have now been reclaimed by the forest.

Eleven miles north of Swanson Bay, the remains of the former Butedale Cannery are testimony to that change. As we approached, we could see a roaring waterfall tumbling into the channel. Then the cannery came into view: a sad collection of collapsed buildings, sagging roofs, abandoned oil tanks, leaning pilings, and scattered old lumber. Founded in 1918, the salmon cannery ceased operations in 1950. Only one person lives there now, renting out cabins and selling ice cream to passing boaters.

As we journeyed north in 2006, I watched the snow on the mountains creeping closer to the water and felt the temperature dropping. When we exited Princess Royal Channel and entered McKay Reach, the body of water between Princess Royal and Grenville Channels, a chill wind came up from the north. We raised sail and tacked north toward Bishop Bay. With its dock and hot springs, the bay promised a pleasant respite. In between tacks, I huddled under the dodger trying to stay warm.

The wind died to almost nothing as we entered the bay, but I still felt chilled from our sail. Fishing boats and powerboats

The bath house at the Bishop Bay Hot Springs is just a short walk from the dock.

A hot bath at Bishop Bay Hot Springs is a relief after a cold day of sailing.

crowded the dock, so we anchored off to the side. We changed into our swimming suits, donned our fleece jackets, and took the dinghy ashore. On the dock a cheerful group of men and women in T-shirts and shorts lazed in deck chairs enjoying the sun, drinking beer and eating crab. "Help yourself," one of the men told us, gesturing to a pot of cooked Dungeness. In its contrast to the cold breeze and snow-capped mountains we had just sailed through, the sunny scene seemed surreal.

We hiked up the ramp and followed a short forested trail along the shore until we came to the small cement cabin housing the hot springs. Inside, sun filtered through a corrugated fiberglass roof, lighting up the steaming water. A faint smell of sulfur drifted in the air. I tested the water with my foot—it was comfortably hot. I slid the rest of the way in, letting its welcome warmth roll over me. If there were negatives to taking the inner channels, they were far outweighed by the opportunity to relax and soak up this heat in these luxurious hot springs.

The Outer Channels

As we passed Klemtu in 2008, the weather radio predicted moderate southerlies: perfect conditions for sailing the outer channels.

"Maybe now we can do some sailing," said Steve as we turned left at Jane Passage, heading for the outer channels.

That night we anchored at Jorgensen Harbour in Meyers Passage. The harbor was deeper than the chart indicated and we spent an uneasy night listening to the sound of anchor chain rumbling across rocks below and transmitted up the chain to *Osprey*'s anchor locker.

The only ripples on the water when we got up at 6:00 a.m. the next morning were from raindrops. Wearing foul-weather gear and gloves, we motored through rock-strewn Meyers Narrows at high-water slack. The kelp that clogs this channel in the summer had not yet appeared, and we passed through without incident.

We found the promised wind in Laredo Channel and raised sail in the rain, sailing wing-and-wing under gray clouds. To the west the rocky shore of Ariztabel Island presented an unbroken barrier, while to the east Princess Royal Island teased us with glimpses of inlets and coves. I remembered the cruise ship MS *Veendam* once again. Since we had seen it heading south off Helmcken Island, it would have returned to Seattle twice and now would again be somewhere in Alaska. The vacation memories of two shiploads of passengers would already be fading in the everyday world of offices and homes, while we were still weaving our way northward and experiencing every mile of the passage to Alaska.

As the wind died and clouds cleared, we motored along Campania Island, where mist swirled around stunted cedars on its rocky heights. Only low-lying islands separate Campania Island from the open waters of Hecate Strait. Fog and mists can move in quickly here. The year before, on our way south, we had watched as a thick fog bank rolled across the island, quickly changing it from a slumbering sunny rock to a mist-enshrouded enigma.

For the third year in a row we were heading north on my birthday. That night, anchored in a small cove called Dunn Passage, we celebrated by cooking a vacuum-packed beef tenderloin. The aroma of roast beef and herbs wafting out of the oven, the warmth from the diesel heater, and the light from kerosene lanterns all conspired to make *Osprey* warm and cozy. Even Jigger seemed content, curled in a ball in front of the heater, his stomach full of kibble. When we sat down to eat, Steve reflected, "Today was a good day. We got to sail and nothing broke!"

Hardly a breath of wind stirred the water the next morning as we motored north through Principe Channel. The land there is low and irregular with a forest of red cedar trees with bare snags poking through green branches. When we had passed through here on our way home the year before, it had looked to me like a land of jewel-green islands. Now, gray skies gave it a look of desolation.

We had just turned into Petrel Channel at Anger Island when water temperature and oil pressure-gauge needles started jumping back and forth. "Turn off the engine," Steve yelled as he ran below.

"We must have a loose connection to ground." Wielding wrenches and screwdrivers, he tightened every connection. "This damned boat—doesn't anything work right?"

While Steve tinkered, *Osprey* drifted. A lifeless gray sea stretched around us in all directions. I could see low-lying islands in the distance. I thought about how helpless we would be without our engine; it might be hours before a wind came up and we hadn't seen another boat all day.

From down below, Steve's voice interrupted my thoughts. "Try it again!" But when I restarted the engine, the needles still bounced chaotically and now the tachometer joined the dance, accompanied by a string of swearing from Steve. "Maybe we've got a bad battery switch." He retreated into the engine compartment and switched the batteries from "2" to "1" then back to "2" and the jiggling stopped.

"It's okay for now. But I'll have to order a new switch from Seattle when we get to Prince Rupert."

A few minutes later the blower motor for the engine started roaring like a jet engine. Steve had installed a new one in the spring after I complained about the noise. Now this new blower motor made a louder racket than the old. "Can't we just turn it off?" I pleaded. "No," replied Steve. "We've got to get air to the engine."

The hillsides above Petrel Channel, one of the outer channels, are covered with artistically twisted bare trees.

Since leaving Port McNeill, we had ignored the warning given by the carver in Alert Bay that a breakdown was our creator telling us to slow down, and had instead struggled to make as many miles in a day as we could. Were these latest problems part of the same message? Or was it just *Osprey* telling us that after two years of cruising in Alaska, more maintenance was required?

We anchored in Captains Cove at the top of Petrel Channel that night, once again the only boat in the anchorage.

The next morning we turned east into Ogden Channel, joining a stream of powerboats coming out of Grenville Channel into Arthur Passage. Fog moved in, turning our world a uniform gray. I peered anxiously through the mist. Lawyer Island with its off-lying dangers of Liar Islet and Client Reef were out there somewhere. They finally emerged from the mist as shadowy blobs. We knew we had entered the outflow from the Skeena River only because the water changed from green to brown and an obstacle course of floating trees confronted us. The fog lifted to reveal massive piles of black coal, tall grain silos and the huge cranes of Prince Rupert's new container terminal. With a population of 13,000, a trans-continental railroad and direct road access to interior Canada, Prince Rupert promised supermarkets, restaurants, and internet and cell-phone access. We were in civilization again.

1.7 PRINCE RUPERT
A Visit to the North Pacific Cannery

"Plan for at least 3 to 4 hours of fun!!!" read a flyer for the North Pacific Historic Fishing Village, the site of the former North Pacific Cannery, now a Canadian national historic site. Because we stop at Prince Rupert going both north and south, our northbound stop in 2008 was our fifth visit to the city. In my quest to slow down and enjoy our journey, I was looking for something different. The brochure promised just that in antique machinery, live theater and home-cooked meals at a "Mess House." We could get to the cannery, in nearby Port Edward, on a city bus that left around noon and returned in late afternoon.

The next day the bus took us through suburbs of modest houses, many up for sale. Like so many towns dependent on lumber and fish, Prince Rupert was struggling. The town's early growth had been inspired by the Grand Trunk Railway, built in 1914. But the line never attracted the freight anticipated. We had glimpsed the latest attempt to take advantage of the railroad, Prince Rupert's new container terminal, on our way into the harbor.

Just past the village of Port Edward, I caught my first glimpse of the old cannery town through the trees—a large complex of white-painted buildings with red roofs, looking neat and clean from a distance. The bus left us and two other passengers in an empty parking lot across a railroad track from the cannery. A guard at the railroad crossing directed us to a ticket booth constructed from the discarded cabin of a fishing boat. The woman at the ticket window told us they didn't have the staff to give tours and wouldn't be doing the historic play but we were welcome to look around by ourselves.

"Is the 'Mess House' open?" I asked.

"No. It's closed; the cook called in sick."

I was dismayed. We hadn't eaten lunch before leaving Prince Rupert and the next bus back was several hours away.

We crossed the tracks to the main building. Inside, we found a large factory with light filtering through small windows. A sign gave a brief history of the cannery. It had been built in 1889, the last salmon was packed there in 1972, it became a museum in 1985, and was designated a National Historic Site in 1989.

Another significant event had been the building of the railroad in 1914. This had made it possible for canneries, in both Prince Rupert and nearby southern Alaska, to market their products across the continent.

Salmon canning was a vital industry in both coastal British Columbia and Southeast Alaska. According to Dianne Newell, author of *The Development of the Pacific Salmon-Canning Industry* (McGill-Queen's University Press, 1989), salmon canning started in Sacramento, California, in 1864, then moved steadily up the coast to Oregon, Washington, British Columbia and, finally, Alaska. Alaska became the world's leader in canned salmon with BC a close second.

The canning process was ideal for summer salmon runs with their short,

The North Pacific Cannery National Historic Site is undergoing renovation. A new dock is in the foreground.

intense bursts of activity. The ability to quickly preserve massive amounts of fish in a few short weeks allowed the canneries to distribute salmon worldwide. Fishermen could easily catch the fish when they congregated for spawning in nearby inlets and river mouths.

Through my reading I had learned much about the biology of salmon, yet knew little about what actually happens inside a cannery. I hoped the North Pacific Cannery would fill that gap in my knowledge. We toured the cavernous building, studying the various machines for sorting, cutting and canning. We also came upon the infamous "Iron Chink" that had replaced Chinese workers on the slime line (where fish are cleaned and cut). It was as if

The North Pacific Cannery National Historic Site provides an opportunity to see an old-fashioned salmon cannery in almost intact condition.

we had been given a chance to tour Namu or Butedale before they rotted away. We tried to piece together the canning process from the signs identifying the machines but soon gave up in frustration. It was clear: the process had been complex and needed someone to explain it. The immensity of the place brought home the fact that the salmon industry wasn't just a few hardy fishermen braving the sea in small boats. It was an industry with a huge need for capital, transportation and supplies.

The more time we spent exploring the building, the harder it became to ignore the squishy floorboards and musty odor. And the white paint that had looked so clean from the road was actually peeling. Was the North Pacific Historic Fishing Village a ghost town or a real museum?

In our explorations of both British Columbia and Alaska, I had gotten used to seeing the remains of past booms and busts in the form of rusty boilers, collapsed buildings and rotten pilings. Fur traders, whalers, herring and pilchard fishermen, miners and, more recently, salmon canners and loggers, have all come and gone. Namu, Swanson Bay and Butedale are some of the more significant examples of industry's transience on this coast. In Southeast Alaska we had seen abandoned canneries in only slightly better shape than Namu and Butedale in the towns of Craig and Kake, while rusty boilers littered the beaches in countless small bays.

An interpretive sign in the cannery explained the decline of that industry in four words: transportation, automation, refrigeration and consolidation.

I looked at this sign in consternation. Where did overfishing and the destruction of fish habitat by deforestation fit in? The sign suggested that the cause was more business-logistics oriented and that even if the fisheries had been managed for a sustainable yield from the beginning, canneries would have gone out of business as fresh and frozen products became more feasible.

We went outside and walked along a boardwalk lined with offices, stores and former workers' cottages. We wandered into empty offices with antique adding machines and typewriters, and into workmen's cottages with kitchen tables and Victrolas. I almost expected to see workers walk by, carrying nets and boxes of fish. The few other tourists on site were shadowy figures emerging from distant buildings. I wondered how the museum could possibly make a go of it with so few patrons. Then I remembered Prince Rupert's new cruise-ship dock. It had been empty when we left on the bus. If a ship had been in, perhaps the scene would have been very different.

In the old general store, I took pictures of empty salmon cans and wished they were full so I could eat. I fumed at the frustration of being marooned.

I had come here to learn about salmon canning and instead had been given a lesson in the challenges of being a tourist in remote locations. It was a lesson I was to revisit in the months ahead.

It was time to move on to Alaska.

Epilogue

In 2010, curious to know what had happened to the North Pacific Historic Fishing Village since we visited it in 2008, I called the Port Edward Historical Society, which owns and operates it. Several days later, Andrew Hamilton, director of the Port Edward Historical Society, responded to my queries with an email. The facility is now called the North Pacific Cannery National Historic Site. The Society's vision for the site is to create one of the most recognizable historic sites in Western Canada. Since we visited, the society has sought and received significant grants for conservation work, added many new interpretive signs, and built a new dock for visiting boaters and tour boats. By the end of 2010 they expect to have completed conservation work on 65 percent of the site. They also plan more interpretive efforts in collaboration with university-museum programs. In fact, Northwest Community College's culinary-arts program will run the food service.

I look forward to visiting a restored cannery on our next trip to Prince Rupert. But, just in case, I'll bring emergency rations and a good book.

1.8   CROSSING DIXON ENTRANCE
Heading for a Snowbound Country

We left Prince Rupert the morning after visiting what is now the North Pacific Cannery National Historic Site, motoring through the calm waters of the winding narrow channel of Venn Passage and passing the Native reserve of Metlakatla, BC, with its rows of neat government-issued houses. As we entered Chatham Sound, the dark hazy forms of Alaska's mountains loomed out of the clouds ahead of us. Already the waters looked more open, the horizon more extensive and the sky brighter than in the forested shores we were leaving behind.

The *US Coast Pilot* warns that "Dixon Entrance is exposed to the rigors of the nearby Pacific." Gale-force winds, fog and heavy seas can make the passage around the rocks and islands of the entrance hazardous.

None of the conditions for a rough crossing existed that day. Although hazy gray clouds obscured the sun, only a light southwesterly blew up Chatham Sound. For the third year in a row we would have an easy crossing.

Our route took us out Chatham Sound, past Dundas Island and across the Dixon Entrance to Alaska's Cape Fox area. Three hours into our passage, we passed Green Island lighthouse with its red-and-white buildings and clean-cut lawns. At 2:30 Steve looked at the chart plotter and announced, "We just crossed the border." While he changed the depth sounder and chart plotter to read fathoms instead of meters (a fathom equals 1.8288 meters or 6 feet), to match US charts, I went below to move the ship's clock back an hour to Alaskan Daylight Time. Then I lowered the Canadian flag from the spreaders and hung the Alaskan flag in its place. We aren't required to fly Alaskan colors; the American flag on our stern was sufficient, but Alaskans are proud and give the blue flag with gold stars approving looks when they see it on our spreaders.

The sun had burned off the clouds, but the air remained chilly. To the north we could see the forested slopes of Cape Fox, while to the west snow-capped mountains seemed to float on the sea, their lower slopes hidden by the curvature of the earth. "It really does look like we're heading for a snowbound country," I said to Steve.

Soon the Art Moderne lighthouse on Tree Point came into view—a tall white line standing proud in the green forest, so different from the red and white lighthouses of British Columbia. At 4:30, I went forward to drop the anchor in Foggy Bay, the only anchorage short of Ketchikan approved by US Customs for boats crossing from British Columbia.

Many of Southeast Alaska's lighthouses are in an unusual Art Moderne style like this one at Tree Point.

In the 19 days since leaving Seattle on May 12, we'd sailed and motored roughly 680 miles. I felt a sense of accomplishment. We'd navigated through tricky channels, slogged through rain and fog, and made numerous repairs along the way. And although we had felt rushed for much of the trip, we'd made the journey in a sailboat, a slow mode of transportation. If we'd come by cruise ship, we would have been here in two days; by plane, two hours. The time it took us to get here helped to remind us of how far Alaska is from the lower 48.

Now the real adventure could begin.

Foggy Bay is a popular anchorage for boats crossing to Alaska from BC and the only one approved by US Customs.

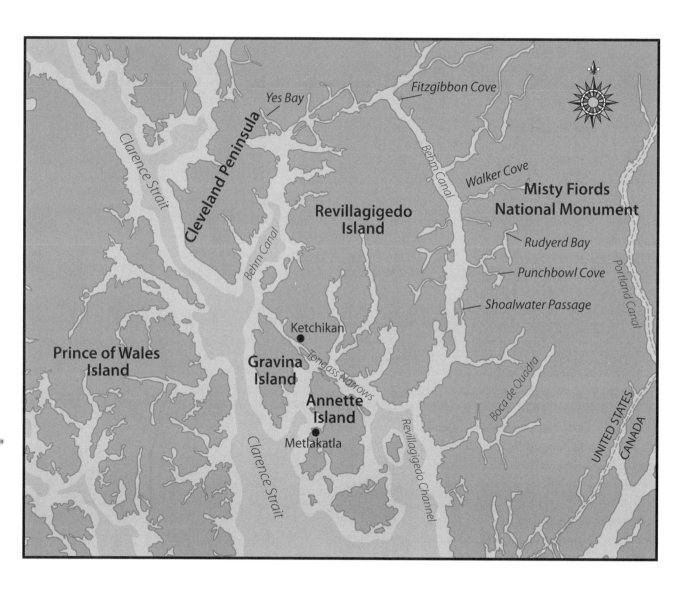

Yes Bay

Fitzgibbon Cove

Cleveland Peninsula

Clarence Strait

Behm Canal

Revillagigedo Island

Walker Cove

Misty Fiords National Monument

Rudyerd Bay

Punchbowl Cove

Shoalwater Passage

Portland Canal

Ketchikan

Prince of Wales Island

Gravina Island

Tongass Narrows

Annette Island

Boca de Quadra

Metlakatla

Clarence Strait

Revillagigedo Channel

UNITED STATES

CANADA

CHAPTER 2

KETCHIKAN AREA

2.1 KETCHIKAN
Is Alaska Real?

Porpoises played in our bow wave under sunny skies as we motored up Tongass Narrows to Ketchikan harbor in 2006 on our first trip to Southeast Alaska. After three weeks of sailing north in the Inside Passage, I was glad to finally be in Alaska and looking forward to our first Alaskan city. I had heard that Ketchikan was a major cruise-ship port, and wondered what would be left of "old Alaska" and how the town would be affected by the huge ships.

Soon, I had a hint of that impact. Ahead, I saw three large white ships at dock, towering over Ketchikan's downtown waterfront and dwarfing nearby buildings. Their size and number startled me.

Steve radioed the Ketchikan harbormaster to request moorage and they gave us a slip assignment in Thomas Basin, the first of several marinas in the harbor. Marinas in Alaska are built for fishing boats but as they are typically away for fishing in the summers, their slips are available for transient boats. It's an arrangement that works well for all: the fishing boats get winter moorage subsidized by summer rentals, visitors get a place to tie up for a reasonable price, and the towns benefit from the business brought by both.

I regarded the cruise ships nervously as we approached, realizing we were going to have to pass within a few yards of one to enter the marina. Although the ships were tied to docks, their sheer size and bulk make them intimidating. What if they

As many as eight cruise ships call at Ketchikan on some days: four in the morning and four in the afternoon.

suddenly got underway? As we passed between the breakwater and the first ship, I had to tip my head back to see the ship's top decks, far above *Osprey*'s mast.

We entered Thomas Basin and tied up between a large motor yacht and an equally large salmon seiner. Steve got out his cell phone and called US Customs. We were officially back in our own country, but far from home.

On the seaward side of the boat basin, the white hull of the cruise ship with its rows of balconies looked like a string of modern apartments. To the south and east old-fashioned wood buildings in various states of repair lined the streets. To the north stood a stadium-like structure from which cheers and roars of applause traveled across the water. The Great Alaskan Lumberjack Show was in full swing.

An old-fashioned rowdy Alaskan town dominated by huge modern cruise ships promised an interesting contrast. I looked forward to exploring the town.

The sound of revving engines woke us the next morning. I got up to see tourists in L.L.Bean outfits boarding sport-fishing and whale-watching boats on a dock across from *Osprey*. To seaward I saw that a different white-hulled cruise ship had replaced the one of the afternoon before.

After breakfast we set out with the goal of seeing the town and collecting our mail from the post office. We headed north along the waterfront, passing the old-fashioned New York Hotel with its white-curtained windows, and crossing over Ketchikan Creek on a rust-colored steel bridge. From the bridge we stopped to look back at Creek Street, Ketchikan's former red-light neighborhood billed in tourist brochures as "where fish and fishermen go up the creek to spawn."

Tourists were strolling the boardwalk, taking photographs of the seductively dressed tour guides at Dolly's House, the museum dedicated to Ketchikan's former brothels. A brothel as a tourist attraction reminds me of something a character in the movie *Chinatown* said: "Politicians, ugly buildings and whores all get respectable if they live long enough."

Ketchikan Creek, also called Fish Creek, with its massive schools of spawning salmon, attracted the first white settlers to this area in the 1880s. Tlingit fish camps already lined the creek and early settlers established salmon salteries, driving pilings and building a wooden city along the creek bank. When gold and copper were discovered on Prince of Wales and other nearby islands, Ketchikan became a supply center for the mining industry. When Prince Rupert, less than 90 miles away, became the terminus for a continental railroad, astute businessmen saw the opportunity to ship fish back east and built salmon canneries and cold-storage facilities. In 1930 Ketchikan claimed it canned more salmon than any other city in the world. Ketchikan's welcome sign, seen by cruise-ship passengers as they disembark, announces the city as the "Salmon Capital of the World."

With fishermen came prostitution. Ketchikan was the

Dolly's House, a museum dedicated to Ketchikan's former brothels, is a popular tourist destination.

first port of call in Alaska for fishermen heading north and the last port for them heading back home with pockets full of money. Fleets of fishing boats stopped at Ketchikan, not just for the brothels, but to spend money on provisions and boat repairs.

But as the city prospered, wives and children joined the male settlers and churches and schools were built. The city council felt they needed to do something about the brothels, but rather than banning them, they consolidated them at Creek Street.

June Allen and Patricia Charles, authors of *Spirit: Historic Ketchikan Alaska* (Historic Ketchikan, 1992) described

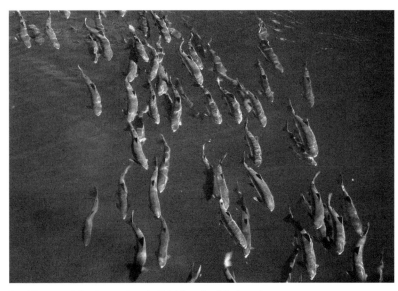

Tourists can watch salmon return to Ketchikan Creek in August.

Creek Street then as a lively place with a dance hall as well as brothels. Its residents called themselves "sporting women" and the street acquired a reputation for fights and brawls that led to the occasional body floating near the mouth of the creek. Creek Street's rowdies became so famous that early tourists made a point of walking by to catch glimpses of the neighborhood's bawdy inhabitants.

Reform pressure finally closed Creek Street's brothels in 1954. The inhabitants went underground or moved to friendlier cities. A few retired to live out their days quietly on Creek Street.

Since those wild times, Ketchikan's economy has seen booms and busts. Overfishing drove the fishing industry down. And although fish stocks partially recovered when the state of Alaska took over their management, less labor-intensive fresh and frozen seafood products now dominate the market. In 1954, Ketchikan became a timber town with the opening of the Ketchikan Pulp Mill. Pulp markets dried up and the mill closed in 1997. The town then turned to tourism, especially tourism by cruise ship.

Evidence of that tourism was everywhere as we approached what was once the center of downtown Ketchikan. Newly renovated buildings lined the street, painted in eye-catching colors probably never seen in old Ketchikan. Looking for a business establishment that might have something useful in it, I passed one jewelry shop after another before finally coming to a drugstore—one of the last strongholds of old Ketchikan was now selling shampoo and Lipitor to tourists.

A tourism office occupied a plain metal building next to a cruise-ship dock. We walked in and were confronted with a long line of desks, each occupied by a clerk selling tours: charter fishing trips, whale- and bear-watching trips, helicopter and seaplane tours of Misty Fiords National Monument and totem-pole viewing at Ketchikan's two totem parks. This was industrial-strength tourism, designed to reap tourist dollars and move cruise-ship passengers in and out fast.

The real Ketchikan started north of the cruise-ship docks. Weather-beaten storefronts with mossy roofs held marine supplies, life-raft and seaplane services, fish processors and the occasional seedy-looking bar. Farther on, we came to a new mall with a supermarket. Walking through it quickly, I saw everything one would expect to see in Seattle—even a Starbucks.

We found the post office in a nondescript building near the ferry terminal, collected our mail and returned to the boat. That afternoon we toured the Totem Heritage Center and wandered through shops in the immediate neighborhood. Above Creek Street we found Parnassus Books, a small shop up a set of varnished stairs and on the second floor of an old wooden building. We browsed among volumes on Alaskan history and Alaskan Natives and chatted with the talkative, cheerful owner who was soon telling us of her experiences crossing stormy Clarence Strait.

On Stedman Street we entered a small store called Chinook and Company. Pyramids of colorful cans of salmon and jars of jam lined the shelves behind racks of fleece jackets and vests. A smartly dressed woman with a friendly smile greeted us.

"You're off a private boat." Seeing our surprise, she continued, "It's your clothes, they're just a bit more worn than those of the cruise-ship passengers."

There was no one else in the store so she had time to talk to us.

"We're at the edge of the cruise-ship area. We like it here. We know that the people who take the trouble to walk here will appreciate wild salmon in the can with skin and bones."

Later that afternoon I was putting groceries away in *Osprey*'s icebox when Steve suggested, "Let's go have a beer at the Potlatch."

Conveniently located at the top of the ramp next to the marina, the Potlatch Bar is a famous fishermen's hangout. Jonathan Raban in *Passage to Juneau* (1999) described the tavern as noisy, crowded and violent, a raucous cave that was pitch-dark except for a single light over the pool table. Raban's description didn't inspire me to visit, but I figured drinking one beer there was an Alaskan experience everyone should have at least once!

The Thomas Wash Basin provides humor with its laundry, showers and espresso.

A red-sided wooden building sandwiched between a propeller shop and the Thomas Wash Basin Laundromat, the Potlatch looked innocuous from the outside. We walked through the door and took seats at a booth. Daylight streamed through two large windows on either side of the door. Tabletops and floor were clean and shiny.

A pleasant waitress in T-shirt and jeans served us our Alaskan Amber Ale and we settled back to watch the action—which wasn't much. Groups of men sat around, drinking beer, talking and laughing. From their ponytails and grubby Carhartts, it seemed likely they were fishermen. When we finished our ales, I walked out the door, puzzling over the difference between the Potlatch Raban described and the one we saw. Was it just different people seeing the same bar at different times, or, as Raban himself suggested might happen, was the Potlatch on the way to becoming a sanitized tourist attraction?

Back at the boat, I grilled steaks we had bought that afternoon, while Jigger meowed at my feet. Tired of stepping on his tail, I clipped a leash to his harness and pushed him outside. As he hopped on deck, I poked my head out of the hatch to check on him just as one of the fishermen from the Potlatch strolled by. He looked tenderly at Jigger and in a high-pitched voice crooned "Kitty, kitty, kitty."

So much for rowdy fishermen.

Blueberry Arts Festival

In 2007 we stopped at Ketchikan on our way south, arriving the first weekend of August—just in time for the annual Blueberry Arts Festival.

Located conveniently at the top of the ramp at Thomas Boat Basin, the Potlatch Bar is a favorite fishermen's hangout.

Saturday was a beautiful sunny day and the parking lot of the Methodist Church in downtown Ketchikan, which served as the fair site, was bustling with kids and adults in shorts and sandals. We found seats in front of the open-air stage and listened to enthusiastic music that to our ears was more noise than harmony. Between bands Steve struck up a conversation with a couple sitting next to us and wearing cruise-ship T-shirts.

"Did you learn about this festival on your ship?"

"Oh no. They don't tell us about anything that's free," the woman replied with a sigh. "We found out about it on the internet before we left home!"

We left to wander among the booths, admiring carved wooden bowls and tea towels embroidered with blueberry designs, and sampling blueberry muffins. John Straley, an author of Alaskan mysteries, was signing books at a booth for Parnassus Books, so we said hello to the shopkeeper and introduced ourselves to Straley. "They're all right," the bookstore owner assured Straley. "They've been in my shop."

The next afternoon we arrived at the New York Café for the 17th annual Richard Brautigan and Dick Whitaker Memorial Trout Fishing in America Poetry Slam. My hazy recollection of the book *Trout Fishing in America* was that it was from the hippy era and had almost nothing to do with trout fishing. Its use in the title of the poetry slam promised an amusing event.

The wood-paneled café was already crowded, but we squeezed in and found stools at the long mahogany bar, the remains of what must have been a tavern in Ketchikan's rowdier days.

In the audience I spotted the owners of the bookstore and the fish store, both of whom we had met previously. Recognizing them almost made me feel as if I belonged here. From the rumpled clothes people wore, I deduced that this crowd was predominantly made up of Alaskans, not tourists.

Ray Troll, Ketchikan's humorous fish artist, and John Straley acted as joint masters of ceremony. Troll—wearing Woody Allen glasses, a ball cap, black T-shirt and shorts—introduced the session. He stood beneath his mural, "Absolutely Creek Street," showing scenes of nude women, dead bodies and sea life floating in a blue-tinted world. Troll talked about how far Alaska had come. They now had their own beer (Alaskan), their own coffee (Raven's Brew) and even their own poetry slam.

Troll was followed by John Straley, who introduced each poet, noting that the judges were scattered around the room at various tables. We listened to an "Ode to a Red-necked Friend," "Ode to a Tan" (by someone newly returned from Hawaii), and a tongue-in-cheek poem by a man confessing love for Sarah Palin, Alaska's recently elected governor. The winning poem was read by a young woman dressed head to toe in white with even a white feather in her long dark hair. I was so intrigued by her costume that when her award was announced, I couldn't remember what her poem had been about.

As we walked back to *Osprey*, I reflected that it was wonderful for the city to put on a festival for its residents during the peak of tourist season.

Is Ketchikan Real?

By our fourth visit to Ketchikan in 2008, we had adjusted to life among the cruise ships and grown to like Thomas Basin. Although other cruising boaters prefer the Bar Harbor North marina for its short distance to the new Safeway store, we liked the more central location of Thomas Basin with its touch of Alaskan funkiness and its friendly locals.

One afternoon after the cruise ships had left for the day, we walked to Creek Street, hoping to visit the shops and art galleries when there were fewer crowds. But no one was about, and our footsteps rang hollow along the empty boardwalk as we passed one darkened store after another. A sign in the window of Dolly's House proclaimed it was closed "so Dolly can attend the policemen's ball."

A store next door to Dolly's was open. A sign outside noted that it was owned and operated by a local Tlingit artist. We went inside and found a young man sitting in an easy chair with his feet up. His pale skin told us he wasn't the Tlingit artist. Behind him elegant and expensive Northwest Native masks decorated the wall. No one else was in the store.

"Normally I'm not open at this hour," he told us. "But I thought I'd just stick around today and see if anyone comes in."

"If it's this dead in the summer after the cruise ships leave, what's it like in the winter?" Steve asked.

"I was here last February. It was like a ghost town. Those 15,000 people who are supposed to live here? They're not real. I figure they just register here so they can get their payments from the permanent fund." (The state of Alaska pays all state residents royalty money from oil sales.)

"What about the neighborhoods outside of downtown?" I asked.

"You mean north of town? There are people there all right, but they're just house sitters for the owners who live down south."

The idea of Ketchikan as unreal resonated with me. With all the tourist activity, sometimes it's a challenge to discern the real Alaska below the artifice. Downtown Ketchikan's quaint false-fronted stores selling nothing but jewelry and souvenirs reminded me of the fake town in the movie *The Truman Show*. Locals stay away from the downtown area and at night it is dark and empty.

What about the rest of Southeast Alaska? Is it phony too? As we headed north I was going to have to look deeper to find the real Alaska.

2.2   METLAKATLA
Where Pioneers Came in Canoes

"Dedicated to the original pioneers of Metlakatla."

So reads the inscription on a triangular stone monument in the neatly trimmed yard of the William Duncan Cottage Museum. The reference to "pioneers" intrigued me. The word brought to mind western movies, with settlers traveling in covered wagons and facing attacks from wild Indians. But in Metlakatla the pioneers *were* Indians and they traveled in canoes from British Columbia, not covered wagons.

It's an odd twist on the often-tragic history of Native life in the wake of European settlement, and it made me wonder if the story of the Metlakatla pioneers had a better outcome as well. Was the leader of the settlement, the Anglican missionary William Duncan, viewed in a more favorable light than his contemporaries? Opinions about him ranged from his being a savior who rescued the Tsimshians from poverty to his being a destroyer of the Tsimshian culture. I wanted to know if the lives of the Metlakatla residents differed from those of inhabitants of other Native Alaskan towns. So on our first trip to Southeast Alaska, in 2006, we were determined to visit this intriguing place.

The settlers of Metlakatla, Alaska, arrived by a circuitous route. In 1862, Duncan sought a mission site free from "heathen practices" and easy alcohol, and led a group of his Tsimshian followers from Port Simpson, BC, to present-day Metlakatla, BC, 20 miles south. More Tsimshians followed, and the village grew to include a school, sawmill, cannery, neat rows of European-style houses, and an 800-seat church. Other missionaries traveled to Metlakatla to study Duncan's methods, and the village became known as a model Native community, a place where Natives were industrious, religious and temperate, and—on the surface at least—lived very much like Europeans.

Problems began in 1879 when a new bishop arrived in British Columbia and insisted that Duncan follow High Church rituals like drinking wine at communion. When he refused, he was dismissed. Metlakatla residents became divided with the majority supporting Duncan.

He fought to regain control of the Metlakatla mission by arguing that the Tsimshian people had rights to the land on which the church stood. When Canadian courts sided with the Anglican Church, Duncan traveled to Washington, DC. With the help of influential supporters he persuaded congress to authorize an Indian reserve for the Tsimshians on Annette Island, near Ketchikan in Southeast Alaska.

In August and September 1887, about 800 of his Tsimshian supporters ventured 70 miles across the perilous Dixon Entrance in a flotilla of canoes, fish boats, and small steamboats to found a new settlement of the same name: Metlakatla. They left behind the villagers who supported the Anglican Church and others who didn't wish to leave their home. Today, there are two communities of Metlakatla: Metlakatla, BC, and Metlakatla, Alaska.

We left Ketchikan on a sunny June morning in 2006, motoring *Osprey* south through the calm waters of Tongass Narrows, into Nichols Passage, and anchoring in Port Chester near a cluster of small islands close to the town of Metlakatla, Alaska. To the east, we could see the twin towers of the William Duncan Memorial Church standing out against the rocky, green mountains of Annette Island. To the west, across the blue waters of Clarence Strait, stood the snow-capped mountains of Prince of Wales Island.

The imposing steeples of the William Duncan Memorial Church are clearly visible from the water off Metlakatla.

We took our dinghy ashore through a new stone breakwater and tied up at the town marina. The first sight we saw when we stepped ashore was a longhouse painted with Tsimshian designs. It was locked, so we headed for the church towers that we had seen from the water. From the church, also locked, we went in search of the William Duncan Museum. But it was closed too, with no sign to indicate when it would open. A woman in the school-administration building, who had given us directions, had warned us that it might be closed. "There are no tour boats today," she explained. I began to wonder if it was possible to be a tourist off the cruise-ship route.

There was still the town to explore and its people to meet. The white clapboard buildings of the cannery across the street looked deserted; fishing season had not yet begun. We headed back toward town, following an asphalt road through a hodgepodge of housing styles: bungalows from the 1920s, ranch houses from the 1950s, prefabricated houses from the 1990s, and trailers, each on their own square of grass. We saw no sign of the Victorian houses Metlakatla had once been known for. Fires and the unforgiving damp of Alaska had taken their toll.

We passed two men sitting on the doorstep of a small white trailer. Tools and lumber surrounded them, and a young boy played in the surrounding yard. They were turning the trailer into a store, they told us. When we mentioned our frustration over the closed museum, one of them asked if we had seen the fireworks stand. "You can't get fireworks like those anywhere else." Then he laughed. "Except maybe on the reservations near Seattle."

That reminded me of something I'd pondered since learning that Annette Island was the only reservation in Alaska where the US had not signed any treaties with the Natives. In 1971, the Alaska Native Claims Settlement Act (ANCSA) gave land and money to a dozen Native corporations as part of a process to resolve land claims. (A thirteenth corporation for Natives living outside Alaska was added later.) Although the act was passed

to expedite oil drilling in the Arctic, its architects also hoped it would help assimilate Natives into the mainstream culture and be an improvement over the system of Indian Reservations in the lower 48. Those covered by ANCSA are classified by the US Bureau of Indian Affairs as Natives, not Indians. I asked the men if Metlakatla had been included in ANCSA.

"No, because we have the island." One of them explained that they had their own fisheries and forest. They also had the right to implement their own fisheries laws if they wished, but had chosen instead to adopt those of the State of Alaska. I thought it ironic that due to having a reservation, this group of Native Alaskans

The Tsimshian artist Aaron Horne carves a totem pole.

most known for assimilation into the mainstream culture was in actuality the only one to hang on to its "Indian" classification and eligibility for services from the US Bureau of Indian Affairs.

Continuing our walk, we stopped at a grocery store. In a cooler at the back, I searched the bottled waters for the least-expensive brand. I was astonished to find one that cost only 40 cents for 20 ounces, a size that can cost as much as $2.50 in Seattle. The label, with a Northwest design and mountains in the background, said "Purple Mountain Pure," bottled in Metlakatla. Early Metlakatla had a reputation for creating its own industries, and the trend was obviously continuing. By the late 1800s, Metlakatlans had built a cannery, a number of sawmills, and stores serving the residents. From 1900 to the 1950s it was the major manufacturer of small boats in Southeast Alaska, famous for the "Davis boat," a double-ended rowboat.

Back at the waterfront, we found two men carving a totem pole under a covered area. One man was tall and thin, the other short and stocky. They were the Horne brothers, they told us, members of the Wolf Clan. They had a third brother, also a carver.

"If we ever open our own shop, we'll call ourselves the Three Bad Wolves," one said with a deadpan expression.

The air was thick with the pungent aroma of cedar shavings. As the brothers worked, we could see the shape of a wolf's head emerging from the wood.

In their Canadian homeland, the Tsimshians had carved magnificent house poles, masks and other ceremonial objects. When they left British Columbia, Duncan had advised them to leave their old life behind, as he had. The Tsimshians built a bonfire on the beach and burned many ceremonial objects, a tragic loss of cultural artifacts and works of art that had been passed down for generations. When Metlakatla artists seriously turned back to carving in the 1970s, they had to visit museums to see examples of their own ancestral art.

The long Alaskan day stretched into evening. We took a walk along the shore of Nichols Passage to Cedar Point and ate hamburgers at a bazaar in the community center. On our way back to our dinghy, we stopped to talk to a couple walking three dogs. Dan Leask, a thin man with graying black hair, had a quiet demeanor, and his young wife, Roxana, did most of the talking.

Steve gestured toward a totem pole that included a figure of a man clothed in a black suit and holding a bible, and asked them if Duncan's church was still important in Metlakatla.

Roxana explained that while religion was still important in Metlakatla, there was no longer just one church. They had a Mormon temple up on the hill, a Jehovah's Witnesses Hall out toward the cemetery, and a Presbyterian church in town. She thought there were seven churches all together.

I asked Roxana what the people of Metlakatla thought of Duncan now.

"Opinions of Duncan differ. Some say they have forgiven him."

There are both pro-Duncan people and anti-Duncan people in the town. Roxana and Dan's family is pro-Duncan. "Nobody forced people to come to Metlakatla," she said. "They came because they thought it was best for them."

According to Peter Murray, author of *The Devil and Mr. Duncan: A History of the Two Metlakatlas* (Sono Nis Press, 1985), Duncan's missionary methods were based on the twin foundations of providing livelihoods for Native villagers and requiring a strict code of conduct. Residents of both the Metlakatlas had to attend church and give up alcohol and gambling. They also had to renounce Native dances and potlatches, the very cornerstones of their culture. In his later years, Duncan became increasingly autocratic, controlling the town's schools, stores and other businesses long after a new generation of Metlakatlans was ready to take over. Parents in Metlakatla wanted a better school for their children, but Duncan obstinately refused, making it necessary for them to appeal to the US Commissioner of Education.

Dan and Roxana later paddled out to the *Osprey* in a red canoe to join us for tea in our cockpit. Dan gave us a necklace of cedar-bark strips and a greeting card with a Tsimshian design of an eagle with wings surrounding a circle of fish. Roxana had made them both.

While I poured tea, Roxana and Dan told us more about themselves. Roxana is a weaver and a printmaker of traditional Tsimshian designs, while Dan is a retired school-teacher who now works in his father's store, Leasks' Grocery, which we had visited that same afternoon. I told them about buying the Purple Mountain Pure water.

"It's called 'Purple Mountain' after the way the mountains turn purple in the sunset," said Roxana, as she motioned to the peaks that rose up on Annette Island to the east. On them we could see evidence of logging. Dan told us that like many small Alaskan towns, Metlakatla's economy was suffering from a decline of the fishing business. The Purple Mountain bottling plant helped but wasn't enough to sustain the town so it had also turned to logging.

We talked until the sun set. As Dan and Roxana paddled back to shore, the mountains above them turned purple.

A Celebration

Steve and I returned to Metlakatla the following August, arriving the day before the town's 120th anniversary celebration. This time we took *Osprey* into the marina, tying up at a vacant slip near the entrance.

Ashore, we found Aaron Horne, the thinner of the two Horne brothers, frantically carving a small totem pole. The pole was for the Fourth Generation Dancers, he told us, and he had to finish it by the next morning. The two side-by-side figures at the bottom—one holding a Bible and the other holding a cross—portrayed the first generation of Metlakatla, the founders. The next figure up represented the builders, and the third the carvers, the first generation to gravitate back to the Tsimshian traditions. The top figure depicted the Fourth Generation Dancers.

We left with an invitation to the pole's dedication the next morning.

Earlier that week I had read in the *Ketchikan Daily News* about a show of historic photographs in the Metlakatla Service Center, a modern building on the outskirts of town. We were greeted there by a Native woman elegantly dressed in contemporary clothes, and she handed each of us a cloth bag printed with a black-and-white photograph of canoes and the words, "Looking at Our Past to Inspire Our Future." She was Mique'l Icesis Askren, a graduate student in art from the University of British Columbia who had put the exhibit together.

We joined the crowd of mostly Native visitors viewing photographs taken in the late 1800s and early 1900s by Benjamin Haldane, a local Tsimshian photographer, and assembled by Askren for her master's thesis. In 2003 many of the pictures had been rescued from the fire of the local waste facility, where someone who didn't understand their value had thrown them away, and they had never before been shown.

As I gazed at a picture of Victorian houses, I heard a woman's voice behind me. "Look at that!" she exclaimed. "They're beautiful. What happened? They tore them down and put up trailers?" I remembered the assortment of houses we had seen in town and understood why she had asked the question. Several people standing nearby murmured agreement but no one explained what had happened to the houses. Moving on, I came across a picture of the original William Duncan church. It was similar to the current church but much more ornate with additional windows as well as turrets on top of the two towers. A man standing next to me pointed to the picture. "That's the old church. It burned down." I could see the awe in his face and realized that many of the residents were catching a glimpse of their town's history for the first time.

That evening on *Osprey*, I read through a copy of Askren's thesis that I had picked up earlier in the day. Askren, a Tsimshian from Metlakatla, argues that Duncan supporters, campaigning for land rights from the US government, made exaggerated claims that the Tsimshians of Metlakatla were assimilated. The success of their campaign fueled the notion that Metlakatlans were no longer true Indians and led to Metlakatla becoming a "spectacle of progress" among travelers in Alaska. Looking only for evidence of progress, visitors failed to see the Tsimshian practices and beliefs that ran through the daily lives of the Metlakatlans. For example, one visitor had described the entrepreneurial skills of a Metlakatla silversmith yet neglected to mention the cultural value of the art he produced. Meanwhile, elsewhere in Alaska, similar artwork received accolades for its representation of Native culture.

Even the Tsimshians of Metlakatla had bought into their assimilation into European culture, focusing on the loss of the dances and potlatches they had relinquished, and losing sight of the many Tsimshian practices and beliefs retained. According to Askren, the view that Metlakatlans had revived their culture only a generation ago was inaccurate. Metlakatlans have sustained their tribal affiliations, and all Tsimshians in Metlakatla could name their tribe and clan. Metlakatlans also maintained carving and weaving skills, even if they first focused on making curios for tourists. Haldane's photographs—many of which include artifacts like miniature totem poles with family crests, and paddles or button blankets—are further evidence of the continuity of Tsimshian culture.

No First Nation or Native American community in British Columbia or Alaska escaped the push for assimilation, says Askren. But each adapted and maintained its culture in its own way.

The kaleidoscope through which I had been looking at Metlakatla shifted. I thought about the stone monument in front of Duncan's cottage, "dedicated to the original pioneers"—not to Duncan. As pioneers, Metlakatlans were in control of their own destiny.

Askren's thesis reminded me that when we visited the village of Klemtu in 1999, villagers told us they didn't know the stories that accompanied a totem pole in their village because as children they had been taken from their homes and forced into residential schools. Only seven years later, however, we had toured Klemtu's magnificent new Big House and been regaled by tales of the wily raven.

At nine o'clock the next morning, we arrived in front of the Metlakatla Administration Building in time to watch four men in traditional black-and-red button blankets lift Aaron Horne's totem pole from a truck. Behind them a line of Fourth Generation Dancers, in button blankets and cedar hats of traditional Tsimshian design, prepared to escort the pole to the longhouse. As leader of the Fourth Generation Dancers, Mique'l Askren directed the operations. At the last minute, she called for substitutes to help carry the pole. No one else stepped forward so Steve and another white man volunteered. With the dancers drumming and chanting, the

Steve helps carry a new totem pole to Metlakatla Alaska's longhouse in celebration of the settlement of the town by Tsimshians of Metlakatla BC.

procession moved past the modern schoolhouse with its colorful plastic play structures, past the rows of small houses, and downhill toward the longhouse.

As the line moved forward, I ran ahead to photograph it. Looking back I could see the men carrying the totem pole framed between the two towers of the William Duncan Memorial Church.

2.3 MISTY FIORDS
A Perfect Fog

Raindrops formed tiny circles on the water of Thomas Harbor as we left Ketchikan for Misty Fiords National Monument in June 2007. As I went below to fetch foul-weather gear, I wondered if we would regret visiting one of the wettest places in Southeast Alaska during a week of forecasted rain. Would rain bring out the moody mists for which the area is named, or hide from sight its waterfalls and magnificent cliffs?

New Eddystone Rock, named by Captain George Vancouver for a lighthouse in England, is Misty Fiords most famous landmark.

Good winds and quiet seas had hastened our trip north from Seattle, putting us several days ahead of schedule. We decided to use that time to our advantage and sail south to the east entrance of the Behm Canal. There we would circumnavigate Revillagigedo Island counterclockwise, a 150-mile trip that would take us into the heart of Misty Fiords, the second-largest wilderness in the United States (the largest, also in Alaska, is the Wrangell-St. Elias area). I was interested in seeing Misty Fiords not only for its spectacular scenery but because of the history of its exploration by Captain George Vancouver in 1793. The British Admiralty had directed Vancouver to search for the Northwest Passage, a waterway between the northwest coast and the east coast of the continent. Only by following the continental shore could he be certain to find the waterway if indeed it existed. To accomplish this, Vancouver and his men took their small boats up every inlet on this coast. In Behm Canal Vancouver followed the edge of the continent.

From Thomas Harbor we motored south in the Tongass Canal and into Revillagigedo Channel. There we raised sail in a light northwesterly. A steady parade of cruise ships, tugs, fishing boats, and yachts heading to and from Ketchikan kept our eyes glued to the radar and chart plotter. When we finally passed Cape Alava at the entrance to East Behm Canal, it was a relief to leave the traffic behind.

In the canal, the wind died down to almost nothing and the rain turned to a fine mist—the kind that works its way into foul-weather gear and gives a clammy cold feel to every surface. *Osprey*'s speed slowed to under 2 knots so we dropped the jib and started the engine. Within minutes, the warm air from our Red Dot heater wafted up the companionway. I sat at the top of the steps under the dodger and watched as the mist-streaked evergreens on the sloped shoreline unfolded before me. Ahead, the black fins of porpoises sliced through gray water. Only a single high-speed tour boat interrupted our peace. We had entered the wilderness of Misty Fiords.

At Smeaton Island, the clouds lifted briefly to show glimpses of the white-capped mountains of the Coast range, teasing us with hints of what better weather could bring.

We ended our day's voyage in Shoalwater Passage, a narrow body of water between Winstanley Island and the mainland. That night rain pattered on our cabin roof and I lay awake wondering if it would ever stop. On our first trip to Alaska, the previous year, we had experienced days of rain without pause. I had hoped for better weather for this trip.

By morning the rain had stopped, replaced by a thick fog. I peered through the port lights, hoping to see out into the canal.

"We've got radar," said Steve, reassuringly. "We'll get there."

"I know we'll get there. But I want to see something along the way!" I had most hoped to catch sight of New Eddystone Rock, the 230-foot lone spire that rises out of the center of the Behm Canal just before the entrance to Rudyerd Bay. Named by Vancouver after a lighthouse off Plymouth, England, this rock is probably the most-photographed feature in Misty Fiords. Vancouver described this part of the coast as "dreary and uninteresting," but "the remarkable rock resembling a ship under sail . . . invited our curiosity." They stopped for breakfast at the foot of the rock where friendly Natives in three small canoes visited them.

But by 9:00 a.m. the fog had lifted, replaced by low clouds that hid the mountains but not the shore. As we motored out of the anchorage, I could see the rock ahead, a big green thumb sticking out of the water. Consisting of the erosion-resistant core of a lava conduit that had once moved molten lava to the earth's surface, the rock was left behind when glaciers had scoured away the basalt flows that covered the canal.

In the canal, I was surprised to see streaks of yellow enlivening the gray waters all around us. The streaks were windrows of pollen, similar to what we sometimes see on a car parked underneath a tree. I had never before seen pollen in the water and marveled at its volume.

Punchbowl Cove and Rudyerd Bay

The entrance to Rudyerd Bay appeared as a chasm cut into the rocks of the mountains. Once inside, massive cliffs blocked the wind from all directions. Almost immediately, the seas flattened to a glassy sheen, so smooth we could see individual tree branches reflected in the water's surface.

I was looking in amazement at these perfect reflections when I saw two columns of mist rise from the water, linger in the air, and then drift away. A minute later, two sleek black shapes surfaced: whales feeding near shore.

Following the shoreline on our right, we turned south into Punchbowl Cove. Sheer black walls, glistening with water from hundreds of small waterfalls, climbed into the clouds. We couldn't see the top, but our charts told us the walls were over 3,000 feet high. Trees clung to crevices in the walls, and patches of white snow lay in shady nooks. At the head of the cove, basalt columns soared above a fringe of spruce.

Geological history explains Misty Fiord's spectacular features. More than 250 million years ago, the land masses we now know as Southeast Alaska's Alexander Archipelago arose from the sea floor in the equatorial Pacific and began a long slow journey north, eventually (between 165 and 100 million years ago) colliding with the edge of what would become North America. That collision and subsequent folding, upthrusting and volcanic activity formed the Coast Mountains and provided the clay for the next artists: glaciers. During what is known as the late Wisconsin Glaciation, snowfields a mile thick covered Misty Fiords. When the glaciers finally began their retreat between 10,000 and 12,000 years ago, they left behind dramatic carvings in the rockbound mountains of the continent: deep fjords, U-shaped valleys, striations in rock walls, and high cliffs.

When we reached the center of the cove, Steve turned off the engine. With almost 150 fathoms below us, there was no hope of anchoring, no fear of running aground. As we drifted, I listened to the peaceful sounds of the cove: gulls mewing, loons laughing, water rushing. Then we heard the drone of a seaplane. It entered the cove, flew up and over the cliffs, then disappeared into the clouds to the south, the sound of its engine echoing off the rock walls. We watched with dismay as another plane followed, then another, in a steady parade. Ketchikan with its hordes of tourists, was just a few miles away.

Above the cove, clouds had given way to sunshine. Despite the onslaught of the planes, calm water and sunlight invited relaxation. I sat in the cockpit and gazed in awe at towering black cliffs while Steve got out his fishing pole. Jigger sat at Steve's feet, eagerly watching the pole go up and down. When Steve pulled in a copper rockfish, Jigger

Numerous waterfalls pour down the cliffs of Rudyerd Bay.

Mist adds a touch of mystery to the steep cliffs of Punchbowl Cove.

meowed with excitement and paced back and forth. "Don't worry," Steve told him. "You'll get your share."

Two more rockfish and a lunch later, we headed *Osprey* up inlet to explore the rest of Rudyerd Bay. Sheer rock walls, almost barren except for patches of yellow-green moss, lined the lower inlet. Braided waterfalls, cascades that divided into separate streams only to join and separate repeatedly on their way down, spouted from every crevice. With each turn, we passed more cliffs and waterfalls. Five miles into the bay, it split into a T. We looked right and saw another sailboat anchored in the shallows near the head of the inlet. We took the left branch, winding past meadows, creeks and cliffs, and maneuvered into a beautiful little nook at the head of the bay. Dark-green hemlock and spruce trees blended with the bright greens of marsh grass and the olive greens of moss—all contrasting with white snowfields on the upper slopes. Patches of snow at the water's edge cooled the air, and I zipped up my fleece jacket and pulled on some gloves. Looking up the valley at the bay's head, we could see snowfields on distant mountains. I marveled that Vancouver had dismissed this bay as an "insignificant body of water."

As we headed back down the inlet, dark clouds gathered above us. Soon, a hard rain fell, turning the surface of the water white. But as we swung *Osprey* around to return to Punchbowl Cove, the sun broke through the clouds and a rainbow spanned the bay.

We tied up for the night at a Forest Service buoy. After a dinner of blackened rockfish, I took the dinghy for a row, enjoying the solitude of the wilderness and the serenity that only a rowboat or a kayak in quiet water can give. The sun had broken through again, bathing green trees and black rocks in warm light. The seaplanes were gone and over the roar of hundreds of waterfalls I heard the two clear notes of a varied thrush. I was glad we had come—and happy it wasn't raining.

Walker Cove

The next morning found us motoring north through thick fog and drizzle. Because of our schedule we didn't have the luxury of waiting for the fog to lift. The mainland appeared as dark shadows while Revillagigedo Island, even farther away, hid in the mists. Our first destination was Walker Cove, billed as a smaller version of Punchbowl. I wondered if we would be able to see anything except fog.

But in the more confined area of Walker Cove, trees began to emerge from the mist. From the top branch of one of the tallest trees, a bald eagle watched over the cove's entrance. Beyond the trees, smooth gray walls ribboned with waterfalls disappeared into the fog above. We could only guess at the height of the cliffs and source of

View from Green Island Anchorage, Fitz Hugh Sound.

Big House at village of Klemtu, BC.

Winds are often stronger in the outer channels of BC. This is Principe Channel.

A variety of brands of canned salmon, North Pacific Cannery Historical Site, BC.

Inside North Pacific Cannery National Historical Site, Port Edward, BC.

Metlakatla's William Duncan Cottage museum, built in 1891, is often open when the cruise ships are in town.

Carrying a new totem pole to the long house, Metlakatla, Alaska.

Grave marker in the shape of a bear, Kasaan Totem Park, Prince of Wales Island.

Hammer Slough, Petersburg, Alaska.

A humpback whale dives near *Osprey* in Holkham Bay.

Drifting in ice in front of South Sawyer Glacier, Tracy Arm.

Eagles perched on bergy bit at entrance to Tracy Arm.

Mother seal with pup, Tracy Arm.

Jigger watching drifting ice, Tracy Arm.

Osprey anchored in West Arm, Fords Terror.

Former cannery buildings, Taku Harbor.

Downtown Juneau, near the cruise-ship docks.

Fourth of July parade, Hoonah.

A Russian Orthodox Church sits on a hill above Hoonah.

Fog swirls around Walker Cove, almost hiding a sailboat on a buoy.

the waterfalls above the clouds. We rounded the bend into the final basin, intending to tie up at a Forest Service buoy shown on the chart. Bands of thick fog streamed out of a river mouth, hugging the water and swirling around the bay. Steve kept his eyes on the radar and chart plotter while I stared into the white fog looking for the buoy. Finally, where the buoy should be, I caught glimpses of a sailboat, like a ghost boat whose presence I couldn't be sure of. With the only buoy taken by the sailboat and water too deep to anchor, we once again turned off *Osprey*'s engine and drifted. The fog, combined with the still water and sound of hidden waterfalls, gave the cove an eerie feeling. I was both entranced by the bands of swirling fog and frustrated by the lack of visibility.

We left the cove as the fog turned to drizzle. In the canal, a 15–20 knot wind from the south promised good sailing, and we raised sail, heading north under gray clouds. On either side of us, hundreds of birds with black-feathered heads dotted the water. I watched them through binoculars as they took flight, and saw the black-and-white stripes of loons, more loons than I had ever before seen gathered in one place.

That night we anchored in Fitzgibbon Cove near the top of the Behm Canal, our trip through Misty Fiords National Monument almost over. It was here that Vancouver smelled sea breeze and concluded that Revillagigedo was an island. He had proven that Behm Canal followed the edge of the continent.

As we turned south toward West Behm Canal the next morning, I gave thanks that except for rain in the Behm Canal itself, we had enjoyed an almost-perfect trip: we had seen towering cliffs and waterfalls in Punchbowl Cove and experienced the mysteries of a fog-shrouded landscape in Walker Cove.

2.4 YES BAY
Through the Lens of a Fishing Lodge

We knew we were approaching the Yes Bay sport-fishing lodge when we saw clusters of identical white runabouts bobbing among the rocks. The Alaskan fishing lodge is the lens through which many visitors see Alaska and I was curious about that perspective. The Yes Bay Lodge, one of only a handful that serves meals to drop-in boaters, promised an opportunity to see a lodge operation up close. And after almost a week in the wilderness of Misty Fiords National Monument, I was ready for a meal cooked by someone else.

We entered the bay under high cliffs and soon saw the low-profile brown lodge next to the mouth of the Yes River. In the distance, green marshes gave way to mountains topped by snow.

The name "Yes" sounds like an affirmation of the worth of the river and bay, but it comes from the Tlingit word *Yaas*, meaning "mussels," and refers to the numerous blue mussels that carpet the bay's rocks at low tide.

We motored past the lodge and anchored in a small cove a short distance from the dock, then took the dinghy over to the resort. As we walked to the lodge, a burly man with a neatly trimmed beard and the red face of an outdoorsman overtook us. He introduced himself as Kevin Hack.

"This is my home," Kevin said, as we entered a large room with a cathedral ceiling, knotty-pine walls and polished floors. He motioned us into an office, where he pointed

The Yes Bay Lodge attracts sports fishermen from all over the world.

to a black-and-white picture of cannery buildings on the wall. "Twelve hundred people used to live here." He pointed to another photograph. "That's my father. He started this. I grew up here, now I'm raising my kids here."

A young woman registered us for dinner. "We have a wonderful chef. He's from Las Vegas."

Kevin encouraged us to look around and suggested we walk the nearby Forest Service Trail. We exited the lodge through a room full of brown boots and khaki-colored rain gear and found the trail behind the lodge. In the last week we had taken in a lot of scenery but all from the deck of our boat so I was glad to be walk-

A US Forest Service Trail leads along the Yes River.

ing in the forest. Sunlight filtered through a canopy of spruce and hemlock, lighting up a natural garden of devil's club, ferns and skunk cabbage. The trail's rough-hewn planks and its stepping stones neatly outlined by moss delighted me. As we walked we heard the constant gurgle of rushing water from the nearby Yes River, a prime source of salmon.

In the early days of the salmon industry, overfishing almost emptied Alaska's rivers of salmon. A hatchery on Lake McDonald at the head of the Yes River was part of the struggle to preserve those runs. The story behind that hatchery and the cannery business that it served is intriguing. I consider it a prime example of politics triumphing over common sense.

When the United States bought Alaska in 1867, American cannery companies were quick to see the potential of Alaska's salmon. By 1900, thirty canneries were operating across Southeast Alaska. By 1920 there were more than a hundred—most owned by corporations from outside Alaska. At first the canneries purchased salmon from Native fishermen, but they soon switched to using their own fish traps, massive structures of logs and nets placed to take advantage of known schooling and migration routes. The traps were so efficient they threatened the very existence of the salmon runs.

The traps became the symbol of outside interests raiding Alaskan resources. Alaskan fishermen, Native and white alike, considered these traps a threat to their livelihoods. The territorial legislature lacked the authority to act, though, and while the US congress introduced legislation and held hearings in Washington DC, it never limited traps, largely because of opposition from cannery companies.

Some fishermen turned to fish piracy, disguising their boats and stealing fish from the traps. As the Robin Hoods of fishermen, fish pirates are celebrated today in *Fish Pirate's Daughter*, a theatrical play shown regularly in Ketchikan.

Instead of limiting fishing, officials from the US Bureau of Fisheries turned to hatcheries as a solution to the rapid depletion of fish stocks. The hope was that hatchery

Workers built the Yes River trail without power tools.

culture could achieve a greater percentage of survival from egg to fry than wild spawning, so that fish runs could be increased without restricting harvesting.

The Yes Bay Hatchery, established in 1906, was the first US government hatchery in Alaska. Old photographs show an impressive operation: large wooden buildings, a tramway up the hillside to the lake, a pipeline to bring water to the hatchery, and houses for the workers.

The Yes Bay Hatchery operated until 1933 when a new US Commissioner of Fisheries, Frank T. Bell, made a tour of Alaska and ordered it closed, along with a hatchery on Afognak Island, Alaska, and seven others across the country. Bell believed that at a time of national economic hardship, hatcheries were a waste of public money and an unjustified public subsidy of a private industry.

Whether the Yes Bay Hatchery was effective is not known as no comprehensive analysis was made during its operation. Commercial salmon catches, which had peaked in the 1930s, declined steadily until the 1950s. One of the first actions the new Alaska legislature took after gaining statehood in 1959 was to ban fish traps. In 1977 the state limited the number of fishing boats. Under state management, the salmon rebounded and today the Alaska salmon fishery is considered an excellent example of sustainable resource management. When sport fishermen bring in their limit of salmon, they can thank good fisheries management by the State of Alaska for their success.

That success was visible on Yes Bay's docks when we returned from our walk to see sport-fishing boats arriving with their afternoon catches. As we watched guides expertly cleaning salmon on the dock, I remembered the last time we had caught a salmon and cleaned it on board. Splatters of fish blood had peppered the cockpit and the boat smelled of fish for days afterwards.

At 5:30 p.m. we entered the lodge, following the clink of glassware and sound of voices into the bar, a large comfortable room with sofas, armchairs and a stone fireplace. Casually dressed men of all ages stood talking in front of the fire or relaxing on sofas. I looked around with dismay to see that I was the only woman in the room.

I was gazing out a window at the water when one of the men came up to me.

"I saw your boat come in. Beautiful."

I opened my mouth to tell him what kind of boat it was, then closed it when he asked, "What kind of engine does it have?" Leave it to a man, I thought, to ask only about the engine. I referred him to Steve.

A few minutes later, Steve and I moved into the dining room where a young woman led us to a table beside a window overlooking the water. Crisp white cloths and sparkling glassware graced the tabletop. Aromas of cooking salmon wafted from the kitchen. A waiter brought Caesar salad with crab followed by teriyaki salmon, wild rice with sour cherries and butternut squash. The finale: hot baked bananas in a sauce topped with ice cream. I thought about our last dinner on *Osprey*—spaghetti with sauce from a jar—and was glad we had stopped here. And although the price ($40 each) was more than we usually paid for restaurant meals in our Seattle neighborhood, for Alaska it was quite reasonable.

When we went to pay our bill we met Kevin again and told him how much we had enjoyed the dinner.

"I tested 42 chefs and spent $8,000 in airfare and hotels before I found one that was good enough. It's hard to find a chef who knows how to cook fish."

I was curious about the challenges of running a fishing lodge in Alaska, so we arranged to meet with Kevin in the morning.

The building was quiet when we entered the large front doors at 9:00 a.m. the next day; all the customers were obviously out fishing. We stopped at the entryway to look at photographs of happy fishermen with their catch, then met Kevin in the office. He took us into the bar where we sat at a small wooden table.

Kevin explained that his family bought the lodge in the 1970s. The cannery at the site had closed in 1936.

"It isn't easy running a lodge in an isolated location. Our family spent 30 years figuring out how to do it. We don't hire anything out; we even own our own plane and tugboat. We have five different communication systems including three phone systems that together work only a third of the time."

Their season is short: May 31 to September 28. "In the winter, we fix all this." He gestured around the room. I looked at the deer head above the fireplace, the polished floor and the massive amounts of woodwork. Everything I looked at was immaculately kept.

"We have a diversity of customers."

I looked up in surprise when he said this, for the only diversity I remembered seeing in the customers last night was in their age and the size of their bald spots—hardly

The remains of the old Yes Bay Cannery can still be seen near the mouth of the Yes River.

the gender, racial and ethnic mix I thought of when I heard the word "diversity." Then I heard him say, "Investment bankers, soybean farmers, even a film producer."

Kevin next told us about the time he spent training his employees. "Our guides are professionals. But sometimes they come from places like Florida and don't know our ways so we have to teach them.

"Fisheries enforcement officers are here all the time. We follow all the rules strictly. In fact, we try to do better than the rules—for catch and release we allow only 25 percent of what the rules permit."

I had one more question for Kevin as we got up to go. "Are all your guests men?"

"This week was a Father's Day special: fathers and sons. The next group will be couples. We're family based."

Before we left Yes Bay that morning, we motored *Osprey* up the bay looking for the old tramway to the fish hatchery. But all we saw were a few rotting pilings. As we passed the lodge area on our way out, I saw rusty machinery across the river mouth from the lodge: the remains of the old cannery. Like many canneries it had been a victim of not just overfishing but also of changing technologies and economics.

Our visit to Yes Bay Lodge had given us a glimpse into another life: gourmet meals with gracious service, space to roam—and someone else to clean our fish. I looked forward to coming back in *Osprey* in future years for more good dinners. But the idea of spending a whole vacation here didn't appeal to me. The Yes Bay Lodge had created its own very pleasant world, but it wasn't the real Alaska. Many of its employees weren't even from this area. I thought of the small towns we would visit on the way north and the Alaskans we had yet to meet. Those experiences would help us see this rugged land through more than one lens.

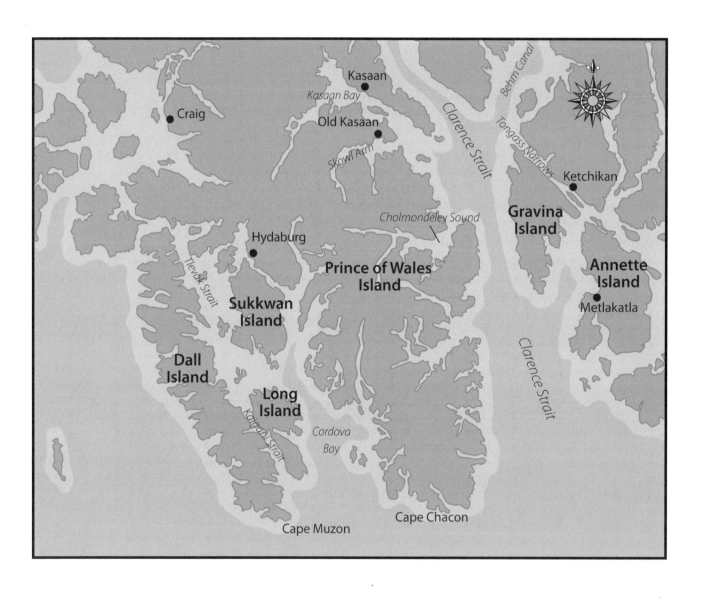

CHAPTER 3

IN THE LAND OF THE KAIGANI HAIDA

3.1 OLD KASAAN
Returning to Nature

Warm sunlight poured through the skylight at Ketchikan's Totem Heritage Center, lighting up totem poles with shapes of ravens, eagles and bears in weathered wood. Looking up at the poles, I admired their grace and art. But how much more exciting it would be, I thought, to find old totem poles in the forest.

Steve walked over to me and pointed out one of the interpretive displays. "Some of these poles come from Kasaan, a Haida village," he told me. "I think that's just a few miles from here on Prince of Wales Island."

That night we looked up Kasaan in the *US Coast Pilot* and learned it was three miles up the north shore of Skowl Arm on the southeast side of Prince of Wales Island. "No evidence of the village remains," reads the *Coast Pilot*, "other than a few weathered totem poles and a few graves."

Steve and I have been fascinated with Haida art and culture since a trip to the Haida homeland, Haida Gwaii (Queen Charlotte Islands) in British Columbia, in 1999. For centuries, the Haida had maintained a complex culture rich in artistic expression. At the time of first contact with Europeans, they were master mariners whose canoes were traded up and down the coast, and sophisticated and artistic carvers of totem poles, mortuary poles, masks and other ceremonial regalia. We knew that the Alaskan Haida, called Kaigani Haida, still maintained ties to their homeland.

We thought it would be fun to explore a Haida site in Alaska. My former college roommate, Julie, a biology professor from Pennsylvania, was joining us the next day for the leg of our trip north to Petersburg and I looked forward to sharing the experience with her. And while we were in the area, we would visit the totem park in New Kasaan a few miles away.

Two days later we left Ketchikan in a brisk northwesterly wind, crossing Clarence Strait close-hauled in boisterous seas that flattened to ripples once we

The Kasaan Totem Park in New Kasaan consists of replicated and renovated poles from Old Kasaan. The park has some of the finest examples of Haida poles in Southeast Alaska.

sailed into the lee of Kasaan Peninsula and into Skowl Arm. Forested islands dotted the denim-blue water while in the background snow-topped mountains rose in the island's interior.

We anchored off the village site in water exposed to the south and deeper than we would have liked. Like many Native towns, Old Kasaan offered good landing sites for canoes but poor anchorages. But the calm, sunny weather made a perfect day for exploring the old village. Although Haida occupied Old Kasaan from the 1700s to 1900, the name "Kasaan" is Tlingit in origin and means "pretty town," most appropriate on such a sunny day.

In the late 1800s Old Kasaan was a frequent stop for steamships. Tourists were treated to a scene of carved poles standing guard over large square houses backed by the dense forest while graceful canoes lined the beach. Kasaan was also known for its powerful chiefs, including Chief Skowal for whom Skowl Arm was named. In front of Skowal's house stood a very unusual totem pole; its top figure was that of a Haida Eagle while carvings below represented white men, depicted with curly hair and beards. Researchers have collected two different stories about this pole: The first says it mocks the Russians for their failure to convert Skowal to Christianity; the other that it commemorates his conversion.

Most of the poles were sold to museums, traded for favors, burned by vandals, or stolen by collectors. Chief Skowal's pole is now in the basement of the Totem Heritage Center. The Civilian Conservation Corps removed the best remaining poles for preservation and copying in the 1930s. We would see those reproductions the next day at New Kasaan.

From our anchorage we could see silvery gray poles through a fringe of trees. We motored ashore in the dinghy and landed on a pebble beach, then pushed aside branches to get to the poles: they towered above us, their smooth surfaces polished gray by age and weather. Near the top of one of the poles, a small carved face peered down at me. Amorphous shapes enveloped in moss and brush topped the poles. Unrecognizable now, those forms might once have been of eagles, ravens or whales.

Steve and I marveled at the massive poles, tilted but still firmly anchored after 100 years. Meanwhile, Julie was contemplating the trees whose thick trunks towered above the poles. "What are they? They're huge!"

"I think they're spruce," I told her, pointing out the scaly bark and straight trunks. The trees were massive. From their size, I would have guessed they were old growth, but as they were located in the midst of a former village site where houses would have crowded out the trees, they were probably second growth.

I went back to inspecting the poles. They puzzled me. Lacking carvings, their smooth surfaces looked like house poles, but if that was the case, the houses would have been immediately behind them. In Haida Gwaii we had learned to recognize longhouse sites by depressions in the ground outlined by fallen timbers. Nothing like that was visible or even possible here. Inland of the poles the ground rose steeply in a tangle of trees and undergrowth.

"These can't be house poles. Where are the house sites?"

"You're right," said Steve, looking uphill. "These must be freestanding memorial poles. But it's odd they have so little carving on them."

We knew that the Haida would not want strangers among their memorial poles so we decided to look for the village site. I had seen what might be a midden (a Native refuse heap that looks like a grassy mound) around a small point to the east so we climbed back into the dinghy. At the midden site we clawed our way through brambles and scrambled under overhanging branches until we reached a point where the ground leveled out. We found a horizontal beam about 30 feet long supported by two nearly vertical posts at each end that told us we had found the house sites. Exploring further, we found the telltale outlines of fallen houses hidden under blankets of moss. Nearby lay a full-length totem pole, face up, with bumps and notches of carvings still visible under moss. Whether the figures were bears, wolves or people we couldn't tell. The pole once stood in front of somebody's house, perhaps telling a story of their ancestors. Raising the pole would have been a great occasion with feasting and gifts—a potlatch.

As we stood looking at the fallen totem pole, a raven clonked above our heads and another answered from the beach below.

The Haida of Kasaan tell a story of how a raven saved them from starvation and eventually led them to Kasaan. Sometime in the 1700s food became scarce on Graham Island, the northernmost island of Haida Gwaii (Queen Charlotte Islands) and the closest to Alaska. A group of Haida, called "muddy mouths" because they were forced to eat food from the ground rather than the sea, looked north and saw land. They built large rafts and crossed the Dixon Entrance, landing at Cape Muzon on Dall Island (west of Prince of Wales Island) near Kaigani. There they prospered. When word of their success got back to Graham Island, more of their people followed them. But this party met bad weather, rain and wind, and missed Cape Muzon, landing instead on Cape Chacon on Prince of Wales Island. They moved north in search of food but found little. With winter coming they grew worried. They noticed that every day a raven came to their camp, flew in figure eights, then soared off in the same direction. Finally, the Haida sent two canoes after the raven, following him to a stream full of dog salmon in Cholmondeley Sound. Later they found (Old) Kasaan one sound farther north, and relocated there.

The houses and totem poles that once graced Old Kasaan are slowly returning to the forest from which they came.

We lingered for awhile, listening to ravens croak and enjoying the peace and quiet of the forest. Awed by the vestiges of this ancient village, I felt as if I had been touched by another era.

When we got back to *Osprey*, we sat in

the cockpit, basking in the sunlight and gathering energy to pull up the anchor to move to a more protected spot for the night.

"That's a magical place," said Julie. "I could see you and Steve enjoyed exploring the old village site. But I was awed by the trees."

Julie's comment made me think. I was looking for human history while she was searching for natural history. But perhaps the important story at Kasaan was of nature ultimately overtaking history and returning the site to the trees, moss and animals. In just a few years, the remaining traces of Old Kasaan would disappear and only the forest would remain.

In *Out of the Silence* (1971), the Haida artist Bill Reid wrote that "an ugly building becomes a beautiful ruin." On the page opposite these words is a black-and-white photo of a moss-covered house frame in Old Kasaan. Reid wrote about how ruins become a natural and beautiful symbol of the cycle of life—of death, decay and re-birth. "This was not what the creators intended," Reid continued, speaking of our appreciation of decayed Native art. "These were objects of bright pride, to be admired in the newness of their crisp curved lines."

We had seen the beautiful ruins: tomorrow we would go to the totem park in New Kasaan to view these "objects of bright pride."

3.2 NEW KASAAN
Objects of Bright Pride

Had someone taken a crude razor and given the Kasaan Peninsula a bad haircut? Brown gashes of crude roads sliced up the new green growth, while stumps like white pock-

marks scarred the terrain. It was a sobering sight and for a few minutes the three of us said nothing as we took in the new landscape.

Motoring up Kasaan Bay along the Peninsula, we were so intent on inspecting the clear-cut we didn't notice the gust traveling across the water until the boat suddenly heeled over so hard Julie and I both had to grab the dodger for support while Steve struggled with the wheel.

A few minutes later, though, we were gliding through calm water as if nothing had happened. We had just passed by a low valley that cut through the Kasaan

The marina at New Kasaan provides convenient moorage while touring the Kasaan Totem Park but is unsafe in a southerly wind.

Peninsula from Clarence Strait to the north—and the wind was rushing through that gap.

Ahead, the village of New Kasaan (or simply Kasaan as it is known today) was coming into view—a string of modest houses huddled along the shore of a crescent-shaped cove. The clear-cut area looming above gave what would otherwise have been a pleasant town a desolate look.

Clear-cuts near Native villages are something we would see many times in the months ahead. When congress passed the Alaska Native Claims Settlement Act, they transferred forest lands surrounding villages to regional and village corporations, thereby removing them from the Tongass National Forest and its Land Management Plan, a strategy that environmentalists had worked hard to create. Many, but not all, Native corporations have taken advantage of that transfer to raise revenue by clear-cutting.

A small marina with a collection of sport-fishing boats, a tugboat and a seaplane, occupied the center of the bay. Our calls on the radio to the village went unanswered, so we tied up on the outermost float. Several Native children played on the floats nearby.

Residents of Old Kasaan began moving to (New) Kasaan in the late 1800s, first to work in a copper mine on the Kasaan Peninsula, later to log for a sawmill in Kasaan itself, and finally to work in a salmon cannery established there in 1902. The cannery burned down and was rebuilt three times and had six different owners over the years. It finally ended operations in 1953. With the closure of the cannery, many residents moved to Ketchikan. The 2000 census reported 39 people living in Kasaan, of which 20 were white and 15 Native.

We had expected a sign or a map to tell us the location of the totem park, but found nothing. I felt a prick of irritation at the Alaska tourist industry that so often assumed we would be on guided tours in somebody else's boat.

We headed off toward what we hoped was the center of town, following a boardwalk that led along the beach and onto a dirt road. The road passed a row of small houses whose log walls, covered porches extending along the cabin fronts, and yards full of abandoned cars made me think of Appalachia. From the houses, we crossed through the middle of town where we found a small library and community center. There was also a recycling depot with bins for glass and newspapers all painted in uniform gray.

We kept walking toward the shore of Kasaan Bay, passing a cottage surrounded by a lush lawn and well-tended gardens. I was beginning to wonder if we were lost when we saw a burly-looking man

A trail leads to the Kasaan Totem Park over this wooden bridge.

struggling to hitch a trailer to his pickup. Behind him a house still sported its Christmas lights. He stopped working to talk to us.

"The trail to the park starts over there." He pointed toward some trees at the end of the road. "It's about as far to the park as it is back to the marina."

The trail led through a second-growth forest of thin-trunked spruce and hemlock. Skunk cabbages grew in the underbrush, their yellow flowers emitting a strong odor. The ground beneath our feet felt springy from an accumulation of evergreen needles. Twenty minutes later, we reached a small wooden bridge crossing a stream. I walked across first and set the frail bridge bouncing. While Julie and Steve waited for it to settle down, I went ahead. Around a corner stood a tall pole showing the figures of a bear, ravens and eagle. Intricately carved in the Haida style and painted in subtle colors it almost blended into the forest.

"We're here!" I yelled.

A little farther in we found a plain stout pole with a bear figure clinging to its smooth surface. Its unadorned chiseled look reminded us of the memorial poles in Old Kasaan. For the next hour, the three of us wandered around the park, admiring the carvings scattered among the trees: nine all together. I noticed that most, but not all, had two-dimensional figures wrapped around the pole, similar to those in Haida Gwaii. There was also a giant wooden bear rearing out of a patch of salal and a whale swimming atop a short pole—figures that I later learned were grave markers.

Although the poles looked recent to me, many of them are restored originals rescued from Old Kasaan by the Civilian Conservation Corps (CCC) during the Depression. The pole I had come upon among the trees near the entrance to the park, with figures of a bear, ravens and eagle, was a restored original, one of two almost identical poles that had stood in front of Chief Skowal's house at Old Kasaan. We had seen its twin on the ground covered with moss at Old Kasaan the day before. Another restored pole, known as the Spencer Pole, includes a figure of a white man in topcoat and hat. It was commissioned by a woman from Kasaan who had married a white photographer named Spencer. Other poles, including the memorial pole with the bear on top, are replicas. All the poles, restorations or replications originated in Old Kasaan.

An old community house stood almost hidden amongst the trees. Moss grew on its roof shingles and the boards around the fire hole lay askew. An unpainted totem pole stood out front, its carvings gray with age. I gave a door in the building's side wall a push and it swung open with a creak. Inside, sunlight filtered through the fire hole. In the shadows at the far end, three wooden statues stared back at me with large green eyes set in white faces. They were frightening and reminded me of how isolated we were. A shrill shriek from outside interrupted the quiet. My heart racing, I ran outside just in time to see a raven flying overhead.

I was relieved to find Julie and Steve nearby. We walked down to the beach, seated ourselves on logs, and gazed out over a peaceful scene—a shallow bay ringed by forest. Behind us the community house with its tall frontal pole sat silent and empty, a reminder of a past era.

Placed on the exact same site, the community house and its carvings are a re-creation

A replica of Chief Sonihat's Whale House sits at the site of the original house.

of Whale House, built in 1880 by Sonihat, a powerful chief of the Eagle clan. Its surroundings would have been different then, with people going about their daily affairs: women drying salmon, men carving canoes, children playing.

I thought about Kasaan Totem Park in light of what we had seen in Old Kasaan. The designers of the Kasaan Totem Park had re-created the setting of an abandoned village with newer poles that could be seen, to quote Bill Reid, as "objects of bright pride." But something was missing, and that was the connection to the daily lives of the aboriginal people. The original pole had not been carved to just be admired—it had a purpose and held great meaning in this complex society. To see poles in the context of village life, we would have to visit another Haida village: Hydaburg.

3.3   HYDABURG
A Festive Stop on the West Coast of Prince of Wales Island

Two days after we left New Kasaan in June 2006, we picked up a local newspaper in the town of Meyers Chuck and learned of a festival celebrating the Haida culture at Hydaburg on the west side of Prince of Wales Island. The chance to visit a more active Haida village and to meet local people appealed to us. And the date—July 29—was right for a stop on our way south.

The morning before the festival, we left the town of Craig, heading south. It was a rare sunny day with just a whisper of a breeze rippling the water, ideal for motoring through the narrow winding channels of the region. We had timed our departure to pass through Tlevak Narrows at slack water. Known locally as Skookum Chuck, the narrows are famous for twists in the channel including a treacherous 90-degree turn and swirling currents. As we approached the dangerous corner, I watched anxiously for whirlpools, but the water was quiet and *Osprey* glided through uneventfully. From Skookum Chuck we turned east through a maze of tree-covered islands to Sukkwan Narrows. As we exited Sukkwan, the village of Hydaburg came into view, spread along the shore and climbing the hillside. It looked more substantial than I would have expected for a community of only 382 (2000 census). We could see a school

The Hydaburg Totem Park, next to the school, is an important part of the town.

and warehouses on the waterfront, while church spires and a small forest of totem poles rose from the town center.

No one answered our hails on the radio to the Hydaburg harbormaster, and when we pulled into a vacant slip the marina was quiet. It appeared that we were the only visitors. Discarded batteries, piles of abandoned fishnets and rusty crab traps littered the dock.

We locked up *Osprey* and headed up the dock, passing three salmon seiners named *Haida Maid, Haida Girl* and *Haida Spirit.* Their peeling paint spoke of better days. Beyond the seiners floated several neatly painted salmon trollers and a beautifully carved dugout canoe. Finally, near the ramp we spotted people: a group of children swimming under the watchful eye of a young woman weaving a cedar-bark necklace.

"Where are you from?" she asked us, a welcoming smile lighting up her bronze face.

"Seattle," we told her, then asked, "Is it okay to tie up at a vacant slip? Is there a harbormaster?"

"There's no harbormaster anymore. The state doesn't take care of the dock, so the city is taking it back." She looked around at the aging wooden floats with their collection of litter, then laughed. "So it can stay just like it is."

A dirt road lined by tall thimbleberry bushes led toward town. As we stopped to taste the bright-red berries, a raven clonked and clacked raucously from a nearby spruce tree. I wondered if he was welcoming us, warning us, or just chatting.

We continued on past a row of small, prefabricated houses into the center of town where the totem park occupied a prominent position between a small white church and a large modern school building. Colorful totems framed a view of Sukkwan Strait and islands to the west.

The town of Hydaburg was created in 1911 when the Haida villages of Howkan, Klinkwan and Sukkwan consolidated in order to provide their children with better schooling. As at Kasaan, the Civilian Conservation Corps retrieved totem poles from former village sites and hired local Native workers to restore some of them and replicate others. Out of this effort came the Hydaburg Totem Park.

Most of the poles in the park have bold, uncluttered figures, each intertwined with the figures above and below. They possess large prominent heads characteristic of Haida carvings. But one pole caught our attention with its depictions of a man in uniform, an eagle and two nude white men crouching at the top. The crouching men resembled the watchmen we had seen on poles at Haida Gwaii, but with smaller heads and wearing red, white and blue striped top hats instead of traditional conical hats. The pole struck me as a parody of a traditional totem pole. I learned later that nude figures were often a protest against

Carvings of nude white men at the top of a totem pole at Hydaburg may have been placed there to protest non-Native interference in Native affairs.

non-Native interference and that the carvings might have been intended to ridicule the whites.

We were contemplating this strange pole when a stocky man with graying dark hair approached us.

"Those white men have been around for a long time." He pointed to the watchmen. "Some of those poles are over 100 years old." When he saw that he had our attention, he continued. "White men didn't appreciate us. Even in my mother's time, we weren't allowed to speak our own language. I remember my mother and a friend chattering away. When the minister walked by, they switched to English."

This frank criticism of our race was delivered in such an informative tone that I didn't take it personally. Still, I hesitated to ask about the Haida festival. Maybe we wouldn't be welcome. I asked instead about the necklace of blue beads he was wearing over his T-shirt. The beads resembled trade beads, brought to the northwest by fur traders.

"It's for the festival tomorrow."

A middle-aged woman came over and joined the conversation. "I hope you'll come. It starts at one o'clock. The children have been learning skills all week, and tomorrow they'll show them off. And there will be a potluck dinner afterwards. Guests don't have to bring anything."

Back at the marina, a young man with a friendly face greeted us. "I'm in charge of the canoe races tomorrow."

"How many canoes will you have?" I asked him.

"Just the one." He pointed to the dugout we'd seen earlier. "We'll have different crews and we'll time them. That way everything will be equal. We'll start at 10 o'clock."

Although I wasn't convinced that a canoe race with one canoe could be very exciting, we walked to the ramp the next morning. But the marina was quiet; the canoe floating empty.

A wrestling match between two grandmothers was one of the highlights of the 2006 Hydaburg cultural festival.

"Oh well," said Steve. "We'll see what happens at one o'clock. If the festival is a dud, we can always go anchor in the islands somewhere."

When we arrived at the totem park just before 1:00 p.m., I was relieved to see a bustling scene of good-natured activity. A group of older women sat around the base of a pole stringing beads. Children ran amongst the poles chattering excitedly. This was how a totem park should be, I thought—in the middle of a busy village, and surrounded by people, not hidden away in the forest like the one in Kasaan.

In the center of the park the young man who told us about the canoe races was busy organizing wrestling matches.

"Everybody gets to wrestle at least once," he was telling the kids. "You keep wrestling until somebody pins you down."

I watched for awhile as pairs of children turned into maelstroms of arms and legs, then wandered over to talk to a woman stringing beads. Between the beads she placed hollow wood tubes that she told me were branches from devil's club.

"Can I take your picture?" I asked.

"Only if you root for me when I wrestle."

"You're going to wrestle?" I looked doubtfully at her ample figure and gray hair.

"Of course."

"Okay. I'll root for you. What's your name?"

"Eileen."

I looked back at the wrestling ring where two beefy teenage boys crouched next to the young man. In one quick movement, he pinned them both to the ground.

"Time for the grandmothers," he announced.

Eileen and another woman moved into the circle and took positions. Everyone else crowded around, talking and laughing excitedly. This was obviously a big event. Eileen crossed her arms and looked angrily at the crowd. "I don't hear much cheering. I'm not going to wrestle without more cheers." Cheers erupted and the two women faced off. In seconds, both women were on the ground struggling with each other, the crowd egging them on.

"Go, Eileen!" I yelled. In the confusion, I wasn't sure who won, but I think it was Eileen.

Children played tug-of-war, raced across the park carrying sand-filled burlap bags

While children race metal canoes, elders and toddlers paddle around the marina in an authentic dugout canoe.

representing slain deer, and shot paper deer with plastic bows and arrows. After each contest adults handed out necklaces. While Steve took a turn with the bow and arrows I looked around at the other adults. We seemed to be the only tourists but I noticed a curly-haired woman dressed in neatly pressed slacks and a jacket writing in a notebook. Thinking she might be a government official or a reporter, I struck up a conversation with her and learned she was a teacher from Wasilla near Anchorage. Her school had sent her to observe Hydaburg's culture week with the thought they could do something similar.

Just then I heard an announcement about the canoe races. We joined the crowd walking back to the marina where two aluminum canoes now floated next to the dugout. It was to be more than a one-canoe race after all. Aluminum canoes might not be authentic, but they did the job. I watched with amusement as children raced back and forth in shifts from the marina to the beach. Paddles flailing, some of the younger ones took quite a while to make the crossing but they all had a great time. Meanwhile, adults and toddlers crowded into the dugout and paddled sedately around the marina.

When the racers left their canoes and started to disappear up the hill, we followed them to a gymnasium. Inside the children were handing out bottles of Purple Mountain Pure water from Metlakatla while women were putting dishes out on serving tables. A delicious aroma of cooked salmon wafted through the air. We took our places in line at the serving tables and helped ourselves to sea asparagus, dried seaweed, salmon, halibut and rice. The salmon had been prepared in many ways: smoked, grilled, and baked, in cheese with potatoes, and with onions.

I tentatively tried the sea asparagus—thin green branches coated with black herring eggs. Its texture reminded me of crisp spaghetti, while the herring eggs added crunch and gave it a fishy taste. Unsure of how to eat the dried seaweed, I watched the people around me. They were crunching on it like candy. My first bite tasted like paper, so I put it aside and focused on the fish, which was delicious.

Hydaburg schoolchildren dance at the Hydaburg Cultural Festival in regalia they made themselves.

When everyone had finished eating and children had cleared away the plates, a woman walked into the center of the gymnasium and announced a regalia contest. "They made these regalia themselves," she said as children wearing woven spruce hats, button blankets and carved masks filed into the room. There was nothing amateurish about the regalia, which looked well cut and neatly decorated. One young woman wore a black dress in a style suitable for a cocktail party but decorated with buttons and red trim. First place, awarded from the volume of applause, went to a young girl in a cedar-bark hat and button blanket trimmed in sea-otter fur.

As the last winner accepted his award,

the beat of drums sounded from outside, and a small band of adults carrying Native drums entered. This was the signal for the children to begin dancing. I expected the usual slow shuffling dances we had seen at tourist destinations in Alaska and British Columbia, but these dancers moved with sureness and ease, acting out stories from myths. In the final dance, two characters pantomimed gambling and the audience filed by to throw money on a blanket for next year's culture week. It was an event most worthy of a donation, I thought, as I added a bill to the blanket.

The dancers filed out and a woman wearing a button blanket came forward and took the microphone. "Would all the veterans please stand." Men of all ages throughout the room stood up, Steve among them.

"We have been pursuing our culture for the last week. Your willingness to serve gives us the liberty to do that."

As we walked back toward the marina in the evening light, I thought about how Steve and I had been granted a privileged glimpse into the modern-day workings of a culture nearly as old as the ice-carved landscape. Plastic arrows, aluminum canoes, beautifully carved regalia, and enthusiastic dancers had all helped create an educational, fun-filled day.

Near the marina, the raven screeched at us again from the spruce tree. This time I decided he was definitely welcoming us.

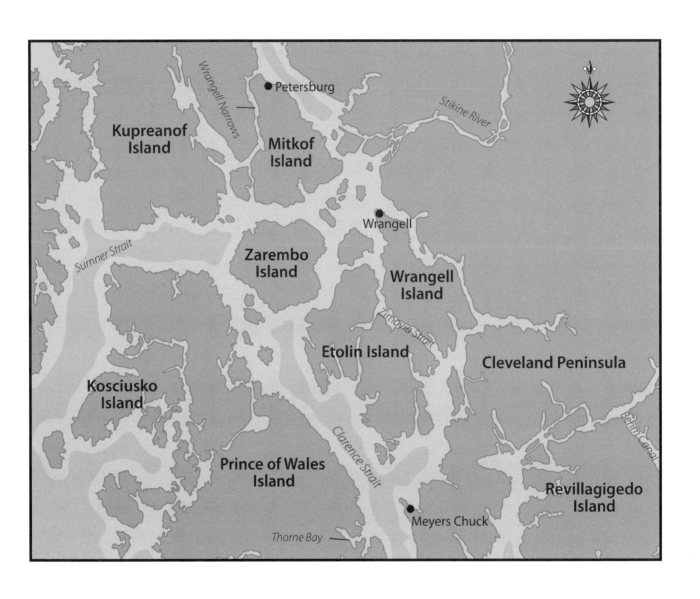

CHAPTER 4

CLARENCE STRAIT TO PETERSBURG

4.1 MEYERS CHUCK
Immortalized by Characters

As twilight darkened into night on our third trip to Meyers Chuck, in 2008, I looked out *Osprey*'s windows, expecting to see lights and to hear the hum of generators. But all around the harbor, dark windows looked back at me. We had arrived on June 7, too early in the year to see any of the summer residents.

Some people might say we had arrived several decades too late.

Meyers Chuck ("chuck" is Chinook jargon for a saltwater lagoon) is a small village in Clarence Strait known for its picturesque houses and attractive island-filled harbor. June Allen, writing for the online paper *SitNews Stories in the News* (*www.sitnews.us*) in 2002, noted that it is also one of those Alaskan towns that has been immortalized by the characters who lived there. With no road access or ferry dock, the access is by private boat or seaplane, and in the past its residents have lived isolated, and sometimes eccentric, lives.

In Meyers Chuck's most colorful years, shortly after World War II, its population consisted mainly of bachelor fishermen of Scandinavian descent. The fishermen, accustomed to living in confined quarters in their fishing boats, were quite happy to bed down in tiny cabins built of scavenged wood. Marian Glenz, a Meyers Chuck storekeeper who wrote a short memoir entitled *Meyers Chuck!* (1994, no publisher given), wrote of her customers, "Their requirements were plain and simple—a loaf of bread, fresh bait and a well-sharpened axe."

The best known of these bachelors was Arndt "Lonesome Pete" Pederson. According to Glenz, Pete would be so busy painting, brewing beer, gardening and telling stories to anyone who stopped at the dock that he didn't have time to chop wood. Instead, he would just shove a log through a window until the end reached the fireplace, then push it farther into the fireplace as it burned. To smoke fish he placed a screen across the top of his chimney and placed the fish on it, retrieving it with a ladder when it was ready.

Fishermen weren't the only residents of Meyers Chuck. Glenz tells of an old couple who sang "Onward Christian Soldiers" while they gardened, a 14-year-old boy who used a Schlitz Beer tray for a rudder on his fishing dory, and a photographer named Joe

Attractive wooden cottages line the shores of Meyers Chuck.

who had long flowing hair, a white beard and thought he was the second coming of Christ.

Retired prostitutes and the occasional fugitive from justice completed Meyers Chuck's populace.

We made our first visit to Meyers Chuck on our way north in 2006 with our friend Julie aboard. After sailing wing-and-wing up Clarence Strait in a boisterous southerly wind, we motored through a narrow channel into the oval harbor. Sunshine glanced off blue water and lit up small wooden houses perched on rocks along the shore and tucked in amongst trees on land. A public dock stretched along one side of the small bay.

Not wanting to maneuver *Osprey* around the dock in the strong wind, we dropped anchor and took the dinghy in. At the top of the ramp we found a bulletin board, a phone booth and a blue mailbox, all in a row.

I looked at the pickup time on the mailbox. There was one pickup a week, at 10:15 a.m. Tuesday and it was already 2:00 p.m. We had missed it.

We followed a trail through the village, passing small wooden houses that peeked out through the trees. One of our guidebooks had mentioned a general store in town

Stairs cut in the rocks lead to this small cottage on the west shore of Meyers Chuck

Meyers Chuck town center consists of a bulletin board, a telephone and a mailbox near the dock.

and Steve was hoping it sold marine supplies: *Osprey* needed a new switch for its bilge pump. So when we met our first resident, a dark-haired man chopping firewood, Steve asked if the store was still there.

"No, the store closed. The population has shrunk in the last twenty years. Only six people live here in the winter now."

Nevertheless, there was an art gallery. His wife would open it for us. She was visiting one of the other residents but would return soon.

We continued our walk, following the trail along the waterfront.

"There's your store," I said to Steve, pointing to an old green building with missing roof shingles and collapsing walls. Faded letters over a door read, "Candy, Pop, Fish Buyer, Gear."

This abandoned store in Meyers Chuck once served a year-round resident population that has now dwindled to only six.

Wandering through the village, I could see what Meyers Chuck's boosters meant by picturesque: there were old log cabins, driftwood fences and stairways built of tree rounds leading up cliffs to houses perched above.

We returned to the clearing to meet a woman in tie-dyed pants and an ochre-colored shirt who led us back to the gallery.

Inside the tiny one-room building, notecards and postcards were displayed on racks, and wooden bowls and pottery occupied the shelves. A quilt hung on a wall.

Julie and I each bought a pair of earrings made from otoliths (halibut ear bones) and several postcards.

"We can still mail them from here," I said, "even if we did miss this week's pickup. What's another week?"

The next morning, Steve looked out *Osprey*'s cabin window. "There's somebody at the post office and I haven't seen the mail plane yet. Maybe we can catch this week's mail after all."

The post office, a square building on pilings with the zip code 99903 printed on the front, was so tiny it seemed lost among the small cottages. Inside, the postmistress, a youngish woman, worked behind a counter. She stood near a large old-fashioned scale with movable weights.

She took our postcards and put them in a pile labeled "Seattle."

"But mine aren't for Seattle," Julie objected.

"We have three categories: Ketchikan, state and Seattle. Mail for New York, New Zealand, wherever, goes in the Seattle

The small art gallery at Meyers Chuck opens upon request and sells local arts and crafts.

pile." Seattle, which once bragged of being the gateway to Alaska, is now the gateway to the rest of the world for Southeast Alaskans.

Half an hour later we were walking up a hill above the harbor when a seaplane circled overhead, and then landed at the dock where several people stood waiting. I watched them walk away with large cardboard boxes and realized what a lifeline the mail plane was for the small village, where just buying a quart of milk required an eight-mile trip across the treacherous waters of Clarence Strait to Thorne Bay. The post office was the center of town.

As we left the harbor that afternoon, I was disappointed that we hadn't met any characters.

That winter, Joyce Swanson—whom we'd rescued from a bear in Glacier Park—gave me the names of two friends who lived in Meyers Chuck and we made our second trip there in 2007, stopping in early August on our way south. I was looking forward to meeting them and learning more about life in the small town. We entered the harbor in a flat calm on a beautiful sunny day and tied *Osprey* to the dock.

"Do you know which houses these people live in?" Steve asked.

"No. I don't. And I don't remember their names either."

"Well, how are we going to find them then?"

"Both are teachers on Whidbey Island. Somebody will recognize that description and be able to tell us where they live." I felt foolish that I hadn't brought their contact information.

We needn't have worried. Walking through the village an hour later, a plump, round-faced woman with graying hair called to us from the porch of a small house.

"Are you the folks from *Osprey*? I saw your boat come in. I'm Cathy, a friend of Joyce Swanson."

Later that afternoon, Cathy and her friend Cheri Meyers, a thin-faced woman with short-cropped hair, joined us for wine and cheese in *Osprey*'s cockpit.

Passing Cheri a glass of wine, I asked her, "Are you related to the Meyers of Meyers Chuck?"

"Yes. I had a couple of great-uncles who lived here and fished. Someone putting names on maps asked them what they called this place. They said, 'We don't call it anything.' The response was, 'Well, what's your name then?'"

Our third trip there, in 2008, was on our way north in early June. Once again we arrived on a beautiful sunny day and took *Osprey* to the dock.

While Steve changed *Osprey*'s engine oil, I took my camera ashore. The old store we had first seen in 2006 was gone, leaving a bare spot on the beach. Its absence saddened me but seemed inevitable.

In a shed next to an empty cabin, a collection of old Coleman lanterns, ranging from rusty skeletons to almost new, hung from a rafter. Alaskans are known for never throwing anything away in case they might need it for spare parts. I was intrigued to learn that even people who didn't live here year-round developed this habit.

The 1940 census counted 107 people living in Meyers Chuck. Just 10 years later, the census reported 51. By 1960 only 27 people lived here year-round. The 2000 census

A portable sawmill provides lumber for construction at Meyers Chuck.

recorded 48 houses in the small town, 39 of which were seasonally occupied, meaning that the majority are summer residences.

I sat down on a log to enjoy the scenery and was immediately struck by the silence. I heard no human voices or any of the other background sounds I might expect in a town—no lawnmowers, chainsaws or doors opening and closing. This wasn't wilderness—there were houses all around me. In fact, the small wooden houses with shingled siding added to the charm of the harbor. The trill of an eagle broke the silence, followed by the clonk of a raven in the forest behind the houses.

The next morning I was out in my kayak when I heard the drone of what sounded like a very large chainsaw. Returning to the dock, I walked up the ramp and found Steve watching a man in earmuffs cutting lumber with a portable sawmill. The blade was slicing through a massive tree trunk, producing solid-looking planks.

"I talked to him before he started sawing," Steve told me as we got *Osprey* ready to leave. "Last year the villagers used the sawmill to cut lumber to replace a house for one of the women."

The notion of a summer village where residents care enough about each other to help build a new house for one of their neighbors in need made me want to know more about them. So when we returned to Seattle, I sent Cathy and Cheri an email. They replied promptly. Several of the year-round residents are commercial fishermen, one works for a dredging company and another is retired. The more than forty summer residents all stay for a good part of the summer, or longer. A few have winter homes in Ketchikan, but most are from down south: Washington, California or Arizona. Some are artists, others commercial fishermen, and some cut lumber to sell to other residents. They all know each other and have community potlucks throughout the summer months.

Although Meyers Chuck is no longer the home of eccentric bachelor fishermen, it is still a memorable place with a strong sense of community—and a true Alaskan spirit.

4.2   WRANGELL
A Western Town

In 2006 we were sailing north up Zimovia Strait to the town of Wrangell when the rain hit. It drummed so hard on the sails and deck that we had to shout to hear each other over the noise. While Steve steered, Julie and I peered anxiously through the torrential downpour searching for the beacons that marked the narrow, twisting channel. This was not a good place to lose visibility. Then, suddenly, we crossed from blue water to brown. The line was so sharp and the color variance so marked that I felt a flash of fear as we crossed it. Could we be entering shallow water? But it was just the plume of the Stikine River, carrying silt-laden waters from glaciers in British Columbia. Its name comes from the Tlingit word *Shtax' Héen*, meaning "cloudy river." Once a major trade route to the

Wrangell's older storefronts with verandas and murals on their walls are a reminder of its gold-rush history.

vast interior of what is now British Columbia, the river is the raison d'être for Wrangell's existence.

The rain slacked off and the town emerged from the mist. When we radioed the harbormaster, he gave us a choice between rafting up with other boats at the town marina or tying up at a summer moorage next to the new cruise-ship dock. We chose the summer moorage because it was close to the town center.

We had only 24 hours to spend there, as we were on our way to Petersburg where Julie had a plane reservation to return home.

The cruise-ship dock was vacant, and when we walked into town we found it quiet. Quaint false-fronted buildings with verandas over the sidewalk providing a covered walkway lined the north side of the street, while 1950s-style sheet-metal buildings dominated the south.

"It looks like a town in a western," said Julie, looking at the north side. "Even its name sounds western."

Despite the light rain, a few people were out on the street. From their purposeful walks, I assumed they were locals rather than tourists. But they all found time to smile at us and say hello.

A woman wearing a jacket unzipped over an arm cast spoke to us as she passed. "When I don't wear a jacket, it rains." I puzzled over this statement since it appeared that it also rained when she did wear a jacket.

We passed clothing shops, a cell-phone outlet, a drugstore, two hardware stores and an insurance agency.

"It's nice to see stores where the people who live here can shop," I said, thinking of the jewelry shops in Ketchikan.

I spotted a grocery store across the street and crossed over to check its hours. A young woman held the door open for me.

"Do you work here?" I asked. "I was wondering when it opens in the morning."

She laughed. "No. I don't work here. But it opens at eight. This is a small town. We all know things like that."

Wrangell hasn't always been such an orderly and friendly town. Exhibits at the Wrangell Museum include quotes describing the horrors of the town's early days: rag-tag buildings, muddy streets, hillsides of stumps, and lawless inhabitants.

Despite these early-day horrors, Wrangell residents are proud of its history—and most particularly of the fact that four different nations have occupied it and three gold rushes spurred its growth.

The Tlingit nation was the first to claim this area. From their village on Zimovia Strait, south of present-day Wrangell, they fiercely guarded their right to trade on the Stikine River. The Russians arrived next. In 1833 Baron von Wrangel, the Governor General of Russian America, sent troops to build a fort, called Redoubt St. Dionysius. His goal was to arrive before the British Hudson's Bay Company to stop them from trading in the Stikine River. In 1839, in exchange for British withdrawal of their claims to Russian America, the Russians leased the post to the Hudson's Bay Company, which renamed it Fort Stikine. The British flag came down in 1867 when the US bought Alaska from the Russians. The US Army, which occupied the site for a few years after 1867, built another fort and called it Fort Wrangell.

The first gold rush was the Stikine Gold Rush, started in 1861 when a French Canadian discovered gold on the nearby banks of the Stikine River. That rush soon dwindled to nothing, and Wrangell with it. The town came to life again in 1873 during the Cassiar Gold Rush at the top of the Stikine in British Columbia. Overnight, Wrangell became a riverboat center. Boats transported hundreds of men to the goldfields and brought them back in the fall. Many of the men overwintered in Wrangell, spending their hard-earned gold in cook tents, taverns, gambling dens and dance halls. It was a time of celebration and rowdiness. For three years, Wrangell was the biggest town in Alaska and the only "white man's town" other than Sitka. But like the Stikine Rush, the Cassiar Rush was short-lived.

When the Klondike Gold Rush started

The plume of the Stikine River, made almost white by its burden of glacial flour, sweeps by the town of Wrangell.

in 1896, Wrangell was ready for it. They knew about stampedes and what gold could do for the town. Wrangell boosters touted the Stikine River route to the Klondike: up the Stikine to Telegraph Creek in British Columbia, then overland to the Klondike. Advertised as the way to avoid the dangers of the mountain passes of White Pass and Chilkoot, it was instead a quagmire of almost-impassible swamps. Those few who made it to the goldfields by this route arrived too late to get any gold. For Wrangell, the boom was soon over.

Today, Wrangell has a population of approximately 2,000 and is primarily a fishing and logging town with a small tourist industry.

A Hike Up Mount Dewey

On our second trip to Wrangell, in 2007, Steve and I found ourselves with time on our hands. Normally when we visit a town we have so many errands—grocery shopping, parts to hunt down, mail to pick up at the post office—that we barely have time to see a town's tourist attractions. But this time everything on *Osprey* was working fine and we planned to do our shopping in Petersburg two days away. As for seeing the sites, we had already visited the museum, totem park and petroglyphs the year before. The only attraction we hadn't seen was the inside of Chief Shakes Tribal House, but that was closed and padlocked.

The identity of the carvers of the petroglyphs on Wrangell's north beach has been lost in time.

We were strolling down the sidewalk, admiring the murals on the western-style buildings, when Steve paused. "I need some coffee."

"There must be a coffee shop here somewhere," I said, although I couldn't remember seeing one.

We crossed the street and entered a small art gallery/adventure-tours office where a woman directed us to a second tour office in a trailer by the cruise-ship dock. There we found a young woman with a ready smile selling sweatshirts, wildlife books and adventure tours of bear watching and glacier touring. The hiss of an espresso machine and aroma of coffee welcomed us.

"Did you come on the ferry?" she asked us.

"No. We came on our own sailboat," Steve answered.

She stopped pouring coffee for a minute and looked at us. "That's quite an accomplishment."

When we told her we were looking for something to do, she picked up a map and handed it to us. "There's a good trail up the hill to Mount Dewey, she said, pointing to a dotted line on the map. "It's not that far and the view is magnificent."

We set off in search of the trail, walking through a neighborhood of older wood houses, nicely painted with colorful gardens. We were standing on a sidewalk puzzling over the map, which didn't seem to match the streets in front of us, when a pleasant-faced woman in her fifties came out of a yellow house and asked if she could help.

"We're looking for the Mount Dewey trail," I said.

She pointed toward a stairway. "Mount Dewey's the hill that John Muir climbed when he scared the Indians by building a bonfire."

I had read the story but hadn't known the name of the hill, or how close it was to town. Muir had described it simply as the "hill in back of the town." I became even more determined to find the trail.

When the naturalist John Muir made his first trip to Alaska in 1879, he got off the steamship at Wrangell. At first he was unable to find a place to stay or camp on the "stumpy, rocky, boggy ground." The town was "the most inhospitable place" he had ever seen. Eventually, a merchant offered him a room in his house, and from there Muir made short trips to nearby forests and streams. One night during a heavy rainstorm, he walked up Mount Dewey unobserved, enjoying "the glad rejoicing storm . . . singing through the woods." At the top he found dry twigs and soon had a roaring bonfire burning. Local Tlingits who could see the flames above the treetops, but not their source, were terrified. They called it a "sky-fire," an evil omen and asked a missionary to pray for them.

Above the stairway, we found a sign for the trail partially hidden in the brush. We followed the trail into the forest where it became a boardwalk of steep switchbacks zig-zagging up the hill. Sunlight filtered through the tall hemlocks and spruce and we could hear the occasional two-note song of a thrush. We enjoyed the smell of evergreens heated by the sun. It felt good to be getting exercise.

From the top of Mt. Dewey we could see over the town of Wrangell and down Zimovia Strait.

"You can tell we don't do a lot of climbing on the boat," said Steve as we paused to catch our breath.

Arriving at the hilltop we found a wooden viewing platform. From there we could see over the town and harbor all the way down Zimovia Strait to the snow-capped mountains beyond.

Nailed to a tree next to the platform was a sign showing a campfire symbol with a red cross-hatch through it and the words "No Campfires" written below.

Apparently the town didn't want any more sky-fires.

Chief Shakes Tribal House

"There goes the town," said Steve, watching a cruise ship tie up at Wrangell's town dock on our second morning there in 2008.

"It's a good thing we're leaving today," I replied, imagining hordes of tourists crowding the sidewalks as they looked for souvenirs. Then, I had a happier thought—maybe Chief Shakes Tribal House would open for the cruise-ship passengers and I would finally get to see inside.

I had wanted to explore the old tribal house since our first visit to Wrangell two years before, but the door had been padlocked both times we attempted to see it, with no indication of hours and no one present to answer our questions. We had to content ourselves with walking around the perimeter and admiring the collection of Tlingit totem poles ringing the island.

Steve interrupted my dreams of visiting the tribal house with a reminder that we needed to leave by noon to catch the tide up the Wrangell Narrows and we still had things to do.

"Okay," I told him. "But if the house is open, I want to see it. If we miss the tide, we can always stay another day."

"We'll see. We've already been here two days. It's time to move on."

From *Osprey*'s spot on the transient moorage dock in the town marina I could see Chief Shakes Island and the Tribal House, a replica of one of the large single-roomed structures originally occupied by an entire clan or extended family. (Common up and down the coast from Puget Sound through Southeast Alaska, these houses are also called longhouses, community houses, big houses and clan houses.)

The location of Chief Shakes Tribal House in the middle of Wrangell's inner harbor struck me as unusual for a tribal house when I first saw it. Historically, Native villages were placed in locations offering good visibility of approaching invaders, and the island did not meet this criteria. But the Nan-yan-yi Tlingits of Wrangell had moved to the island from their original village site on the Zimovia Strait to be nearer the Russian trading post of Redoubt St. Dionysius. In the 1930s, when the Civilian Conservation Corps wanted to build a model longhouse, they chose to build it on Chief Shakes Island because there were still elders in Wrangell who remembered how the old houses were built.

The island and tribal house were named for a series of chiefs, all named Shakes, several of whom had lived on Shakes Island. The first Chief Shakes won his name in a battle against Tsimshians from the Nass River area. The Tsimshians, led by Chief We-Shakes,

Visitors enter Chief Shakes House through this large bear figure.

Chief Shakes House contains many beautiful and historic carvings such as this devilfish (octopus) with abalone eyes.

had raided the Nan-yan-yi, seeking access to the Stikine River for its fish. But the Nan-yan-yi fought back, killing 150 of the opposing warriors. To escape the accustomed fate of a defeated chief, being made a slave, We-Shakes offered his killer-whale hat and his name to the Tlingit chief. "We-Shakes" became a Tlingit name, eventually shortened to "Shakes." (Among northwest Natives, names were considered to be property and could be traded or given to someone else.)

The house sat surrounded by grass in the shadow of a large cottonwood tree. The cottonwood seemed out of place in an area where spruce and hemlock were predominant, but it provided a green haven in the busy harbor. While Steve took the empty propane tank into town I remained at the marina to tidy up *Osprey*, glancing up at the island occasionally to look for activity. I had just finished and was taking some last-minute pictures of the marina when I saw a stream of tourists entering the tribal house.

I hurried up the dock and across to the island to join the line of tourists. Most of them appeared to be in their seventies or eighties, with a few younger people sprinkled among them. I felt out of place in my jeans and sweatshirt among women in neatly pressed slacks and sweaters, and half-expected to be stopped at the door. But no one asked for ID and I crawled through the small oval opening into the house along with the others.

My eyes took a minute to adjust to the darkness. The first thing I saw across the open room was a wooden screen painted with strange faces and figures, including two large green and yellow eyes. On either side of the screen stood two magnificent carved poles with their intricate carvings in warm cedar glowing in the faint light. To my right a large green frog with red spots on its back looked as if it were climbing the wall.

Floorboards creaked and thumped as tourists took seats on bare wooden benches lining the house's perimeter. I looked down to see floorboards dimpled by an adze and worn smooth and shiny from countless footsteps. I had seen similar dimples on boards on the outside of the house and knew it meant the boards were hand hewn, using traditional methods. I was awed by how authentic this house was.

A youngish woman in a red and black vest welcomed us to the tribal house and told us her name was Carol. She introduced an elder, Marjorie, who had come to give us their history.

Dressed in a black button blanket with a red border and a conical cedar-bark hat, Marjorie looked frail but spoke in a clear and strong voice that held the audience's attention.

"When the missionaries came, they thought we were savages. Does this look like the work of uneducated savages?" she asked, pointing to one of the carved posts. Exquisitely carved suction cups of an octopus foot flanked strange faces with beaked noses, abalone eyes and teeth made of the opercula of snails. Although some in the audience might find these figures alien, there was no quarrelling with the quality of the workmanship.

Marjorie went on to tell us how her people migrated down the Stikine River from the interior. When they came to an ice bridge over the river, the tribe sent an elderly couple ahead in a boat, under the bridge. When the couple didn't return, the tribe thought they were dead. Only their nephew had faith. He saw two figures a long way off and knew they were safe. The nephew and the rest of the people followed the couple under the ice bridge to their new home.

Marjorie talked about the totem poles outside the longhouse. The bear pole, a plain one with bear prints leading up to a bear figure on top, was the mayor's favorite. It told the story of how a bear led their people up a mountain during the great flood.

"It proves we had a flood story long before we heard about Noah's Ark. The missionaries didn't know we were already Christians. We just had another name for God."

Presbyterian missionaries were a major influence in Wrangell's history. The first missionary, Amanda McFarland,

An elder of the Stikine Tlingit tells legends of her tribe to tourists in Chief Shakes House.

arrived to start a school in 1877. S. Hall Young, the missionary who accompanied John Muir in his explorations, arrived a year later. Among other activities, Young and his wife established a girls' boarding school in Wrangell. In the Wrangell Museum, I had read a letter from the Presbyterian Church to the Natives of the town apologizing for the behavior of the missionaries, who had banned Tlingit culture and language from churches and schools. Marjorie's comments about missionaries told me the Tlingits had not forgotten the ill treatment they received.

After the cruise-ship passengers filed out, I saw that Steve had arrived during the talks, and we went up to thank Carol.

"It's a beautiful house," I told her.

"It needs restoration badly." She pointed to a hole near the floor where rotten wood had been removed. She explained that the Wrangell Cooperative Association, which owns the house, planned to apply for grants and had arranged for engineers to review its condition. Some solutions, such as pumping

An elaborate painted panel serves as a backdrop to presentations at Chief Shakes House.

epoxy into the rot, aren't acceptable to historic preservationists so aren't eligible for grants. "We're working on a traditional structure with modern methods and an inflexible bureaucracy. It's hard.

"I worry about global warming," Carol continued. I looked at her in surprise at the change in subject, but realized she was still talking about the challenge of melding ancient ways with modern reality.

"The plume of the Stikine River extends farther out into the bay every year" (due to the increased river flow from melting glaciers). "One year we were fishing where we had always fished and we were at the meeting of the river and the bay, where it had never been before. But we caught the best haul of fish ever. I don't know what it meant."

Carol locked the longhouse door and we walked out into the sunshine. Marjorie was standing on the lawn, looking up at the cottonwood tree.

"My grandmother planted it. She brought it down from the Stikine."

We left the harbor at 11:30 a.m., crossing the boundary between the brown water of the Stikine River and blue water of the sea on our way to Wrangell Narrows. We'd finally gotten to see the Chief Shakes Tribal House, but it took the arrival of a cruise ship to do it.

4.3 WRANGELL NARROWS
"Taken at the Flood . . ."

The flood tide surged north, swirling around the pilings of a nearby beacon and pushing *Osprey* almost a knot faster than our usual 6-knot cruising speed. On either side of us, dark green hills brooded under high clouds.

Wrangell Narrows' 60-plus navigational signals have given it the nickname of "Christmas Tree Lane."

We were en route from Wrangell to Petersburg via Wrangell Narrows, the narrow winding channel connecting Sumner Strait in the south to Frederick Sound in the north and called "Christmas Tree Lane" for its 60-plus navigation aids that blink red and green at night.

"Do you want to take us through?" asked Steve.

I gulped, but agreed. Steve takes the wheel in tricky passages more often than I do, a situation I don't mind because it's easier to just ride along and this also leaves me more time to take photographs. But this was our third trip through the narrows and I didn't need many photographs. Taking the wheel would be a challenge and an accomplishment. And I knew Steve would be in the cockpit with me, helping me look for dangers just as I did when he steered.

"Taking us through" meant three hours of being glued to the wheel, anxiously checking the paper chart, the chart plotter, and the water ahead to identify the next green or red beacon. Rocks, islands and mudflats line the channel and a stream of ferries, small cruise ships, tugs with barges, and fishing boats crowd the narrow channel, adding to the danger.

Tidal currents in Wrangell Narrows can reach speeds of 6 to 7 knots, but today, because we were in a period of neap tides, currents would be only 3 knots. The *US Coast Pilot* advises entering Wrangell Narrows toward the end of the flood tide to avoid dangerous currents. The tide floods into the narrows from both north and south, meeting in the middle near Green Point. In our two previous trips through the narrows, we had learned that entering them toward the end of the tidal cycle put us at Green Point just as the flood turned to ebb and we could then ride the ebb north, taking advantage of currents all the way.

Steve looked at his watch. "It's only two o'clock. We're early. We may have to anchor near Green Point to wait for the tide to turn."

As I steered *Osprey* past the Battery Islets, I looked at the chart plotter and saw with alarm that there was a ship coming down the channel toward us.

"We need to get out of the channel," said Steve, looking at our AIS (automatic identification system for ships). "It's a Cruise West ship." Cruise West ships are small cruise ships but in these tight waters there would be little room to pass. I looked anxiously at the chart. There was room off the right side of the channel so I slowed down and stayed right, waiting for the ship to pass. An easy thing here, I realized, but in faster currents or a tighter part of the channel, keeping *Osprey* from being swept on a rock while we waited could be tricky.

The ship passed, leaving the odor of diesel exhaust in its wake. A few minutes later, we entered a dredged channel where Beecher Pass joins the narrows. My arms ached as I struggled with the wheel to keep *Osprey* on course as currents sweeping across the channel tried to push us ashore. Around us, small sport-fishing boats darted among the rocks and islands. I envied the ease with which they moved; their powerful engines and shallow drafts giving them free rein where *Osprey*'s keel constrained us to the channel.

As we followed the channel curving to the northeast, majestic white mountains came into view. We continued on, *Osprey*'s engine thrumming as the current picked up speed. Ahead I could see a field of green and red beacons where the channel passed between the shallows of Boulder Flats on the left and the broad delta of Blind Slough on the right. Navigating should have been easy: we just had to go "red right returning"—putting the red beacons to starboard and the green to port. (In the Inside Passage boats are "returning" when they are heading north.) But we were moving so fast up the twisting channel that identifying the next beacon before the current swept us by was difficult.

"Don't look too far ahead," said Steve, as we took a curve that first went right, then left. By heading for the next green far ahead, I could have missed the next red close by and steered into a mud flat. Even when finding the next beacon was easy, steering was still a challenge as currents threatened to sweep us out of the 150-foot-wide channel.

Just as the end of the constricted part of the narrows approached and I could think about relaxing, Steve looked at his watch. "If we don't anchor soon and wait for the tide to turn, we'll be fighting the flood after Green Point."

I motored *Osprey* into a small bight in the tide flat off the east side of the channel where four- and five-fathom soundings provided depth for anchoring. But crab-pot buoys and moored skiffs clogged the water and the flood tide ripped through. I imagined us being swept down on the buoys as we tried to anchor, wrapping their lines around our propeller. "I don't feel comfortable anchoring here," I told Steve. "Let's go on. There are places farther north where the channel widens."

Steve agreed and we motored on, still being pushed north by the tide. We exited the dredged part of the narrows and approached Green Point, passing it at 4:25 p.m., almost exactly at maximum flood. According to the current tables, the flood tide should have been flowing south here, against us. But when I looked at our speed on the chart plotter, I was surprised to see we still had a knot of current with us. Like an urban bus schedule, tide and current tables aren't always right. I was glad the tables were wrong in our favor.

"It would be a shame to waste this good current," said Steve. "Let's forget about anchoring and just keep going."

A line from Shakespeare's *Julius Caesar*, learned in high school, popped into my head, "There is a tide in the affairs of men, which, taken at the flood, leads on to fortune." If Shakespeare had been a sailor he would have kept going.

With the tight twisty part of the narrows behind us, I could relax and enjoy the scenery, especially the mountains that towered over everything, dominating the landscape and turning quaint cabins and attractive fishing lodges lining the waterway into inconsequential ornaments.

Five miles beyond Green Point, we rounded a curve into Scow Bay, where in the early days of the region's halibut fishery old ships ("scows") anchored during the winter in order to purchase halibut from the fleets of fishing schooners. Old pilings and rustic warehouses with piles of crab pots on their aprons now lined the waterfront, interspersed with the occasional lodge or dwelling.

Two tugs with barges stacked high with containers pulled out from a landing ahead of us. Afraid the current would sweep us into them as they maneuvered their tows, I throttled back to let the tugs into the channel. By the time they were far enough ahead for us to pick up speed again, the current was racing south against us. *Osprey* crawled past the land as the engine worked to buck the tide.

Finally, we rounded Turn Point to see the town of Petersburg spread along the waterfront. I handed the wheel over to Steve so I could take photographs of the picturesque wharves and canneries. I felt a sense of accomplishment in having successfully navigated the fearsome Wrangell Narrows. A flood tide taken at the right time—and a good engine—had gotten us through the narrows in time for dinner in Petersburg.

4.4 PETERSBURG
Making a Living from the Sea

"Petersburg is a town that still makes its living from the sea," boasts Petersburg's Chamber of Commerce on its website. Elsewhere on the website, the Chamber asks, "Why come to Petersburg?" The reasons include mountains, glaciers, whale-watching, sport-fishing, reasonably priced accommodations, and avoiding "the large cruise-ship crowds." The tight quarters and shallow waters of the Wrangell Narrows keep the big ships away.

Steve and I like to visit towns off the beaten path and away from tourist centers. We enjoy the friendly atmosphere of a small town. At least, that's what we're envisioning until we look for a restaurant.

"Are you sure you want to eat out?" asked Steve as we walked up the dock at Petersburg's North Marina. In previous visits we had discovered the pizza restaurant was primarily takeout, the Mexican restaurant served bland food on Styrofoam plates and the seafood restaurant was expensive. But seeing all the fishing boats around us made me hungry for seafood.

Steve stopped in front of a small wooden powerboat with Idaho registration. A man and woman, both wearing John Deere ball caps and nearly identical green khaki jackets, were hosing down the boat's deck. A row of rods on the boat's stern told us they were most likely here for sport fishing.

"How's fishing?" asked Steve.

The view from the northern end of Wrangell Narrows includes the seafood processing plants of Petersburg.

The man glanced up at us. "Good. We fished in the channel today and got a mess of rockfish."

Chatting for awhile to exchange stories of fishing and boating in Alaska, we learned they keep their boat at Petersburg and fish here every year.

As we started to turn away, the man reached into a white plastic icebox and pulled out a fish fillet in a plastic bag.

"Why don't you take this yellow-eye rockfish."

Cooking a fish wasn't exactly what I had in mind for our seafood dinner, but nevertheless we took the fillet and returned to our boat. Blackened rockfish would do nicely.

This was our third trip to Petersburg. In our previous two we had checked off all the tourist attractions, visiting the museum, walking across the muskeg, gawking at the replica of a Viking ship outside the Sons of Norway Hall and poking among the shops on main street. This visit would mainly include errands: parts to buy for *Osprey*, laundry to wash, groceries to stock up on and email to check at the Petersburg library.

The next morning as we walked up the dock toward the ramp, a cacophony of sounds greeted us. Hammers tapped on wood, sanders roared, drills whined, and fishermen called to each other. In the background a symphony of ravens clonked and croaked as they hopped across docks or peered down from the funnels of fishing boats. The pungent smell of yesterday's fish wafted around the vessels.

A young boy wearing a life jacket was jigging off the dock with a small fishing pole. We peered into his bucket to see several herring swimming in fresh sea water.

"What are you going to do with them," I asked.

"Use them for bait in my crab trap," he replied with a tinge of scorn in his voice, obviously thinking, "What else?"

They start them young in Petersburg.

We walked up the ramp and past the harbormaster's office where fishermen sat on sofas and chairs, talking and drinking coffee. At the top of the dock a row of refrigerated trucks hummed outside the Trident Seafood plant. Half a block farther, we were in downtown Petersburg.

Rows of one- and two-storey buildings lined both sides of the street. From where we stood we could see two hardware stores, a department store, a small grocery store, a deli, a pharmacy and a laundromat. From the standpoint of a traveling boater, Petersburg, with just 3,100 residents, is a perfect small town: almost everything we need is within walking distance of the marina.

On our first trip to Petersburg in 2006, we visited the Clausen Memorial Museum where we admired the Fresnel lens from

Businesses in downtown Petersburg support the local fishing industry.

an old lighthouse, inspected the model of a fish trap and scrutinized an "Iron Chink," the fish-processing machine that displaced Chinese workers. A standard collection, I thought, and not very exciting. Then we watched a 20-minute video of Petersburg history called *The Town that Fish Built*, and my interest was piqued. Here was a town that understood its place in history and the forces that created it.

Petersburg was established in 1897 by a Norwegian immigrant named Peter Buschmann. Buschmann was attracted by the site's level ground, its location on the steamship route to Seattle and the plentiful supply of ice floating just outside the harbor from the Le Conte Glacier. At a time when most newcomers to Alaska were thinking of gold, Buschmann was thinking of fish.

By 1901, Petersburg sported a cannery, sawmill, wharf and warehouses. The wharf made regular steamer service to Seattle possible, which in turn made a fishery for fresh halibut practicable. Soon, a few miles south in Scow Bay, scows were buying halibut from fleets of schooners. Halibut doesn't can well and in the days before refrigeration it could be fished only in the winter when it could be kept cold and fresh. Fishermen accustomed to longlining for halibut in the rough winter seas off Cape Flattery in Washington State were quick to move to Alaska's protected waters.

The town grew, attracting more immigrants from Norway and elsewhere, while the canneries imported Chinese, Japanese and Philippine workers mostly to work on the slime line: gutting, cleaning and sorting fish. (Today, Petersburg boasts of its diverse population yet still calls itself "Alaska's Little Norway" and its Little Norway Festival celebrating Norwegian Independence Day every May 17 is the town's biggest event.)

At the town's peak, eight canneries operated in Petersburg, processing herring, clams, shrimp, cod and crab, in addition to the more traditional harvest of salmon and halibut.

According to the video, Petersburg might have evolved into just another cannery town controlled by Seattle owners if not for the perseverance and independent spirit of its residents. During the reign of the canneries, Petersburg residents fought to establish their own store, the Trading Union, which competed with the company store. In 1926, a group of local businessmen organized a cold-storage company to produce ice and freeze fish, expanding the halibut fishery from an exclusively winter to year-round enterprise.

In 1965 Petersburg faced a decisive moment. Six years into Alaskan statehood, with fish traps banned and salmon catches on the decline, canneries controlled by out-of-state owners started closing down. But while corporations from down south saw the cannery tide ebbing, the Petersburg business community saw opportunity flooding in. They purchased a local cannery, calling it Petersburg Fisheries. Then disaster nearly struck during the new company's very first year of operation. Salmon runs failed all across Southeast Alaska, and while other canneries could weather this slow period due to corporate connections, Petersburg Fisheries faced bankruptcy.

Then a miracle occurred. After the Seattle-based canneries closed for the season and sent their summer workers home, a late-season run of chum salmon flooded through Southeast Alaska. Petersburg Fisheries—ready with its full team of local workers—rode the run to solvency.

By adopting innovative strategies including year-round processing and floating processors that can follow the fish, Petersburg Fisheries grew, eventually expanding to become Icicle Seafoods, Inc., with permanent plants in Petersburg, Seward, Homer and Kodiak in Alaska, and in Bellingham in Washington State. (The Petersburg plant is still referred to as Petersburg Fisheries.) Today, Petersburg credits its success as a town to the brilliance of its business community in purchasing the cannery and selling shares of its stock to Petersburg residents—and to the hardworking wives who typically tend Petersburg's stores.

"We get along so well because we're hardly ever together," said one Petersburg wife on the video. And because their wives run the businesses on Main Street, the fishermen spend their earnings there—hence Petersburg dollars stay in Petersburg. "That's better than a third going to Seattle," noted a fisherman. As a Seattleite, I wasn't quite as convinced but nevertheless liked the mental image of Petersburg residents working together in such a cohesive way.

We were grateful for the success of this community as we went about our errands. In the Hammer & Wikan hardware store, Steve searched for new ground wire for *Osprey's* still-jiggling gauges while I looked for vinyl cement to repair a see-through chart bag. Inside the store, we wandered down aisles of plumbing, tools and cooking gear—anything and everything a household or fishing boat might need. Steve located his wire while I found rolls of vinyl but no vinyl glue. We hit upon it in the second hardware store—in a quart can, sized for fishermen.

Visits to the drugstore for vitamins and Sing Lee Alley Books in a comfortable converted house, completed our day.

As I walked out of the drugstore, I noticed the sign over the door: "Rexall Drugs." So it is part of a chain, as is the Hammer & Wikan hardware, a True Value entity—apparently all the stores here aren't 100-percent local even if they are owned or managed by fishermen's wives.

Rain and dark clouds greeted us the next morning as we finished our errands, reminiscent of our first visit when it rained solidly for three days—a not uncommon occurrence in this area where the annual precipitation is 106 inches. That year Steve overheard a fisherman on the telephone to his wife: "I didn't bring enough dry socks." And in the laundromat another stuffed his foul-weather boots into the dryer. Thirty seconds later they kicked open the dryer door and landed on the floor. On the docks, work had continued even in the rain. "Some years we don't get any dry days at all for painting," one fisherman told us.

But today the rain stopped by evening. Because this was our last night in Petersburg, we treated ourselves to a dinner at the Northern Lights Restaurant. We left the marina and walked south along the waterfront, admiring the scrolls and flowers of Scandinavian rosemaling imprinted in the sidewalk. Taking a shortcut through a parking lot, we passed a dormitory for cannery workers. "Comedor," read the sign outside one of the doors, Spanish for dining room. As we walked by a group of workers smoking outside the door, I caught words of Spanish. A new group of immigrants for the slime line.

In the restaurant the varnished wood tables and booths ringed a large room with picture windows overlooking a boat harbor. Groups of people in jeans and sweatshirts ate hamburgers and fish and chips, and the odor of fried food drifted through the air. While we munched on iceberg lettuce and freshly boiled shrimp, we looked out the window at workers stacking rows of crab traps on a boat's aft deck.

As we left, the evening light was glancing off old wooden buildings on Hammer Slough. We walked to the bridge to see a perfect reflection in the water below. The view was an artist's dream of a nature that would have attracted rows of painters with easels and brushes in places like Gloucester, Nantucket or other East Coast ports. Here, camera in hand, I was the closest thing to an artist.

The video *Petersburg, the Town that Fish Built* attributes the town's survival as a fishing port to the resources (fish) and hard work of its people. Alaskans like to brag about their state as a land where independent and hardy workers conquer the wilderness without interference from government. But others point out that this is not the whole story. Sustainable management of Alaskan fisheries by state government and the International Pacific Halibut Commission (US and Canada) ensures there are still fish to catch. And it is outside capital that gave Alaska's resource development—including Petersburg's canneries—a significant boost. And then there are all

Fishermen prepare for the upcoming crab season by loading traps on a boat in Petersburg harbor.

those Seattleites who staff the offices down south. Petersburg Fisheries' parent corporation, Icicle Seafoods, Inc., is based in Seattle, as is Trident Seafood, owner of another Petersburg plant.

From Hammer Slough, we walked back to the marina, passing the dock where the fishing-boat crew we watched during dinner was still loading crab traps. The stack now reached above the vessel's cabin top. There's no doubt that Petersburg's fishermen work hard—and while that may not be the whole story, it's undeniably worth a lot.

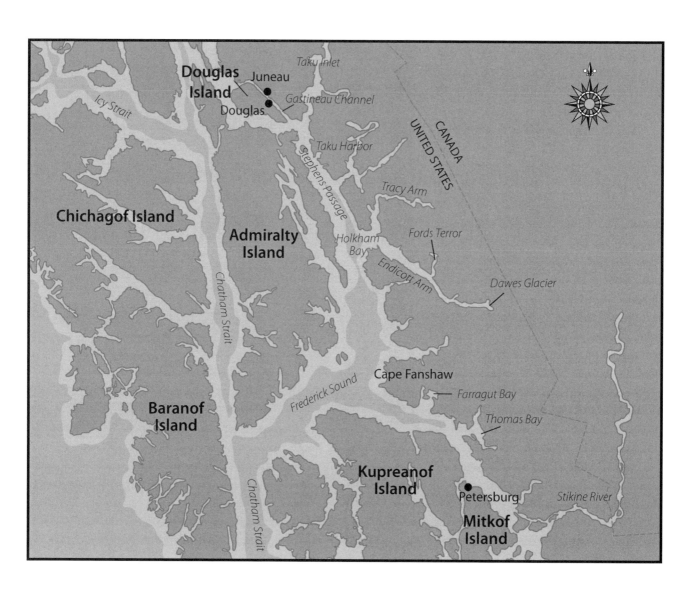

CHAPTER 5

FREDERICK SOUND TO GASTINEAU CHANNEL

5.1 THOMAS BAY
A Fanciful Tale

"A visit to Thomas Bay isn't complete without reading *The Strangest Story Ever Told*." I looked with dismay at this note in the guide, *Evergreen Pacific: Exploring Alaska & British Columbia, Skagway to Barkley Sound* by Stephen Hilson. The day before in Petersburg's bookstore, I had thumbed through the blue booklet by Harry D. Colp but hadn't purchased it, dismissing it as a fanciful tale dreamed up by prospectors who spent too much time in isolated rain-soaked cabins. Now I regretted not paying more attention. I like to know as much as possible about a place before visiting, and feared I had missed a critical piece of history.

Still, we were going to Thomas Bay because of its scenery and glacier, not for the history. Baird Glacier at the north end of the bay is surrounded by a large outwash plain that offers a rare opportunity to walk on newly created land and view a glacier up close.

We left Petersburg with the last of the ebb, riding the tide out Wrangell Narrows and into Frederick Sound. It was a beautiful clear day, free of fog and mist and almost warm. As we entered the sound, I looked with astonishment at a jagged wall of snow-covered mountains across the water. Now I understood why residents of Southeast Alaska put up with all the rain. A chance to look even occasionally at a stunning sight like these mountains was worth a lot of gray days.

Only a few cat's paws of wind ruffled the water as we motored the 10 miles north to Thomas Bay. Several people had told us

Small fireweed plants and moss grow on glacial sediments on the Baird Glacier outwash plain.

Currents move fast through the entrance to Thomas Bay.

the "real" Alaska begins north of Petersburg. Seeing this area in good weather confirmed that notion for me. Here in Frederick Sound the vista was wider and the mountains, which are closer to the water and steeper than farther south, looked taller and more rugged.

The first Europeans to explore this area were Captain George Vancouver's lieutenants James Johnstone and Joseph Whidbey, in 1794. More than 100 years later in *Appleton's Guide-Book to Alaska* (1897), travel-writer Eliza Scidmore noted that "these lieutenants made plain to their chief the 'uncommonly awful' and 'horribly magnificent' character of the scenery along Prince Frederick shore; and Vancouver began the lavish use of adjectives which is in vogue in Alaskan narratives today." Now, 110 years after Scidmore, I continue the custom, struggling with adjectives to describe the mountains. How many different ways can I say "rugged"?

We entered Thomas Bay through a narrow channel between two rocky spits. A strong flood surged into the bay, heeling the entrance buoys and carrying *Osprey* forward. For a few terrifying moments I worried that the current would push us into the shallows off Wood Point. Steve, at *Osprey*'s wheel, steered toward the center of the channel so that we headed sideways as we swept through. Seconds later we were past the shallows and in the deep bay with its slower currents. Two large powerboats followed us, their powerful engines allowing them to negotiate the entrance with ease. Ahead, I could see a sharp line in the water where blue waters from the sound met milky green glacial waters. Sunlight falling on the green-white of the glacial water gave the scene an almost tropical look.

As we rounded Wind Point and headed north, thoughts of the tropics dissolved in

Striations carved by the Baird Glacier in earlier times can be seen on rocks above the outwash plain.

a blast of cold air off Baird Glacier. At the head of the bay we could see massive cliffs sculpted smooth by ice. The long tongue of the glacier emerged between two headlands, with craggy snow-capped mountains framing the scene. In front of the glacier stretched a low flat area, the glacier's outwash plain that we hoped to explore.

Baird Glacier was once a great deal larger than it is now. The rocky spits that we motored between mark the farthest extent of the glacier, 2,700 years ago. They are the remnants of the terminal moraine, deposits that accumulate at the end of a glacier's path.

As we moved up the bay, we could see impressive effects of past glacial action on the cliffs around us: striations where the glacier dragged rocks against walls and rounded surfaces scoured by glacial action.

We were motoring toward the glacier but still a long way from it when I glanced at the depth sounder and saw it jump from 20 fathoms to 12 fathoms in a few seconds. "Getting shallow," I said to Steve, pointing to the instrument. As the numbers dropped to 11, 6, 5 and then 1.4, Steve turned the boat away from the glacier and in a few minutes we were in deep water again. Were the depth readings accurate or a result of the thick glacial flour clogging the water? We couldn't see bottom to tell.

The water in front of the glacier is too exposed for anchoring, so we headed to Scenery Cove, two miles away on the east side of the bay. With its steep, tree-covered sides, green marsh and views of distant mountains at its head, the cove lived up to its name. Another sailboat had taken the shallowest spot off the marsh, so we anchored farther out in 100 feet, letting out all 270 feet of our anchor chain.

We waited for the tide to come in, then climbed into our dinghy and headed for the glacier. A cold wind and a short chop sent spray across the dinghy bow, making me wish I had worn foul-weather gear instead of a windbreaker.

The chart showed a broad mud flat extending into the bay from the outwash plain with a blank area in front of the flat labeled "shoaling." Would we be able to find our way across the flat? Even at high tide, it might be too shallow to navigate.

As we approached it, glacial flour turned the water a milky brown so opaque we couldn't tell six inches from six fathoms. "I can't tell where to go," said Steve. "Look, there are rocks way out here." He pointed ahead and I saw black mounds dotting the water's surface. But a minute later the mounds disappeared, replaced by different mounds farther away.

"They're seals, not rocks!" I said. Steve turned the dinghy toward them and a few minutes later a wide channel between two cobble spits opened up. We had found the river that drains from under the glacier (or at least one of its branches). So steep were the riverbanks that motoring between them was like navigating between two jetties. The current increased as we moved upstream until soon we were running in place, our outboard barely keeping pace with the current. We turned and ran back to the river's mouth. There we found a minuscule cove, just large enough to shelter our dinghy.

"I think we discovered a new navigation tool," I said, as we walked the anchor up onto shore. "Seal navigation: if the water's deep enough for seals to dive, it's deep enough for an outboard."

The cold wind we had battled in the bay now blew warm over the land. From the top of the cobble spit, we could see across a large plain stretching toward the glacier whose looming white presence squatted just a short distance away. The plain reminded me of a desert: reddish-yellow soil interspersed with sparse vegetation and shallow arroyos where the river once flowed. But a second look showed that the reddish-yellow soil was actually carpets of dry moss. Swaths of luxurious blue lupines waving in the breeze cut across the moss. Small pink foxgloves grew in dry patches of glacial flour. The moss and lupines were growing among cobbles six inches in diameter or more. These were pioneer plants, laying down soil for other species to come.

We started walking toward the glacier, our feet crunching on the dry moss. Bare gray walls rose above us, giving way to forest-covered slopes and then white-capped mountains. I was amazed that a scene could be so desolate and beautiful at the same time.

While I stopped to take pictures, Steve walked ahead, disappearing in a deep arroyo. Alone, I looked around uneasily. Could a bear be waiting behind the next bush? I listened to the wind rustling across the sand and regarded the stark gray cliffs looming above me. A cloud moved across the sun and I shivered.

Suddenly, the beating of wings and a cry of keek, keek, keek startled me. A solitary tern flew up in front of me, screeching a warning, then flying in circles overhead. My heart pounded from the suddenness of the noise. "It's just a bird defending her nest," I reassured myself; nevertheless I hurried to join Steve.

In the city I long for wilderness, to be away from people and surrounded by nature. But here, far from civilization, I felt uneasy. Was it the "horrible magnificent character" of the scenery or just our extreme isolation? The setting was certainly different from the low-forested hills I had grown up with in Puget Sound. There the mountains and glaciers keep a polite distance, mere scenic backdrops to our daily lives.

We walked across barren plains, steadily moving toward the glacier yet never seeming to get close. Distances can deceive in Alaska, and we soon realized the glacier was larger and farther away than it first appeared.

I began to worry about our dinghy. What if the river carried it away? We could be stranded here for days, alone on this alien plain.

Steve was concerned about the dinghy too, but for another reason. "We're not going to make the glacier before the tide goes out. We'd better turn back before the dinghy goes high and dry."

We turned back toward the dinghy. We hadn't reached the glacier, but we had gotten close. As we approached the shore, I picked up my pace, anxious to see the dinghy and its assurance of safe passage back to the *Osprey.*

"What's your hurry? The tide's not going out that fast."

I didn't want to tell Steve how the vastness of the plain made me uneasy, so I mouthed something noncommittal about wanting to get back to start dinner. When we crossed the last pile of cobbles, though, and saw the bright yellow of our waiting dinghy, I breathed a distinct sigh of relief.

A couple of weeks later in Juneau, I bought a copy of *The Strangest Story Ever Told.* That night I sat down to read the 30-page booklet, which tells the tale of four prospectors who pool their resources to look for gold in the hills above Thomas Bay. One by one, they—and others who visit Thomas Bay—go crazy, insisting they have seen strange hairy creatures that resemble devils. My scalp prickled as I read about one lone trapper following strange tracks in a circle, coming back to where he had started and realizing then that whatever was making the tracks was now following him.

I put the book down feeling my original suspicions that the story was simply the fanciful notions of prospectors isolated in alien scenery had been confirmed. Yet—remembering the uneasiness I felt on the glacial plain—I was glad I hadn't read it until after we left Thomas Bay.

5.2 FANSHAW
A Very Short Boom

As we rounded the rocky point of Cape Fanshaw where Frederick Sound turns north, I looked at the thick forests on the surrounding land and reflected that this was real wilderness: no houses, no clear-cuts, just trees as far as I could see. Then, just a few miles farther north, we entered Cleveland Passage to find rows of old pilings and a large rusty boiler on the beach.

The pilings were remnants of the former village of Fanshaw. First settled in 1902 as Cape Fanshaw, it was renamed Fanshaw in 1932. Several salmon canneries and salteries were built in 1918 and 1919, but by 1920 only one remained open and it closed a year later—a cycle of boom and bust common to Alaska fisheries and dictated as much by corporate decisions down south as by the fish in Alaska. Crab and fish were processed there sporadically thereafter but most of the town's approximately 25 residents earned their living by serving the fishing fleet in the summer. As fishing declined, Fanshaw's fortune diminished with it and in 1953 the post office closed. Robert Hassler, author of *Traveler's Guide: Southeastern Alaska* (1973), visited there in 1969 and reported grassy clearings with colorful but overgrown flower gardens around abandoned cabins. By the time fishing improved again in the 1980s, time had passed Fanshaw by.

Abandoned townsites like Fanshaw and the remains of former salmon canneries are common in Southeast Alaska. Thinking these relics were the full extent of this village, we didn't venture ashore on that first trip in 2006. But over the winter I saw a note in *Exploring Alaska and British Columbia* by Stephen Hilson about a fox

A small cruise ship motors into Cleveland Passage at Fanshaw to anchor for the night.

farm on Whitney Island near Fanshaw across Cleveland Passage.

The history of fox farming is one of boom and bust. Fox farming grew exponentially in Southeast Alaska after World War I. Stylish flappers were wearing fur coats, stoles, muffs and hats, and fur prices were soaring. Fur farming seemed poised to grow—as one of Alaska's fur-animal veterinarians expressed it, ". . . the advances of civilization will diminish the catch in the wilds and increase the demand for the product of fur farming." Where better to farm furs than in the wilds of Alaska with its vast acres of available land and a populace already invested in fur trade? Alaska territorial officials promoted the growing

Rockweed covers old machinery on Whitney Island across from Fanshaw.

industry by funding special veterinarians and the Forest Service supported it by leasing whole islands to fox farmers for only $25 a year.

Islands were appealing as farm sites because they could be cleared of predators and foxes could be allowed to run free. By 1924, 140 permits were in force for fox farms in the Tongass National Forest (covering most of Southeast Alaska). The farms accelerated the transition in Southeast Alaska from raw wilderness to cleared land, a process already underway with the growth of salmon canning.

Armed with this information about Fanshaw and its nearby fur farm, we returned to Cleveland Passage in 2007. This time I noticed pilings across the passage from Fanshaw, on Whitney Island, the site of the former fox farm.

A light but persistent rain was falling so we donned foul-weather gear before getting into the dinghy. A small white seal perched on a rock just off the beach watched us go by. We stepped out of the dinghy onto a field of golden-brown rockweed emitting the pungent smell of seaweed. Under the rockweed we saw the outlines of a veritable junkyard: engine drive shafts, rusty chains, miscellaneous engine parts, and a small round boiler. Exploring further, we crossed a line of beach grass just above the high-tide line and ducked underneath spruce branches to enter the forest. There we found the remains of a cabin, its wooden walls collapsed under a sheet-metal roof. Nearby we came across a small cart and some rusted rails. Hilson had reported that a rail system had been used on nearby Storm Island to transport food to the foxes. Apparently one had been used here too.

Jack O'Donnell, author of *Alaskan Panhandle Tales or Funny Things Happened up North* (Frontier Publishing, 1996), writes of visiting this fox farm when it was still operating. According to O'Donnell, the owners were a couple who, through hard work, had made the farm into a comfortable home.

At the time of his visit to Whitney Island, O'Donnell was on his way north to work

Collapsed buildings on Whitney Island across from the former town of Fanshaw may mark the location of a former fox farm.

on a fox farm on Dorn Island, off Admiralty Island in Seymour Canal. Just out of high school, O'Donnell saw the job as an adventure and a way to escape the expense of town living. That the only pay would be a share of the sale of furs in December didn't concern him at the time. For six weeks he worked alongside the farm's owners, Ed Ramstead and "Cranky" Nels (who wasn't cranky at all), living in a one-room cabin without running water or electricity. He raked herring, fished for halibut, sawed firewood, and cooked fox food of cereals and fish on an open fire and then rowed a heavy boat around the island to deliver it to fox-feeding sites. The work was exhausting and unrelenting. When the farm's fox pups started dying, he realized his share of the proceeds would be minimal so he quit and returned to Petersburg, glad to reclaim the comforts of town.

O'Donnell's experience was not unusual. Foxes weren't native to Southeast Alaska and couldn't adjust to the wet climate. Many farmers, former trappers or fishermen, weren't knowledgeable about raising animals. Foxes died of distemper, lungworm, botulism, dysentery, encephalitis, rickets and pneumonia. Farmers whose foxes survived had only a few years of strong earnings before oversupply, changing fashion and the Great Depression pushed fur prices down while the increasing costs of shipping and food pushed expenses up. The industry never recovered and by the end of World War II, almost all the farms were deserted. Today, no foxes live on the islands of Southeast Alaska and only abandoned machinery and rotting cabins remain to tell the tale of this brief boom.

We poked around the woods and beach for a while longer, finding more machinery and abandoned work sheds surrounded by the stumps of former spruce trees and the tall thin trunks of their subsequent replacements. There was something both sad and comforting in the way the trees were covering the traces of the old farm: sad that an era would soon be forgotten, comforting that nature could so readily cover our mistakes.

We returned to *Osprey* for a dinner of crab pesto made from our catch of the day before. Just as we finished eating, sunlight burst through the cabin window. Moving to the cockpit we could see a beautiful triple rainbow arched over Fanshaw. Several powerboats and two other sailboats had anchored near us and their crews were out enjoying the view. As we watched, the small cruise ship MS *Spirit of '98* motored into Cleveland Passage and dropped its anchor, sending the rumble of its chain across the quiet water.

There were more people in the harbor that night than had ever lived at Fanshaw.

5.3   TRACY ARM
"White Thunder Bay"

The Sumdum Glacier hung in the mist above us and monstrous icebergs rested on bare rocks at the bay's entrance. Holkham Bay seemed too tame a name for this magical place; the Tlingit name, Sumdum, for "white thunder," the thundering noise calving glaciers make, sounded more appropriate.

It was 2007 and we were making our second trip to Holkham Bay on Stephens Passage 32 miles south of Juneau. The bay is famous for its three tidewater glaciers, two in Tracy Arm and one in Endicott Arm. On our first trip we had made the 44-mile round trip up Tracy Arm, picking our way through floating ice to the face of Sawyer Glacier. But pack ice had stopped us from approaching the arm's second glacier, South Sawyer. Now Steve was determined to make a second try to get close in to both glaciers.

"We made it to Sawyer and we saw South Sawyer from Sawyer Island, only three miles away. Wasn't that good enough?" I asked.

"No. I want to get close. And it's a fantastic trip. Don't you want to see it again?"

"It's beautiful. But shouldn't we go somewhere else instead? How about Dawes Glacier in Endicott Arm?"

"It's too far. And it's not the same."

The truth was I was conflicted about going back to Tracy Arm. The arm's plunging cliffs, imposing headlands and towering blue-white glaciers had been awe-inspiring but navigating in the ice was unnerving. The *US Coast Pilot* warns that calving ice in Tracy Arm can generate waves high enough to swamp a small boat or to crush a frail hull between icebergs. And although Steve had pointed out that the *Coast Pilot* also says that a small boat can ride the waves safely by keeping away from the glacier face and avoiding getting packed in the ice flow, the warning still made me nervous.

We had made the trip up the inlet and back safely but I feared it would be tempting fate to go again.

Steve won the argument by both his sheer determination and by inviting two new friends, Lynne and Bill of the sailboat *Capsella,* to accompany us. I could hardly act scared in front of other boaters eager to see the glaciers. One boat instead of two would save fuel and two extra sets of eyes would help spot floating ice. *Osprey*'s full keel, with an aperture for the propeller, was a better design for ice than *Capsella*'s fin keel and un-protected propeller.

That night we anchored near the entrance to Tracy Arm in a small unnamed bay called Tracy Arm Cove by boaters. From our anchorage we could see icebergs drifting in the open water, flocks of eagles resting on the shore, and a grizzly bear browsing among sedge grass.

The next morning we left the cove at 9:00 a.m., stopping briefly at *Capsella* to pick up Lynne and Bill. They came on board with extra clothes, camera gear, and a bowl of freshly caught salmon.

It was a perfect day for looking at glaciers: light clouds let through just enough light to illuminate the steep slopes without blinding us on the ice fields. The four of us sat in *Osprey*'s large cockpit, enjoying the mild weather and views of forested hillsides. Navigation was easy here as only a smattering of icebergs drifted in the quiet water.

At 10:00, I looked ahead and saw the cruise ship MS *Zaandam* coming toward us. Steve took *Osprey* over to the side as the huge vessel glided past. Rows of passengers standing along the ship's bow looked down at us as we looked up at them.

Farther on, we passed a cliff so steep it seemed to rise straight up from the water's edge. Across the inlet, more sheer rock walls dwarfed a small cruise ship at their base. Beyond the cliffs, rounded headlands and U-shaped valleys reminded me of photographs of Yosemite Valley in California. "It's incredible," said Lynne, and I had to agree with her.

These formations were evidence of recent glaciation. Rivers cut valleys into V-shapes while glaciers, moving down those valleys, carve them further into U-shapes.

The rounded headlands in Tracy Arm, similar to the famous features of Yosemite in California, were created by glaciation.

The naturalist John Muir, who traveled here in a dugout canoe paddled by Tlingits, was the first to note the resemblance between Yosemite and Holkham Bay and attribute it to the process of glaciation. Like us, Muir journeyed here two years in a row. On his first visit, in November of 1879, solid pack ice prevented him from seeing any of the bay's glaciers.

Muir returned in August of the following year, hunting for what he called his "lost glaciers" in Holkham Bay. This time, he explored both Endicott and Tracy Arms, and saw the glaciers in both. Somewhere in the middle reaches of Tracy Arm, Muir encountered "bergs from shore to shore, which seem to bar the way against everything but wings." Muir urged his paddlers forward, enjoying the "extraordinary grandeur of the wild unfinished Yosemite."

At 11:00 a.m. we passed another sailboat coming toward us. We motored over to talk to its crew and they told us thick ice had turned them back. "Wimps!" said Steve after we pulled out of earshot. A small tour boat zoomed past us shortly after and Steve pointed to it, "If they can do it, we can at least try."

Half an hour later we arrived at a sharp bend in the fjord. A massive gray cliff rose above us; its surface dimpled as if someone had carved out spoonfuls of rock, then polished the remainder. As we turned, a blast

U-shaped valleys such as this one in Tracy Arm are a sign of past glaciation.

of cold air hit us and a fleet of bergy bits (medium-sized icebergs) sailed toward us. Bill, who had volunteered to steer a while back, turned the helm back to Steve, saying, "I'd rather you be the one to run into an iceberg."

Steve wove *Osprey* through the ice. Bill stood at the mast and Lynne at the bow, ready to warn of low-floating ice. Some of the growlers (very small icebergs) were more transparent than others and difficult to see because they were made of denser ice and rode low in the water. As the growlers became more numerous, it became impossible to miss all of them, and our progress through the water was accompanied by a cacophony of crunches and cracks from the ice and cries of "Damn!" from Steve. But, still he forged ahead.

Bill had gotten out his video camera and was filming our progress. I heard Lynne ask him, "Do you think we'll make it to the glacier?" Bill replied into his microphone. "It looks iffy but Steve is pretty intrepid."

We were approaching the Y at the top of Tracy Arm when I noticed brown dots on the ice up ahead: seals resting on ice floes. It was the pupping season, and soon we could see mothers nursing their pups all around us. Steve steered *Osprey* away, trying not to scare them. I watched, dismayed, as a tour boat roared by, sending ice floes rocking and seals sliding into the water. When seals are forced from the safety of their floes they use valuable energy swimming that is better saved for nursing and growing.

When we reached the Y, we looked south to the South Sawyer Glacier, its massive blue wall towering over the inlet while dark mountains loomed above it. Sawyer Glacier to the north was still hidden around a bend.

We could see two tour boats working their way across the fjord in front of South Sawyer Glacier. Steve steered toward it.

We had made good time up the inlet. Muir, 117 years earlier, had not been so fortunate. It wasn't until "toward 9 o'clock, just before the gray darkness of evening fell," that Muir's party arrived in front of the glacier. "'There is your long-lost friend,' said the

Watching glaciers requires jackets, gloves and hats. Facial hair doesn't hurt either.

Indians to Muir, laughing; 'he says, Sagh-a-ya' [how do you do]?" And Muir watched as berg after berg calved from the glacier's face.

Muir rejoiced in the beauty of the glaciers and in the magnificent geological formations, seeing in them evidence of God's handiwork. In his amazing discoveries of glaciers in the very process of sculpting mountains and valleys, Muir saw proof for the theory that glaciers had a role in creating the landscape. This glacial theory, first proposed by the scientist Louis Agassiz, was considered radical by many scientists, who believed features such as U-shaped valleys and rounded headlands had been formed either by slow erosion and deposition or cataclysmic events.

As *Osprey* advanced, we could hear the occasional boom of icebergs peeling off the glacier's face. The sound of ice banging against the hull was continuous.

Finally, we came to a place where the ice looked impenetrable. Two tour boats were still ahead of us, but both had metal hulls and stronger engines.

Steve turned off the engine. "Let's drift."

The wind had died down but the air was chilly, cooled by the ice. By now all of us had added layers of jackets, hats and gloves. As we drifted, we could hear the floating ice clicking, clacking, cracking, crunching and dripping, interspersed with an occasional boom as the glacier calved. We sat in the cockpit and gazed at the scenery, amazed by the beauty of the huge glacier and the mountains above it—and by the sense that we were seeing creation underway.

Jigger, who had been hiding in his warm bunk below, emerged on deck and stationed himself at the rail to peer over the side, fascinated by the small growlers drifting by. While we gazed at distant scenery, he focused on the near.

"I'm trying to figure out how to explain this to someone who has never been here." Lynne gestured at the water with its floating ice. "Pictures just aren't going to do it. It's like floating in a huge frozen daiquiri."

"Or a margarita," Bill smiled. "But without the salt."

Lynne and I went below to make sandwiches for lunch. Listening to sounds of ice bumping against the hull below was unnerving, like being inside a drum during a drum roll. We were just drifting and yet the boat resounded with the sound of hundreds of collisions with small growlers; crunches and cracks boomeranged around the cabin. What the comparison to a daiquiri lacked was fear. Were we far enough from the glacier's face to avoid the steep waves caused by calving? I hoped so. Although the ice made me apprehensive I wanted to get close enough to experience the glaciers in all their splendor.

Back on deck with salmon sandwiches in hand, I saw that we had drifted across the inlet and were now gliding quickly down its west side, accompanied by a flotilla of bergy bits, all being swept out to sea by runoff from under the glacier. Several tour boats and a powerboat traveled with us. As one of the tour boats drifted by, tourists inside a glass-enclosed cabin aimed cameras at us.

The current swept us within a boat length of the rockbound shore. I looked at the depth sounder and saw we still had 40 fathoms beneath us. Above us hung brown cliffs streaked with orange from iron ore and dotted with the occasional shrub.

After an hour of drifting, we emerged from the ice and Steve started the engine. As we approached the entrance to the north branch of Tracy Arm, we could see that the ice packing it just an hour earlier was gone, and a clear channel beckoned.

"Let's just take a look at Sawyer," said Steve as he turned *Osprey* north into the narrow fjord.

Sawyer Glacier is hidden from the lower reaches of the north arm by a bend in the fjord, and we all looked eagerly ahead, waiting to catch the first glimpse of it. But when we came around, the first thing we saw was a huge iceberg sitting smack in front of the glacier. Steve motored cautiously around it, keeping his distance. The iceberg sat immobile. "It's probably grounded," Steve concluded. "It's at least 50 feet tall. That means it could be 500 feet deep." Drifting icebergs can be dangerous for small boats as they can roll suddenly, taking the boat with them. If the iceberg was grounded, it would be less likely to turn.

I checked the chart we carried in a plastic case in the cockpit and could see that immediately in front of the glacier, the water was 60 or more fathoms deep, while farther downstream, the bottom climbed to 35 fathoms. A 500-foot deep iceberg could indeed ground as it approached the shallower water, which would explain why it wasn't moving. Still, I wondered if its sheer size could account for its seeming immobility and felt nervous as we passed it.

Beyond the iceberg, in front of the glacier, the water was free of ice. Steve turned off the engine again, and we drifted. We were much closer to Sawyer Glacier's snout than we had been to that of South Sawyer Glacier. We could clearly see the glacier's blue color and the long cracks in its face. The clean blue ice of the glacier contrasted with the bare and almost orange-colored rock-bound cliffs around it.

Both South Sawyer and Sawyer glaciers are retreating, meaning ice is calving and melting at their snouts faster than it is accumulating upstream, causing the position of the snouts to move slowly up inlet. The evidence of retreat is visible in the bare rocks immediately down inlet. If the glaciers were advancing into new unglaciated land, we would see trees and other vegetation at their margins.

As we drifted in front of the glacier, I suddenly glanced at the chart plotter that we keep running on the cabin roof. We hadn't been paying much attention to it, as the water is very deep everywhere and the major navigational obstacle, the floating ice, is not charted. So I was astounded to see the position of our boat, according to the chart plotter, to be sitting very solidly on the glacier, not in water as we actually were. Apparently, the glacier had retreated significantly inland from its charted position (based on a year-2000 chart) and where once there had been ice, there was now navigable water.

"Look at that," I said to the others. "We're aground!"

We all laughed, but as we motored away from the glacier, I watched the depth sounder anxiously. We were in new waters that had not yet been charted; who knew what dangers lurked?

We motored south into the main fjord of Tracy Arm, weaving our way back through the ice. When we finally cleared the ice, Steve said, "That was a successful day. We saw two glaciers and only lost a little bit of paint."

I breathed a final sigh of relief and felt a strong sense of achievement. While I hadn't conquered my fear, it hadn't taken hold of me either. But where Steve rejoiced in the accomplishment of bashing through the ice, I looked back on the magnificent scenery and the impression of having had a front-row seat to an incredible geological process.

5.4 FORDS TERROR
Braving the Narrows

I surprised myself during our third summer in Alaska when I suggested we go to Fords Terror. A destination that had terrified me the year before suddenly seemed intriguing. Two summers of navigating among glaciers and sailing through narrow rock-bound passages had given me more courage.

Fords Terror, a narrow six-mile-long fjord off Endicott Arm, is famous both for its spectacular scenery and the story behind its discovery. In 1889 Harry L. Ford, a crew member on the US Coast and Geodetic Survey vessel *Carlile P. Patterson,* entered the fjord in a rowboat at slack water. There he was trapped by raging currents and floating ice until the next slack tide released him.

Although the tidewater glacier that clogged the fjord with ice during Ford's time has retreated into the mountains, other reasons to fear Fords Terror remain. Deep-keeled sailboats must enter at slack water, but the time of high-water slack is known only vaguely and varies with the height of the tide. Uncharted rocks and reefs are reported near the entrance, and the channel takes a hard turn just after that, obstructing visibility. And,

The west arm of Fords Terror provides the best anchorage—and a magnificent view.

Narrows separating outer Fords Terror from the inner basin can make for a terrifying entrance.

finally, icebergs from Dawes Glacier work their way into the fjord and rush out the exit with the ebb tide.

I knew all this but decided we should visit Fords Terror anyway. How could we fully explore Southeast Alaska without visiting this famous fjord? After all, Southeast Alaska was about adventure and spectacular scenery. Fords Terror offers both.

We made our entry into Fords Terror even more risky by arriving late.

That morning, we left Tracy Arm Cove with plenty of time to motor to Dawes Glacier at the head of Endicott Arm and get back in time to catch the afternoon tide (assumed to be about an hour after high water at Juneau) into Fords Terror. But we'd lingered too long at the glacier's face, admiring the pure blue of the glacier glittering in the rare Alaska sun and watching seal pups on the ice floes. When we finally turned to leave, we found our way partially blocked by ice and had to pick our through the bergy bits and growlers at slower than normal speed.

As we turned into Fords Terror, I looked at my watch: two hours past high tide at Juneau. We were an hour later than we should have been.

"It's better to go through the narrows with the current slightly against us to give us better steerage," said Steve. "Besides, no one really knows the time of high-tide slack in Fords Terror anyway." That didn't assure me; it meant we could be even more than an hour late.

Fords Terror consists of two parts separated by a narrow throat: an outer anchorage and the inner fjord where Ford was trapped. We planned to take *Osprey* through the narrows and to anchor for the night in the inner fjord.

Steve picked up the radio and called, "Sécurité, Sécurité, sailboat *Osprey* entering

Fords Terror." No one responded to warn us they were coming the other way, so we kept on going, passing the charter boat *Pacific Catalyst*, anchored in the shallows.

Before we'd left Seattle, I had printed out directions from a blog for entering the narrows. The directions included a photo of a waterfall with a double stream. From that waterfall, the blog advised to proceed at a course of 290° magnetic to the entrance of Fords Terror. I could see the entrance to our left and scanned the rock wall to starboard for a waterfall. One tumbled down the wall just a few feet away. Was that it?

"I don't think that's it," said Steve, looking at the picture. "It's not double." I had a moment of panic. I hadn't expected more than one waterfall. What if we couldn't tell which was the correct one? We continued on and a few minutes later found the unmistakable braided pattern of the double waterfall.

Steve turned *Osprey* and announced, "There's 290. Go look for rocks." I stood on the bow and looked ahead, but all I could see was swirling brown water. A point of rocky land jutted out into the fjord, and we were headed to the left of that point. A lone kayaker floated in a back eddy to the point's right.

Steve at the wheel was fighting to keep *Osprey* on course. I feared we were entering too late in the tidal cycle.

We were nearing the point at the entrance when I heard over the radio, "Green sailboat, green sailboat, this is the kayak at Fords Terror." Knowing Steve couldn't handle the radio in the current, I went back to the cockpit to answer it. Then I heard, "We've got a group of kayaks coming out, can you turn around?"

I looked at the knot meter, then at the chart plotter. We were doing 6 knots through the water, 3 knots over ground. That meant we had 3 knots against us. With unmarked rocks all around us, turning around could sweep us off course onto a rock.

"We can't turn now," said Steve. "Tell them we'll do our best to watch out for the kayakers."

The kayaker replied that the kayaks would be coming out on the east side. Steve steered toward the west as far as he dared. I looked ahead anxiously, feeling both scared and angry: scared because I wasn't sure we could avoid the kayaks; angry at the kayaker for putting us in this situation by not answering Steve's security call.

Just before we made the turn, a kayak appeared around the bend. Steve pointed toward the east, and the kayak steered in that direction. Three more kayaks went whizzing by, their occupants looking surprised to see us. A small bergy bit followed them, sweeping by so quickly I didn't have a chance to worry about it. I looked at the current rushing by and listened to the engine roaring. Were we going to make it? After what seemed like an eternity, but was probably only 15 minutes, the water depth increased from a few feet to 300 and the current diminished to less than a knot. We had made it.

Now I could turn my attention to the scenery. On our left were steep, almost perpendicular rock walls that climbed straight up—so high we traveled in their shadows. On our right, the walls climbed less sharply, but gave way to great stone slabs where water flowed in sheets. Everywhere I looked I saw rock sculpted by glaciers: gouges, scoops and striations. And across these surfaces water dripped, streamed and gushed. I

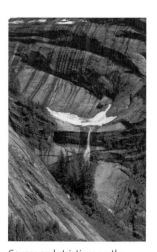

Gouges and striations on the walls of Fords Terror are evidence of past glaciation.

had marveled at similar features in Tracy Arm, but in intimate Fords Terror they seemed more compelling.

Three miles from the narrows, the fjord branched into two arms. Shallows blocked the east arm, so we turned west. Ahead of us, at the end of the inlet, a waterfall tumbled down a green slope with white-topped mountains beyond. We motored in and dropped anchor off a green marsh. A brown bear grazed among the sedge, glancing up only briefly when the clatter of our anchor chain echoed off the hillside.

I set the anchor and Steve turned off the engine. We both sat in the cockpit, looking at the green slopes above us, at the waterfalls tumbling down the hills, and at stripes of snow where the eroded earth formed shadows. This was true wilderness. It was hard to imagine a more beautiful place. It had been worth it to brave the narrows.

5.5 TAKU HARBOR
Real Alaskans

We had just left Endicott Arm in 2008 and were passing the red buoy marking the entrance to Tracy Arm when the buoy's lower half disappeared. I looked at it in amazement, trying to figure out what had happened, when suddenly it vanished completely—it had been swallowed up by fog.

Provided by the Borough of Juneau, this dock offers refuge to boaters waiting out strong winds in Taku Inlet.

"Turn on the radar," Steve ordered. "There are icebergs ahead." I ran below with visions of the *Titanic* in my head. When I came back on deck, icy blue shapes were looming out of the fog and then disappearing as we passed. I grabbed my camera. The scene was frightening but it was also mysterious and alluring.

A few minutes later we reached the open water of Stephens Passage. Fog gave way to gray skies, rain and a light southerly. Icebergs dwindled to a few white blobs in the distance. We turned north, heading for Taku Harbor, 22 miles away. We had been there twice before and although its scenery wasn't spectacular, it has a good harbor, a logical stopover the night before arriving in Juneau.

While Steve went below to write in the log, I stayed on watch, looking out for the cruise ships, tour boats and recreational traffic coming and going between Juneau and Tracy and Endicott Arms. Between dodging other boats, I peered at the shore through binoculars. Even in the rain the scenery was impressive. To starboard I could see caves, sea stacks and arches carved out of jade-green rock. Above the rocks, mist swirled around steep forested hills. To port, in the open waters of Stephens Passage, the spouts of humpback whales hung in the air.

Five miles from Taku Harbor, the wind increased to 20–25 knots from the south. Steve came on deck to raise sail and soon we were scooting downwind, sails out wing-and-wing, rolling in the waves. Rain pelted at my back and damp seeped into my gloves and under my jacket hood. I was glad when Stockade Point at the entrance to the harbor came into view.

The wind died at the harbor entrance and we lowered sail and motored to the large public dock on the far shore. The red roofs and peeling white paint of the former Taku cannery next to the dock were just visible in the mist.

Taku Harbor was once the site of a Hudson's Bay Company fort. That the fort was here at all is a hiccup on the path of history. The land was owned by the Russians, who leased it to the Hudson's Bay Company, which hoped to make the harbor a trading center for furs brought down the nearby Taku River by Native traders. But relations between the Hudson's Bay Company and the Taku Tlingits floundered, and the HBC discovered they could do all the trading they needed from their steamship, HMS *Beaver*. After only two years, they abandoned the fort.

Today Taku Harbor's main attractions are two docks owned and maintained by the City of Juneau. The docks provide refuge away from the fierce Taku winds that blow off the glaciers and down Taku Inlet a few miles to the north.

Since our first visit to Alaska two summers before, I had wanted to meet what I thought of as "real Alaskans," by which I meant rugged individuals who live in the bush all year, eat moose and wild blueberries, and generally live a life of hardship and resourcefulness. But in the small coves and bays we visited, the few houses we saw were mostly vacant, and in the towns and cities everyone seemed in a hurry—not much different from the busy people on the streets of Seattle.

Tiger Olson, Taku's most famous resident, had been such a "real Alaskan." Irving Petite, author of *Meander to Alaska* (1967), visited Olson in 1966 and described him as "a hip-booted, suspender-trousered, battered-hat kind of guy." Olson lived alone by the dock in a small green and red cabin and spent his days prospecting, hunting, fishing, and searching for drift logs for firewood. But when visitors arrived, he would drop everything to welcome them. And visitors came in droves: in small cruise ships, private boats and tour boats. Almost every visitor went away with a gift—a chunk of pyrite, called fool's gold, that Olson packed out from the Sumdum area especially for them.

Tiger Olson is gone now and tour boats no longer make regular stops at Taku Harbor. But a steady stream of visitors on private boats still head into the dock.

We were standing on Taku's main dock looking at a large white megayacht with gleaming anchors when I noticed a small yellow sailboat without a mast approaching the dock. A man and woman, in their sixties or seventies, jumped off the boat to tie up. The man sported a crew cut and chiseled features, and the woman had dark hair tied away from her round face. They both wore regular street shoes, rather than the brown XTRATUF boots so beloved by Alaskans.

"Is that a sailboat or a powerboat?" asked Steve.

The man laughed. "It's a motor sailor. I built it myself and haven't finished rigging it."

We introduced ourselves and learned they were named Andy and Lu. They seemed congenial so we invited them aboard *Osprey*.

They sat at the dinette in *Osprey*'s cabin and told us their story.

"We live in Farragut Bay, about 75 miles south of Taku," Andy told us, accepting the glass of red wine Steve poured for him and leaning back on *Osprey*'s green cushions. "We're heading to Juneau for business."

Thirty-five years ago, they'd moved to Alaska from California where Andy was employed by the defense industry and Lu had been a biology teacher.

"I got fed up with my job and the people I worked with," Andy told us. They sold everything and moved to Alaska.

"We built a 3,000-square-foot house, because that was what we were used to in California," Lu said. "But that was a mistake; we don't need it here."

I was curious about life in such an isolated place and asked them where they bought groceries. They ordered directly from Seattle, they told us, "organic food that's healthy. And we get much of what we eat from our own garden."

"We've sailed these waters for 35 years," Andy said. He went on to explain that they had recently sold a larger sailboat, and in addition to building the little motor sailor had commissioned a hull and deck for a second, a heavy-weather sailboat, from a builder in Port Townsend. "The weather is so bad in the winter that sometimes we can't get out of our bay for five months because of the storms. We need a sturdy boat." Andy planned to spend winters finishing both boats at their home in Farragut Bay.

"We've had to learn new skills for our new life," Lu said. "I've become an artist and sell my paintings at a gallery in Juneau."

Andy told us he was born in Germany. One of his earliest memories was of watching the Nazi SS kill forced laborers for no reason. Lu's story was also dramatic. As a child she was forced to walk from Russia to Germany. She was the only one to survive among five families that started out on the march.

They had time to read in the long winters and took advantage of it to keep up with current events. Andy is a man of firm opinions. "The Iraq war was a mistake, militarily, economically," he told us, setting his wine glass down hard on the table for emphasis.

After Lu and Andy returned to their boat, I realized we had finally met some "real Alaskans." But they'd come via California and live in a 3,000-square-foot house.

5.6   JUNEAU
Lucky Me

"Lucky Me" proclaimed a sign on the south end of Douglas Island at the entrance to Gastineau Channel. As we motored by in *Osprey*, I looked through binoculars to see the sign standing among a collection of small houses surrounded by the usual trappings of rural Alaska: blue tarps, satellite dishes, plastic chairs and aluminum skiffs.

The City and Borough of Juneau owns most of the undeveloped land on Douglas Island and when it decides more private land is needed, holds a lottery for the right

Tourists can rent gold pans at the Last Chance Mining Museum and try their luck at panning in Gold Creek.

Gold Creek, where Joe Juneau made his famous gold strike, runs through Juneau.

to buy it. One winner of a lottery had put up the "Lucky Me" sign. Now the small community around it is known as Lucky Me.

I wondered why someone would cry, "Lucky me!" over the mere chance to buy a lot miles from the nearest road. Was it because they loved Juneau? Or was it because they wanted to get far away from its center while still living there? The view up Gastineau Channel was certainly impressive: steep hills with a faint dusting of snow on their tops rising on either side of the channel. And at the end of the channel we could see the large white blocks of cruise ships anchored and moored at downtown Juneau.

We tied up at the Douglas Marina across the channel from Juneau. We had just finished eating lunch when I heard a familiar voice outside, "Ahoy, *Osprey*!" I looked out the port light to see our friend Gary Parker, who had moved to Juneau from Seattle about 10 years earlier.

"I thought you might be here by now. I got your email," said Gary as he settled into *Osprey*'s cockpit and started telling us about Juneau.

I could see that Alaska had been good for Gary. His black hair was still dark and his waist had thickened only slightly since we had last seen him.

"My office is just five minutes from my boat," he said, pointing to his sailboat, *Erebus*, a few slips away. "And in the winter I can be on the ski slopes half an hour after work. Yeah, it rains a lot, even more than Seattle, but you get used to it," he said, laughing with delight at his new hometown.

Brimming with enthusiasm, Gary listed everything he wanted to show us. "We'll drive out to the ski area and go to the Last Chance Mining Museum. Tomorrow we'll see the Mendenhall Glacier. Let's get going."

As I followed Gary up the dock to his car, I thought he too was proclaiming "Lucky me!"

Hard-Rock Mining

Several hours later, after touring Douglas Island, we stood on a pedestrian bridge looking down on people crouched on a stream bank panning for gold. Dressed in sweatshirts and jeans they looked like ordinary Alaskans, or even tourists—a far cry from the grizzled prospectors who once panned this creek.

We were on the grounds of the Last Chance Mining Museum in the hills above downtown Juneau and looking at Gold Creek, where Juneau's history began.

Towns in Alaska seem to vie for the most notorious history. Ketchikan touts its prostitutes and fish pirates, Wrangell its heavy-drinking miners from the Cassiar

A dramatic cave-in at the Treadwell Mines in 1917 followed by a fire in 1926 turned the town of Treadwell into ruins.

Gold Rush, and Skagway has con man Soapy Smith. Juneau's early history includes two prospectors of questionable reputation and an amusing story about its name.

In 1880, miner George Pilz of Sitka heard rumors of gold near Gastineau Channel and hired Joe Juneau and Richard Harris, veterans of the Cassiar Gold Rush, and three Native helpers, to search for it.

Juneau and Harris took their time getting to Gastineau Channel, working their way up Stephens Passage and finally reaching it in August. Later stories from other prospectors suggest drinking bouts may have slowed their progress. In Gastineau Channel, they found a roaring stream on the east (mainland) side of the channel and, pushing their way through willow thickets and devil's club, panned their way upstream. They found consistent quantities of gold as they went, but instead of staking claims they returned to Sitka. Pilz sent them back, and this time they found a rich gold-bearing vein. For Juneau and Harris, it was the culmination of their careers. Years of prospecting in rain and snow, far from civilization, had finally paid off. Each of the two men may have been thinking, "Lucky me!"

Juneau and Harris quickly formed the Harris Mining District, staked claims for themselves and sponsor George Pilz, and established a townsite that they named "Harrisburgh." The names may have come about because Harris was the only one of the five people present who could read and write English.

Harris and Juneau returned to Sitka with 1,000 pounds of high-grade ore. Soon other prospectors swarmed over Harrisburgh (or Harrisburg) in Alaska's first major gold rush. The Navy sent the USS *Jamestown*, commanded by Charles H. Rockwell, to preserve the peace.

Juneau residents enjoy a Fourth of July on Sandy Beach, created from the tailings of the Treadwell Mines.

This being Alaska, both democracy and pandemonium soon ruled. New arrivals questioned the legality of the Harris Mining District. In February, 31 miners convened a town meeting and declared Harrisburgh null and void. The next day 34 miners voted to rename the town: 18 voted for Rockwell, 15 for Juneau and 1 for Harrisburgh. Meanwhile the US Postmaster General, acting on out-of-date information, recorded the name Harrisburgh for the post office.

Soon ships steamed up Gastineau Channel bringing miners and supplies to the new town, whatever it was called.

The Navy, satisfied everything was under control, left the area. At a general meeting on December 12, 1881, the town's name came up for vote again. Out of 72, 47 were for Juneau City, 21 for Harrisburgh and only 4 for Rockwell. The Postmaster General, perhaps thinking "city" too grand a term, changed the name to just Juneau. Calls for another vote by Harris failed.

In a few years the thud of stamp mills crushing gold-bearing ore echoed off the hills. Juneau, along with the towns of Douglas and Treadwell across the channel, became a center for large-scale hard-rock mining: the extraction of gold from veins by industrial processes. By the time gold mining came to a close with World War II, three major mining operations had come and gone. The Treadwell Mines on Douglas Island put Juneau on the map for their sheer size and country club-like company town—before collapsing in a dramatic cave-in in 1917. The Perseverance Mine won acclaim for its innovative methods. And the Alaska-Juneau Mine turned a mining camp into a stable small city. Together these mines produced a total of 6.5 million ounces of gold at a value of almost $160 million.

As for the prospectors Harris and Juneau, Harris made some money but lost it in legal battles over overlapping claims. Joe Juneau made money too, but spent it in his namesake city's saloons. He died in 1895 at the age of 69 in Dawson City, during the Klondike Gold Rush.

Today, Juneau's economy is based on government services, tourism and support services for logging and fishing. It became the capital of Alaska in 1906 and was combined with the city of Douglas and surrounding areas to become the City and Borough of Juneau in 1970. It has a population of 30,000.

The Last Chance Mining Museum commemorates Juneau's hard-rock mining industry. From Gold Creek we followed a trail uphill until we came to two unpainted corrugated metal industrial buildings.

A musty odor greeted us when we walked through the door of the larger building. As my eyes adjusted to the dim light, I could see gears, cables, tools and other paraphernalia scattered about the room on the floor, on tables or behind glass cases. A pile of gold pans and a sign advertising them for rent stood on a counter. We were the only tourists there, perhaps because it was 6:15 p.m.

A young woman welcomed us. "This was the air-compressor room for the Alaska-Juneau Mine. And that's the air compressor," she said, pointing to a long metal contraption—complete with pulleys, ropes and wheels—that was used to ventilate the mine. "Most of what you see are spare parts. It took years to get delivery and the company couldn't afford to wait so they kept lots of spares."

Thank goodness for priority mail, I thought, remembering parts for *Osprey* delivered to us in Ketchikan from Seattle in two days.

I wandered over to a glass case with a three-dimensional glass model of the Alaska-Juneau Mine. The area had once been honeycombed with mining shafts, some even burrowed underneath the Gastineau Channel.

As we left the museum, what struck me most was not the history of the mines but how so little of them was left: two old buildings and a few spare parts seemed like a small monument to a major industry.

The next morning while Steve worked on *Osprey*'s engine, I went in search of the site of the old Treadwell Mines, curious to see how much of the mines and their company town remained. From the marina I could see Treadwell's saltwater pumping building, a small concrete structure on pilings, on the tidal flats south of Douglas, so I started off in that direction.

Crossing a parking lot and walking along a magnificent stretch of golden-colored sand—tailings from the mines—I came to a stamp machine (called a mill) standing like a sculpture at the edge of a trail. With its vertical metal rods and wooden frame, the machine made me think of a medieval instrument of torture. The workhorses of hard-rock mining, these machines were used to crush ore that was then treated chemically to remove gold. This one, made in Marysville, Washington, and consisting of five stamps, was the original mill that started Treadwell's operations. Later mills were all constructed on the site to ensure the mines were self-sufficient.

Two joggers ran past and I followed them onto the trail and into a grove of young alders. Sunlight filtered through the trees. Rusty machinery lay alongside the trail, and concrete platforms covered with moss and ferns were visible among the branches of salmonberry bushes. Turning a corner, I came to the skeleton of an old building, its steel beams and concrete walls standing among twisted roots and branches of new trees.

At its peak in 1915, the Treadwell Mines employed 2,000 men working in 8-hour shifts, seven days a week, every day of the year except Christmas and the Fourth of July. A reported 960 stamp machines in five mills pounded incessantly, creating so much noise that passengers on ships could hear it as they steamed up Gastineau Channel, and diners in the Douglas Café had to shout to be heard.

All this came to an end on April 21, 1917, during an extreme high tide. By then, 10 million tons of ore had been removed from three major Treadwell Mines, leaving Swiss-cheese holes in the ground 2,800 feet down. Workers first noticed a hole under the firehouse with water running in from the hillside. Just five minutes later, water from Gastineau Channel began flooding into the hole and from there into the mines. In little more than three hours it was all over. All the workers escaped, except possibly one, who may have taken the chance to disappear to a new life. But the economic life of Treadwell was over. Only the Ready Bullion Mine survived and it closed in 1922. Talk of reopening the mines ceased in 1926 when the old wooden buildings and houses of Douglas and Treadwell went up in flames.

Looking at the young poplars growing among the ruins, I thought in amazement of the changes this land had gone through: from a wilderness to an industrial gold mine to a jogging trail. With its pounding stamps and the hills denuded of vegetation by air pollution, Treadwell didn't strike me as a pleasant place to live. Yet, in the midst of this din, Treadwell officials, workers and their families carried on their lives in a company town that had been referred to as a "country club." In addition to mills, foundries and offices, Treadwell had a manager's mansion, stores, dining halls, bunkhouses, and a natatorium. The Treadwell Club, to which all workers and their families were automatically given membership, had a library, auditorium, bowling alley and a Turkish bath. I wondered if any of the workers had thought, "Lucky Me."

I found the answer to my question, not in Alaska but in Seattle, from a fellow writer, Sheila Kelly, whose grandfather had been a machinist at Treadwell. Fascinated by stories of Treadwell told to her by an aunt, Kelly decided to document them. The family history expanded to a history of Treadwell itself, *Treadwell Gold: An Alaska Saga of Riches and Ruin* (University of Alaska Press, 2010). In her research, Kelly heard stories about the good life in this gritty town: swimming competitions with the band playing, ballroom-dancing lessons, picking blueberries in the field behind the town, and fishing and hunting. Among the people Kelly interviewed was Phillip Bradley Jr., son of a mine superintendent. She quotes Phil Jr. as saying, "Treadwell was . . . the damndest most beautiful place for a youngster to grow up in. Gee, what a piece of luck . . ."

An Urban Glacier

"There it is," said Gary, a note of pride in his voice that I would have expected if he were showing us a civic center or the Mendenhall Glacier. But not the Alaskan Amber Brewery in a beige corrugated steel building in the midst of an industrial park.

Our second day of Gary's guided tour had started with errands—the hardware store for a dowel to make a drying rack for foul-weather gear in *Osprey*'s cabin, and the fuel depot to fill *Osprey*'s propane tanks. Now we were getting a tour of new development in the Mendenhall Valley on our way to the glacier. Gary had already pointed out the Walmart, the Costco and the soon-to-be Home Depot. "The Alaska stores have been robbing us blind," he said. " Now I'm saving lots of money and the competition is good."

I was aghast to realize that Walmart and its fellow box stores had conquered the last frontier. From my viewpoint, Walmart was responsible for turning thousands of small towns across the lower 48 into near ghost towns. We hadn't been to downtown Juneau yet, and I wondered what could be left of it now that box stores had moved in. But I held my tongue. We were Gary's guests and I didn't want to get into an argument with him. In Alaska, where often only the most basic consumer goods are available, I could imagine that the residents feel lucky to have any new store.

Our tour of the new shopping areas over, Gary drove up the Mendenhall Loop Road toward the glacier.

Gary owns a house in the Mendenhall Valley. "People worry about mud slides, but it's no more dangerous here than California with its earthquakes," he told us.

Just 12 miles from downtown Juneau, the Mendenhall Glacier is easily the area's biggest tourist attraction. Stretching from the Juneau Ice Fields to Mendenhall Lake below,

A gorgeous backdrop for a wedding gave this bride goosebumps.

the glacier is more than one and a half miles across at its widest and 400 to 1,800 feet deep. And, because it's an urban glacier, visitors can enjoy the amenities of hiking trails, parking lots and a visitors' center built and staffed by the US Forest Service.

Gary had a full list of things for us to see that day, so we bypassed the visitors' center and followed a walkway down toward the lake. The glacier seemed to hang over the lake, a giant white highway sweeping down the mountains. I thought it looked a long way off as I gazed over the expanse of mud and brown water separating it from us.

As if reading my thoughts, Gary said, "The glacier was a lot closer when they built the center. It's been retreating fast."

In fact, the Mendenhall Glacier has been receding at a phenomenal rate of 55 to 110 yards per year since the 1990s. Scientists predict that it will continue to retreat as long as global warming persists.

Global warming or not, the air had a distinct chill from wind blowing off the glacier. Just then a cloud covered the sun and I zipped up my jacket, wishing I'd worn a hat.

Ahead of us, looking very incongruous in the wilderness setting, walked a bride and groom: the bride in a traditional long white gown and the groom in a dark suit. A very pregnant young woman carrying a tripod and a large bag of camera gear walked in front of them. Bringing up the rear was a small girl in a frilly dress partially covered with a parka. They all looked cold to me. Why wasn't that groom offering the bride his jacket?

As they stopped to get into position for a picture, we passed them and I looked closely at the bride's bare arms. They were covered in goosebumps.

Cruise-Ship Town

Throngs of tourists jostled each other on the sidewalk, vying for spots under store awnings out of the rain. Colorful banners and planters full of flowers hung from old-fashioned light fixtures in front of brightly painted storefronts. Waves of tourists moved from one store to another in a frenetic bustle. At the end of the street we could see several cruise ships tied up at the dock.

Steve and I were taking a day to see downtown Juneau.

"I don't like to go downtown. There's nothing for me there," said Gary. "You can borrow my car."

We had spent the morning grocery shopping at the A&P (that's Alaskan & Proud, not Atlantic & Pacific) and the afternoon touring the Alaska State Museum. From the museum we had walked toward downtown, passing the state legislative building. Working our way toward the cruise-ship terminal, we had thumbed through old Alaskan history books at the Observatory bookshop, poked among hiking gear at an outdoor store and walked through several art galleries. We also browsed through the latest bestsellers at Hearthside Books. Now we were on Franklin Street, just a few blocks from the cruise-ship terminal and surrounded by jewelry stores advertising themselves with lines like, "In Alaska and the Caribbean." These we knew were owned by the cruise-ship companies and patronizing them did little for the local economy.

Steve stopped in a T-shirt store with a small sign in the front window announcing it was locally owned.

"We haven't bought any T-shirts on this trip yet," he said. "We might as well see what they have."

We pushed through a crowd of tourists dressed in identical plastic ponchos as we entered the store. I picked out a burgundy T-shirt with a killer-whale design while Steve chose one with a picture of a humpback whale breaching. I added a coffee mug with a Native design as a gift for one of my brothers.

Back on the street I looked around at the nearby stores. "It's not bad," I told Steve. "The stores are attractive and some of them have some good art for sale. And let's face it, with all those new box stores, these storefronts might be empty if it weren't for the cruise ships."

"Yes, but would you want to spend a whole week going from stop to stop seeing the same stores at every port?"

"I guess not. We've already run out of things to do. Let's go get dinner."

We had the name of a seafood restaurant that another boater had recommended. But when we found it, we discovered it was next to a cruise-ship terminal.

"Let's try it anyway. I don't know where else to go," I said to Steve.

We entered a big warehouse of a building. A crowd of people milled around near the entrance. I heard the clatter of dishes and smelled grilled fish. A young woman in a mini-skirt and tight sweater took our names.

"It might be an hour or an hour and a half. You can wait at the bar."

We looked at each other in dismay.

"Forget it. That's too long," Steve said.

We went back to the sidewalk and stood under an awning to look through our visitors' guide. There were only a few restaurants nearby, and those didn't appeal to us.

"Let's just go back to the Island Pub," said Steve, referring to a pub in Douglas where we had eaten pizza two nights ago.

We drove across the Douglas Bridge, parking in front of a one-storey wood building with a row of American flags hanging from its roof. Inside, a comfortable hum of laughter came from customers sitting at tables or around the square wooden bar. Large picture windows overlooked the Gastineau Channel and the welcoming aroma of pizza wafted around the room.

Sipping a glass of red wine, I leaned back and relaxed. Maybe it wasn't a fancy restaurant, but I felt lucky to be away from all those cruise-ship passengers.

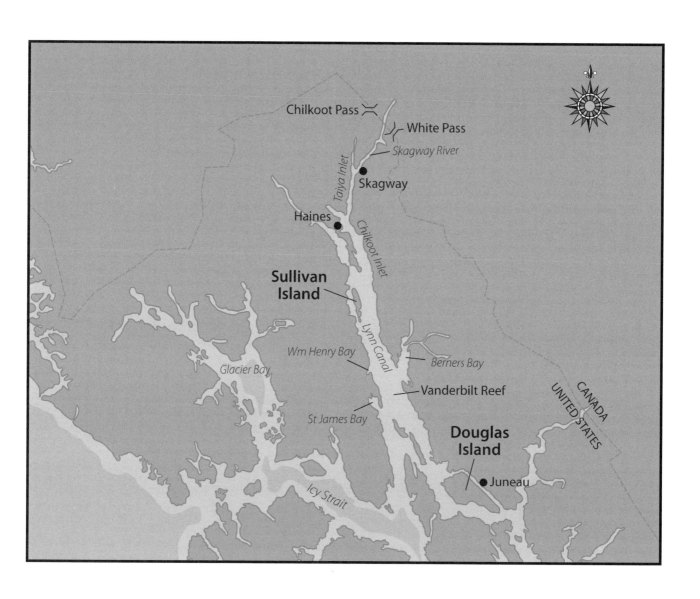

CHAPTER 6

SKAGWAY

6.1 SAILING TO SKAGWAY

As we motored *Osprey* out of the Douglas Marina, heading for Skagway, I wasn't at all sure we were doing the right thing.

"There's no point in sailing to Skagway," another boater had said to us when we told her where we were going. "We took the ferry. Lynn Canal isn't a great place to sail and it doesn't have a whole lot of anchorages."

Skagway is 111 miles north of Juneau. To get there we would have to sail south down Gastineau Channel, around Douglas Island, then north up Lynn Canal, a long narrow body of water bordered by mountains on either side.

"The mountains funnel the wind up and down the canal," said Gary when I asked him about the winds. "They blow mostly from the south in the summer and the north in the winter."

Then there was the question of whether Skagway was even worth visiting. "It's a tourist trap with a mining-town theme. Cruise-ship folks really like it," Gary told us.

We weren't keen on a theme town, but Skagway did have the White Pass and Yukon Route Railroad. The chance to ride it was reason enough to go. As for sailing versus taking the ferry, the easy way wasn't our style. Besides, what would Jigger do if we left him for three days?

The winds that day seemed designed to ease my fears. We motored down Gastineau Channel in a flat calm, then drifted north under sail in Stephens

Osprey sails north in a strong southerly wind in Lynn Canal.

Passage, finally turning the engine back on near the north end of Douglas Island. A clearing sky gave us the first glimpse of sun we had seen in a week. To the east we could see Mendenhall Glacier sweeping down the mountains and glittering in the sun, while to the west a humpback whale spouted. As we motored through a fleet of gillnetters, I watched the crew on one of them pull shiny salmon from their net.

By the time we entered Lynn Canal, we were under sail again. At 5:00 p.m. we passed Vanderbilt Reef. In the high-tide waters, it looked like no more than a small flat rock topped by a steel tower, insignificant compared to the mountains looming in the background. But I knew those waters hid an extensive and dangerous reef.

On the night of October 23, 1918, the Canadian Pacific liner *Princess Sophia* was making its last run of the season, heading south from Skagway to Seattle with a full load of passengers, when gusting winds and blinding snow overtook it from the north. Without modern radar and GPS the ship's captain relied on the compass and whistle, counting the seconds for an echo to bounce back from the shore to tell him the ship's distance from land. We'll never know exactly what happened, but at 2:00 a.m. *Princess Sophia* struck Vanderbilt Reef at full speed. With a horrible grinding and tearing sound, it slid up on the reef and remained suspended, hull partly afloat in shallow water.

The captain radioed for help and soon a fleet of tugs, fishboats, mailboats and other vessels assembled nearby. But in the heavy seas, the *Sophia*'s crew could not launch lifeboats without risking them being dashed to pieces, and rescuers dared not approach. By 7:00 p.m. a full-scale blizzard was underway. Unable to even see the *Sophia* in the dark and snow, the rescuers retreated for cover.

Meanwhile, wind and waves began to move *Princess Sophia* and lift it off the reef. Twisting and grinding, it swung around, and then slipped backwards off the reef. On the radio, her would-be rescuers heard, "For God's sake, hurry!" Then silence. When the storm abated, only a lone mast marked *Princess Sophia*'s grave. Not one of the 353 passengers survived.

The Canadian Pacific Liner *Princess Sophia* ran aground on Vanderbilt Reef with a loss of all on board on October 23, 1918.

Today few people beyond maritime buffs and the descendants of the *Princess Sophia*'s victims know of the sinking. Ken Coates and Bill Morrison, authors of *The Sinking of the Princess Sophia: Taking the North Down with Her*, suggest that the reason for this is the itinerant nature of her passengers—residents of the North (the name for a region that included territory in both Canada and Alaska) who still called towns all across Canada and the United States home and spent most of their winters there. With no center of mourning, no monuments were erected to memorialize the disaster and *Princess Sophia* was simply forgotten.

A gillnetter fishes for salmon in Lynn Canal.

Our weather couldn't have been more different than that experienced by *Princess Sophia*. From Vanderbilt Reef we sailed northwest in a dying wind, drifting toward William Henry Bay on the west side of Lynn Canal. In the bay we anchored off a sandy beach next to a fishboat. From our deck we could see up a river valley to snow-covered peaks in the west and across Lynn Canal to more mountains gleaming in the evening sun.

I went to sleep that night thinking we had escaped the strong winds of Lynn Canal. But when we motored out of the bay the next morning a fresh breeze was blowing from the south, sending waves ricocheting off rock walls along the canal. *Osprey* began to pitch and roll. From below decks we heard a loud wailing meow. Jigger was seasick. I didn't feel so great myself.

Steve raised sail while I steered and soon we were lurching through the waves at 6 knots. The wind whistled through my fleece jacket making me shiver. An overcast sky and dark mountains looming on either side of the canal made for a bleak day.

As the morning wore on, the wind rose. Steve took the wheel and with the wind behind, we sailed wing-and-wing, jib on one side, mainsail on the other. But even with a pole holding the jib out, the erratic rolls of the boat in the rough water would send the jib slamming across the bow with a loud "whump" while Steve struggled to keep us on course.

Ahead we could see Sullivan Island stretching along the west shore. "Let's go inside," said Steve. He hoped that by sailing between the island and the mainland we would get some temporary relief from the seas. A river delta jutted out from the mainland shore across from the island's south end, providing protection from the south. As we entered the channel, the sun burst through the clouds, turning the water, which was thick with

Sullivan Island provides shelter from the seas in Lynn Canal.

glacial flour, green. With a sandbar to port and rocks to starboard, we were occupied with sailing and had no time to enjoy the view. But once beyond the delta, we could relax. I took over the wheel to give Steve a break.

Seeing the island in the sunlight reminded me how far north we were (the 59° N latitude line passes through Sullivan Island); even at 11:00 a.m., so close to noon, the sunlight came at an angle, lighting up the land. Beyond the river delta, huge flocks of seabirds flew in formation, their wings beating the air in a whirring sound as they raced like dark shadows across the water. Cormorants? Grebes? They were moving so fast I couldn't tell. To port, a powerboat rocked at anchor off the river mouth, the first pleasure boat we had seen that day.

As we passed the north end of Sullivan Island at 11:30, we could look west up a valley to a glacier and east to the whitecaps in Lynn Canal. Steve took the wheel back and headed for a passage between Taisani Island and Seduction Point at the south end of the Chilkat Peninsula. From Seduction Point we would be turning up Chilkoot Inlet toward Skagway.

By now the wind blew 30–35 knots, and the least deviation from our course heeled the boat sharply to one side or the other.

"We need to reef the mainsail," said Steve. "Take the wheel and I'll get ready."

I realized he intended me to steer while he reefed, our usual pattern. But normally we reefed going upwind at wind strength far less than this. I imagined myself fighting the wheel while the boat sailed with a mind of its own.

"No. Let me reef. You steer." Although I couldn't remember the last time I had taken a reef, I knew it was the only way we could make it work.

Steve headed the boat just enough upwind to set the sails flapping and I clipped my harness on the jack line that runs along the deck and inched my way forward, clinging to the cabin top in the pitching seas while waves crashed against the side of the boat and sent spray into my face. Hanging on to the boom with my left hand, I used my right to let the mainsail down to the first reef points, crank in the reefing line, then crank the mainsail up tight again. It was done, and it hadn't been as bad as I'd expected.

Without losing a beat from the reduced sail area, *Osprey* surged ahead into Chilkoot Inlet. As we passed a narrow spot between Battery Point to the west and the Katzehin River delta to the east, the waves grew steeper and the boat pitched and rolled. The shallow sandbanks at the river's mouth looked uncomfortably close.

Beyond the narrows, the inlet opened up to a broad water body before forking into two more even narrower inlets. Across the water we could see the town of Haines, a thin line of buildings dwarfed by the mountains above. As we turned into Taiya Inlet, the easternmost of the two, the wind dropped to 12 knots and I breathed a sigh of relief. Just a few more miles and we would be at Skagway. In the narrower inlet, we sailed closer to shore and could see how different the terrain was from farther south. To starboard a waterfall gushed down a steep hillside while to port, on the north-facing slope, short, dry-looking pine trees clung to bare rock.

The lull in the wind was only a brief respite. Soon it was back up to 30 knots and we were racing up the inlet. As the buildings and docks of Skagway came into view, Steve got out one of our hand-held VHF radios and called the harbormaster. No answer. I looked anxiously at the town coming up fast. Would we have to enter an unknown marina in this strong wind without knowing if there was space for us?

We were rapidly approaching the end of Taiya Inlet. Two cruise ships occupied a pier to the west, two others a pier to the east—in the area shown by one of our cruising guides as the only possible place to anchor. Above the roaring of the wind in our rigging we could hear the beat of helicopters delivering loads of tourists from a day of sightseeing.

"My God!" said Steve. "This town really has sold its soul to the cruise ships."

Steve turned into the wind and I raced to the mast to take down the sails. Held up by the force of the wind that was sending it shimmying, the mainsail refused to drop on its own, and I had to tug it down hand over hand.

"It's 42 knots!" yelled Steve over the roar of the wind.

I returned to the cockpit to hear Steve talking urgently into the radio, "Skagway harbormaster, Skagway harbormaster, this is *Osprey*, over." This time the harbormaster answered. He had a slip for us just inside the breakwater.

As we motored though a canyon of white cruise ships, I tied down the flailing sails as best I could and put fenders and lines out on both sides, ready for anything. Steve steered through the breakwater and then turned to starboard into a narrow slipway and past a tour boat. Once there the wind pushed us onto the dock, into the only vacant slip.

With the boat safely moored, we looked around. We were in a narrow slipway, side to the wind and stern to the channel with a very beamy tour boat behind us.

"They've just given a whole new meaning to 'tourist trap,'" said Steve. "We'll never get out of here until the wind dies."

The Town of Skagway

After a hard day of sailing, we wanted a reward—dinner at a good restaurant. Jigger, meowing and pacing the cabin floor next to his empty dish, expected a treat too. We left him a handful of his favorite kibble,

Skagway with its railroad, museum and renovated storefronts, is a popular stop for cruise-ship passengers.

A cruise ship moored at a dock at Skagway looks as if it is cruising down Broadway Street.

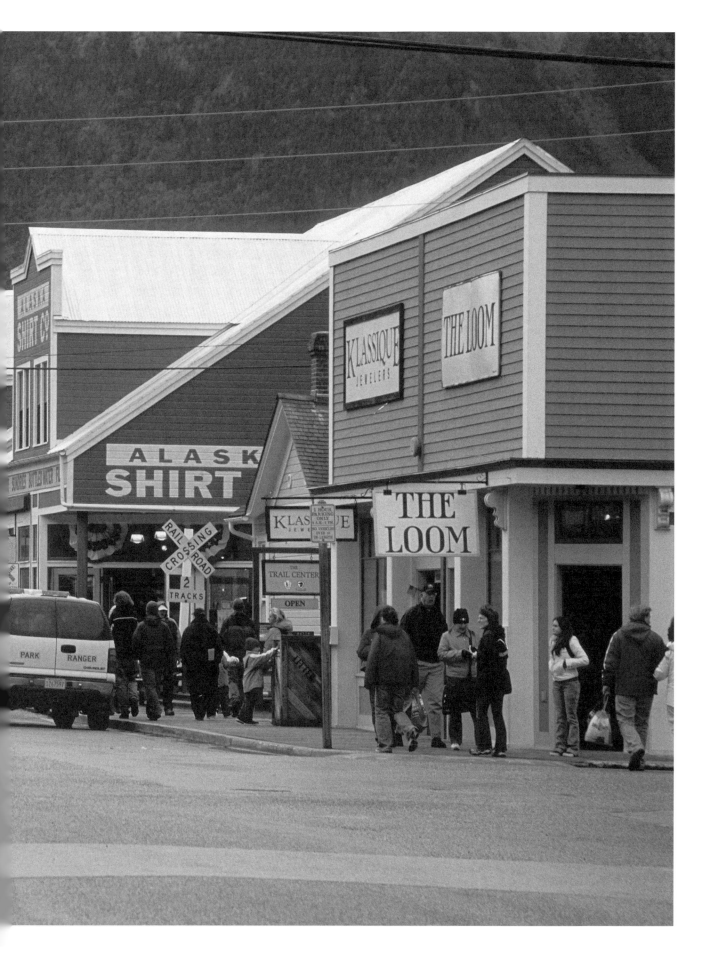

locked the cabin door, and headed up the marina ramp to the road. There we encountered streams of pedestrians, their arms laden with plastic shopping bags.

"Good," said Steve when he saw they were heading toward the cruise-ship dock. "They're leaving. We'll have the town to ourselves."

The name "Skagway" comes from the Tlingit word "Skagua," meaning "home of the north wind." Today, the wind was blowing from the south, but strong enough to make the pedestrians bundle up in fleece and Gore-Tex. The town occupies the delta of the Skagway River, and the flat terrain offers no protection from winds blowing up or down the valley.

In just a few minutes we were on Broadway, Skagway's main street. We looked left, then stopped abruptly, astonished by the view. At the end of the street, a massive white cruise ship looked poised to charge right up Broadway into town. Snow-capped mountains towered above the ships.

We turned north up Broadway, looking at shop windows. A few tourists still wandered in and out of the stores, their footsteps clumping on the wooden sidewalk. The stores had the wild-west look we had learned to associate with Southeast Alaska's tourist towns: false-fronted buildings and colorful paint. The paint reflected restoration by the National Park Service, but this was no theme park. Instead of the outfitters, dry-goods stores, dentists, grocers and other establishments that once served the miners, we passed jewelers, T-shirt shops, linen stores, furriers and more jewelers: many identical to ones we had seen in Ketchikan and Juneau.

We came to a building labeled "Skaguay News Depot." From the old-fashioned spelling, I thought it was an old newspaper office, but then realized it was a modern bookstore.

"Look at that!" Steve pointed to a sign in the window. "It says they have *The New York Times*." At home, we have the *Times* delivered to our house every morning and both of us read it religiously. But we had seen it only twice in the month and a half since leaving Seattle.

"A *New York Times*?" The clerk behind the counter shook his head. "They're all gone by now. Come back tomorrow morning about 10 o'clock."

A young man carrying a guitar leaned against the counter chatting with the clerk. Steve asked them about restaurants.

"Olivia's Garden is several blocks to the right," the young man told us. "It's a new restaurant and has a good chef."

We found it inside the Skagway Inn, an old-fashioned white clapboard building surrounded by a garden. We walked through a wallpapered lobby furnished with antiques, and into the restaurant where we took a table by the window. From there we looked out into a side yard where raised planter boxes sprouted huge green rhubarb leaves, lettuce, herbs and flowers. At a nearby table, stylishly dressed young people, mostly women, were drinking margaritas. No brown XTRATUF boots here.

A waiter in a blue shirt served us green salads topped with delicate purple pansies from the restaurant's own garden, along with plates of delicious spicy Spanish sausages. They were tapas, but big enough for a meal.

"We just opened three weeks ago," he told us.

"Will you be open all year?" I asked.

"Oh no. A place like this always closes in the fall."

"What will you do? Stay here?"

"I'll probably go to Hawaii. I spent a year and a half in Charlotte Amalie (capital city of the Virgin Islands) before coming here. Skagway is nice in the summer but no fun in the winter." Some things hadn't changed since the days of *Princess Sophia*.

We walked back through the town in the deepening Alaskan dusk. We had just eaten the best meal we'd had so far in Alaska, and wondered how the most remote and smallest of all the tourist towns

Many of Skagway's old storefronts have been renovated by the National Park Service as part of the Klondike Gold Rush International Historical Park.

had produced such a nice restaurant. As we passed the Red Onion Saloon, the sounds of laughter and guitar music drifted out into the street. The cruise ships were gone for the night, but the town still hummed. Maybe Skagway wasn't going to be so bad after all.

6.2 THE KLONDIKE GOLD RUSH
The Last Great Gold Rush

"Two things I dislike about Alaska," one of my friends told me once, referring to Southeast Alaska. "It rains all the time and everyone there obsesses about the gold rush."

I confessed to agreeing with her with regard to the gold rush. In fact, when looking for books on Alaska in Seattle bookstores, I was annoyed by the large number on the gold rush and passed them by. We were going to Southeast Alaska, not the Canadian Klondike.

Arriving in Skagway, however, I realized I was overlooking several important points. Gold may have been discovered in the Klondike Valley of Canada, but much of the rush occurred in Alaska. Some of it even happened down south, in my hometown of Seattle. The gold rush opened up Alaska to development and changed it from "Seward's Folly" to "our Alaska," a place as large in the imagination of Americans as it is in geography. Finally, the sheer magnitude of the gold rush as an event helped to weave Alaska into the cultural fabric of the United States.

On July 17, 1897, the front page of the *Seattle Post-Intelligencer* blared, "GOLD! GOLD! GOLD! GOLD!" Newspapers around the world picked up the story and the rush to the Klondike began. Pierre Berton, Klondike expert and author of *Klondike: The*

Last Great Gold Rush, 1896–1899 (Anchor, Canada. 1972), called the rush of 1898 the "last and the most frenzied of the great international gold rushes." Conditions were right for a perfect storm of a stampede. It was the peak of the gay '90s. Thrill-seekers rode balloons and read Jules Verne; anything and everything was possible. The 1893 financial panic left men desperate for jobs and money. Within a few days of the *P-I*'s headlines, stampeders poured into Seattle and other west-coast cities, ready to pay anything for passage north.

The stampeders shared one goal: to reach the town of Dawson on the banks of the Yukon River in the Canadian Klondike. But to get there they could choose from almost a dozen routes, each one with its boosters. Those with money could pick the all-water route: by steamer to St. Michael on the shore of the Bering Sea, then by riverboat up the Yukon River. Canadians touted "all Canadian routes" overland through miles of forests, mud, and mosquitoes, while some Americans touted "all American routes" across glaciers from the Gulf of Alaska. (Boosters of this route apparently forgot that the Klondike itself was in Canada.) But by far the largest number boarded boats for Alaska's Inside Passage to either Skagway or its rival twin city, Dyea, three miles southwest. Few realized until it was too late that they couldn't reach Dawson before winter. And, as one anonymous stampeder said, whatever route they chose, they would wish they had taken another.

Skagway and Dyea offered competing routes over the mountains. Dyea had the Chilkoot Pass. It was steep, ice-covered, narrow, and impassable by pack animals, but an established Tlingit trade route. Skagway had the 45-mile White Pass, 10 miles longer than the Chilkoot but 600 feet lower. A switchbacking, roller-coasting, undeveloped route, White Pass was suitable for packhorses, mules or goats—or so its boosters claimed.

In July 1897 the future town of Dyea consisted of a small but flourishing trading post. Skagway was even smaller: a lone house occupied by the family of William Moore, a sea captain who had purchased enough land there for a townsite in anticipation of the next gold rush. By August, Skagway and Dyea each had become (in the words of Pierre Berton) towns "of swearing men and neighing horses," with streets of black mud and newly formed governments. Soon Skagway had makeshift saloons, blacksmith shops, and rows of tents: the beginnings of what today is the Skagway unit of the Klondike Gold Rush International Historical Park.

A gray day of rain and wind greeted us on our first morning in Skagway. For company on our explorations we had Jennie and Peter of the ketch *Jennie V* from Michigan. Early that morning we had looked out *Osprey*'s windows to see their boat motoring into the marina. We had first met them anchored among icebergs in Tracy Arm, had shared a crab dinner with them in Taku Harbor and had last seen them in Juneau three days before. Both in their sixties, they were cheerful, enthusiastic sailors. We had immediately recognized kindred spirits.

"I hope you don't think we're following you," Jennie greeted us. We were delighted to have their company and be a foursome of private boaters in a town packed with cruise-ship passengers. From the marina we could see four big ships, so we knew the town would be crowded.

Our route into town took us by a small blue house with a National Park Service sign. We decided to investigate. Inside we learned the house once belonged to Benjamin Moore, son of William Moore, the clairvoyant sea captain who first settled Skagway. Only a few other tourists were in the historic house with us, reading interpretive signs and looking at the antique furniture. On the way out we stopped and talked to the park ranger. "Where are the tourists?" asked Steve. "With four ships in town, there must be eight thousand cruise-ship passengers here today."

"Actually," said the ranger, reading from a schedule on her desk, "there are 9,682. But we won't see many of them here. We're off the main street and as the National Park Service we're not allowed to advertise so they don't know we're here."

We found the cruise-ship masses soon enough on Skagway's Broadway Street. Throngs of tourists in raincoats and plastic ponchos crowded the wooden sidewalks, ogled the quaint false-fronted storefronts and wandered in the streets taking photos. At the Klondike Gold Rush National Historical Park Visitors' Center, we squeezed past more tourists to look at black-and-white photographs showing long rows of stampeders struggling up the snow-covered Chilkoot Pass or stumbling past dead horses on White Pass. Then we joined the line to view *Days of Adventure, Dreams of Gold*, a movie made from colorized versions of the same black-and-white photographs. After seeing the pictures of the column of prospectors, the immensity of the gold rush began to dawn on me. Somewhere around 100,000 stampeders joined the rush but only 40,000 reached the Yukon; 20,000 worked claims but only 300 made more than $15,000 ($330,000 in today's dollars). Of those who didn't strike it rich, many still considered the gold rush to be the high point of their lives—an adventure to tell and retell.

In the main room of the visitors' center, our small group stood and stared at a huge

This house belonged to Benjamin Moore, son of William Moore, a sea captain who settled Skagway in anticipation of the next gold rush.

Dead Horse Gulch on the White Pass trail, where thousands of pack animals died in the scramble for gold.

pile of gear: the year's worth of food and supplies the Canadian government required of each prospector. There were bags of flour, rice and beans, boxes of canned goods, galvanized buckets, pickaxes, hammers, saws, nails, blankets, a tent—all together weighing roughly a ton. The idea of carrying this load over a snowy mountain pass was mind-boggling. Although some prospectors hired Tlingit porters, most toiled alone or in the company of partners. Able to carry only about 65 pounds a trip, some prospectors trekked back and forth as many as 30 times.

Through the fall and winter of 1897, at least 52,000 stampeders crossed the Chilkoot, shuttling goods up stairways cut through ice. Meanwhile, on the trail to the White Pass, 5,000 men set out, but only a handful reached the top. Alaskan rain turned the trail into mud. Packhorses with crushing loads stood for hours as the long line of closely packed prospectors labored up the trail, so desperate for gold they wouldn't let anything stop them—including severe risk to their horses. Soon dead animals lined the trail in tangled masses. By September, the route turned into impassible mud and thousands retreated to Skagway to wait for a freeze before setting out again. Chilkoot, the steeper and higher of the passes, stayed frozen longer and turned out to be the better choice.

Jammed with stampeders with nothing but time on their hands, Skagway grew into a true American wild-west town—with pawnbrokers, dance halls, gambling halls, vigilantes, hustlers and shootouts. And behind all this stood one infamous con man: Jefferson Randolph Smith, commonly known as "Soapy." We were to learn more about him later, but first we had a train to catch.

6.3 THE WHITE PASS AND YUKON ROUTE RAILROAD
In the Path of Stampeders

The diesel locomotive roared and chugged up the mountain. Inside the first passenger car, where I sat by a window behind Jennie, the passengers were silent except for an occasional "Wow!" as the train traveled up a narrow ledge cut out of the steep rocky mountainside. Far below, the Skagway River snaked its way through thick green forests as a thin white line.

Ahead a metal bridge cantilevered over a narrow canyon. As the train approached, I could see the bridge's spindly supports were darkened with rust. I told myself that thousands of tourists made this trip every day. Surely it was safe. But when the train veered right at the last minute and headed toward a tunnel instead of over the bridge, I breathed a sigh of relief. As we passed the bridge, I caught a glimpse of broken ties and bent rails and realized it was no longer in use.

We had just passed Dead Horse Gulch on the White Pass trail, where thousands of pack animals died in the infamous scramble for gold. A perilous trek was now an easy train ride.

Construction of the White Pass and Yukon Route (WP&YR) Railroad began on May 28, 1898, shortly after the first winter of the gold rush. A total of 35,000 men, up to 2,000 at a time, worked on its construction. New gold strikes lured men away while others grew discouraged by the hard work, heavy snow, and temperatures as low as 60°F below zero. Falling rock, steep slopes, and dangerous blasting powder took their toll; 35 men lost their lives on the project. But by February 1899 the railroad had reached White Pass, 20 miles from Skagway, and by July 1899 Lake Bennett, another 20 miles. The contest between Skagway and Dyea for the best route to the Klondike was over—Skagway had won.

We had boarded the 4:00 p.m. train at the WP&YR depot, a newly renovated building in downtown Skagway. It looked just like a train station should, with ticket windows, benches, and old-fashioned luggage carts decorated with planter boxes. Lines of passengers snaked through the lobby in front of the ticket windows, waited for coffee at the snack bar, and purchased T-shirts and hats in the gift shop. More passengers milled around the platform watching two-toned green and yellow locomotives shuttling lines of UPS-brown cars back and forth on the tracks. The scene appeared chaotic but railroad employees had it under control; they seemed to be everywhere, carrying clipboards and wearing uniforms with the initials WP&YR.

"Listen carefully," cautioned a voice over a loudspeaker, "or you'll end up on the wrong train." When our train was finally called, a cheerful young woman led us down the tracks and around the corner to where a train sat waiting. I glanced up at the sky. The rain, which had been coming down steadily earlier, had finally ceased, and I could see patches of blue among the clouds.

A man in a gold-braided hat directed us to the first car after the locomotive. We found seats on the left—the side of the car we figured would have the best view—and settled in for the ride. The car was simply furnished with padded bench seats, wooden-paneled walls, large windows, and an oil-burning heater at one end. Around me sat families with children, oldsters with graying hair, and everybody in between. The young couple behind us told us they were off a cruise ship. Most cruise-ship passengers purchase their tickets on board

A White Pass and Yukon Route train crawls along the steep face of a mountain.

Falling rocks, steep slopes and freezing temperatures made construction of the White Pass and Yukon Route Railroad a challenge.

and ride special trains that deliver them directly to the cruise-ship docks. By buying their tickets at the station, they saved money but risked missing their ship if the train was late.

Soon the train was chugging through the outskirts of Skagway. I caught glimpses of white gravestones among trees as the old miners' cemetery flashed by on our right. Cottonwood trees gave way to hemlocks and spruce as we left the river delta behind.

The farther from Skagway we traveled, the steeper and more twisted the route became. The WP&YR's narrow gauge, with only 3 feet between rails compared to 4 feet 8½ inches of a standard gauge, made construction easier and allowed for sharper turns, a necessity on the steep and twisty trail. The sharper turns also made for a more exciting journey.

Steve and Peter went out to ride on the open platform between our car and the locomotive. After awhile I followed, but the constant roar of the locomotive and the stench of the diesel exhaust combined with a cold wind drove me back inside. There I stayed glued to my seat, listening to the announcer point out the sights: sections of the old wagon road, a black cross marking the grave of workers buried in a rock slide, and whirlpools in the Skagway River below. The trees became shorter and less abundant as we climbed; sub-alpine firs replaced hemlock and spruce and then low bushes replaced the firs.

As we came out of the final tunnel before the summit, we gazed down on a narrow rocky trail, barren except for a few patches of yellow lichen. A sign marked it as the '98 trail. On this day, 108 years after it had last been used, we could still see where the stampeders and their pack animals had tamped down the rocks.

At the summit of White Pass, we waited for the locomotive to switch to the other end of the train and for the train behind us to catch up. We gazed out on a scene of desolation: bare gray rocks against gray clouds. Alongside the track, in bare rocky ground, five flagpoles flew the flags of Canada, the United States, Alaska, British Columbia, and the Yukon Territory: a reminder that the gold rush was an international event. Beyond the flagpoles sat a small log cabin with a metal roof and a white sign with the initials NWMP. From

The White Pass trail is still visible where the stampeders and their pack animals tamped down the rocks in their rush to reach the Klondike.

just such a small cabin, the Canadian Mounties watched over the pass in 1898. Americans in Skagway might be lawless, reckless and anonymous, but from here on, they would be under the watchful eye and protection of the Mounties. Mounties would enforce the laws, record names and next of kin, rule on whether boats were safe enough to brave the Yukon River, and mediate conflicts. Any American con men that dared to enter Canada were sent marching back home.

The White Pass and Yukon Route Railroad, which once carried gold ore across White Pass, now operates as an excursion railroad.

Still ahead for the stampeders who crossed the White Pass on foot that first winter of '98 were freezing temperatures and the back-breaking work of cutting trees to build crude boats. When the spring thaw came, they would navigate through rapids, whirlpools, and swarms of hungry mosquitoes to reach Dawson City and the goldfields.

Thanks to the White Pass and Yukon Route, future travelers would have an easy trip. In addition to the railroad, the company operated paddlewheelers, stagecoaches and sleighs—providing transportation all the way to the Yukon. And as the Klondike evolved from a land of stampeders to one of mining corporations, the WP&YR provided the transportation to open the country.

Working steam engines can be seen at the White Pass and Yukon Route railyard.

The White Pass and Yukon Route Railroad carried gold ore, supplies and people across the pass until 1982 when gold prices dropped worldwide and mines closed. It reopened in 1988 as an excursion railroad, operating during summer months only and drawing most of its passengers from the cruise ships. The gold may have been gone but for the WP&YR Railroad, the scenery was the new gold.

On the return trip, our car, which had been at the front of the train just behind the locomotive, became the rear car. I joined Steve and Peter on the platform and watched the track roll out behind us as we glided downhill. For a short time I had felt as if I had joined the stampeders on their great adventure. We pulled into the station just in time for the cruise-ship passengers to make their ship. Impressed by the efficiency and cleanliness of the train, I looked forward to our next adventure in Skagway: *The Days of '98 Show with Soapy Smith*.

6.4 SOAPY SMITH
The Musical

"We'll start our play in just a minute," said the actor, addressing the audience. "But we're missing an important prop. Can anyone spare a dollar bill?" The audience in Skagway's Eagle Hall laughed uneasily. No one raised a hand. We knew the musical was about a con man and weren't about to be taken in.

The actor, in a black suit, string tie and white broad-brimmed hat, paused and looked over the audience. "All right, I'll tell you what I'll do. Give me a one and I'll give you a ten." As he said this, he drew out a wallet from his back pocket and waved it in the air.

Finally, a man several rows back held up a dollar.

"Now I'm going to keep my promise," said the actor as he handed the man a dime.

We had just seen how Skagway's famous con artist Jefferson Randolph ("Soapy") Smith worked.

Soapy acquired his nickname in Denver, Colorado, where he would gather a crowd, wrap a $100 bill in a package with a bar of soap, mix the bar in with others in a basket, then offer the soap for sale. No one ever got the lucky bar.

Soapy arrived in Skagway determined to be the town boss. He recruited a gang of scalawags and set about winning control of the town. Dance halls, saloons and gambling dens quickly appeared—all run from "Jeff Smith's Parlor." Bogus businesses thrived: ticket offices selling passages on ships that never arrived; information offices selling misinformation, and Soapy's most famous enterprise—a telegraph office without telegraph lines.

Some said Soapy wasn't all bad. He gave money to widows (whose husbands his men had killed), supported a local church, and ordered his men not to fleece Skagway's permanent residents. When the Spanish-American War broke out, he organized a militia and marched as grand marshal of the town's July 4th parade.

But then Soapy's men went too far: they stole gold from one of the first miners to bring his riches back to Skagway. Afraid that news of this theft would drive returning prospectors (and their gold) elsewhere, Skagway's merchants formed a vigilante group to stop the con men.

Soapy's reign ended in an Alaskan version of a western scene: a shootout at the end of a wharf between Soapy and Frank Reid, the city engineer. Soapy, shot in the heart, died instantly. Reid, shot in the groin, died twelve pain-filled days later. His gravestone reads "He gave his life for the honor of Skagway."

The day Reid died was the same day the White Pass and Yukon Route's first steam locomotive chugged through town. It was the end of one era and the beginning of another. Mining corporations soon replaced stampeders as the rush became a slow steady business.

Frank Reid died a hero but today few remember him. Soapy, however, is famous. *Amazon.com* lists a play and eleven books about him, the latest published in 2006. Soapy's great-grandson maintains a website dedicated to his memory and invites readers to join his family in toasting Soapy's ghost on the anniversary of his death. And then of course there's the musical, *The Days of '98 Show with Soapy Smith*, which we were about to see.

The day before we had been walking down Broadway Street with Peter and Jennie when a colorful poster of actors in gay '90s outfits lured us inside a theater. While the others bought tickets, I prowled the entryway. A small contraption of steel and leather straps hanging on the wall caught my attention. A sign underneath said, "This place is a genuine tourist trap."

A man dressed in a broad-brimmed black hat and a black suit walked by and saw me smiling at the notice.

"I like your sign," I told him.

"We tell it like it is here."

"Be sure to come at seven o'clock," the ticket seller was saying to Steve and Peter. "With the evening show you get gambling."

"I'm not so sure about this gambling," I told Jennie as we entered the theater the next night. "When other kids were playing cards, I had my nose in a book."

The gambling den was a low-ceilinged room off the theater entryway with three large green felt-covered tables. We could choose between blackjack, poker and roulette. Jennie headed for the poker table while Steve, Peter, and I chose blackjack.

I needn't have worried about my inexperience. At the blackjack table a red-headed woman with heavy makeup and huge breasts that hung over the table doled out instructions with the cards. She gave us each a pile of both red and blue chips and then dealt us each two cards. The object, she explained, was to get the highest hand totaling twenty-one or less. When each player's turn came, they could choose to say, "hit," which meant "give me another card," or "stand." I had a seven and an eight and chose "hit."

"I wouldn't do that if I were you," said the dealer.

I looked at her suspiciously. This was Soapy Smith's gambling den so I figured it would be a mistake to take her advice.

"Hit." I repeated.

"I *really* wouldn't do that."

"Okay. Stand."

She was right. Had I taken another card I would have lost that hand. As others experienced similar plays, we all began to accumulate tall piles of chips that mysteriously doubled or tripled in value at various times. The dealers, I realized, were making us all winners. In between hands, our dealer quizzed us about Alaska. For each correct answer, she gave us more chips.

"How many stars on the Alaskan flag?" (Eight)

"What's the Alaskan state flower?" (Forget-me-not)

"When did Alaska become a state?" (1959)

I was curious about the dealer who seemed so enthusiastic about Alaska and Skagway.

"Do you live here year-round?" I asked her.

"Oh, no. I come every summer but I'm from New York."

"What do you do there?"

"Look for acting jobs."

After the gambling, we filed into the theater, laughing at our winnings as we took our seats on red-plush chairs. On the stage was a re-creation of Soapy's saloon, complete with a bar, tables and a piano.

"We have one more thing to do," the actor announced after the dime trick. "This isn't a regular theater, it's the Eagle's Hall. We need to raise some money for the Eagle's scholarship fund for Skagway High School students."

At that point a winsome young blonde in gay-'90s costume came on stage, jumped up on the bar, smiled seductively and hiked up her skirt to reveal a frilly blue garter on her right leg.

"The gentleman who bids the most for this garter will get to remove it from this lady's leg." The woman waved her leg in the air.

"Who will give me five?"

Silence.

"All right, who will give me a dollar? Fifty cents?" A lackadaisical bidding pushed the price to four dollars.

"Ladies can bid for their husbands."

I suddenly thought it would be fun to have that garter as decoration in *Osprey*'s cabin. I offered five dollars. My entry spurred the bidding war and soon we were in the teens, with Steve whispering, "Go for it."

"Twenty dollars!" I bid. Silence.

"Going once, going twice. Twenty dollars it is!"

To the crash of chords on the piano, Steve climbed up on the stage and slid the garter off the woman's leg.

"That twenty dollars gets you the garter," said the actor to Steve. "Anything more is between you and her."

Soon the audience was laughing and clapping to rousing ragtime music. The musical, mostly about Soapy and his mistress, was not only entertaining, it involved the crowd. The actors recruited a man in the audience as a customer for a dance-hall girl and a woman to join in the cancan.

We walked out of the theater laughing, Steve with his garter and Peter with a tape of ragtime music he had earned for winning the most chips at gambling. "I'm glad we did that," said Jennie and we all agreed. I reflected how different Skagway seemed to be from Ketchikan, where the streets emptied of people promptly at 5:00 p.m. It was as if Skagway had looked at all the tourists streaming off the cruise ships and instead of retreating had said, "Let's have a party." By providing a consistent flow of tourists, the cruise ships made it all possible. I thought of the people we had met: the waiter from the Virgin Islands, a laundromat operator from Florida and the actress from New York. They were all summer residents. And they were here to give us a good time (and take our money doing it).

I had dismissed the town of Skagway as being too touristy and not the real Alaska. But in Skagway, tourism *is* the real Alaska. The gold is gone but the rush remains.

The next morning the wind had dropped to less than 10 knots in the marina and we motored easily out of the harbor.

"I'm glad we sailed to Skagway," said Steve as he steered *Osprey* down the inlet. "But if we go again, let's take the ferry."

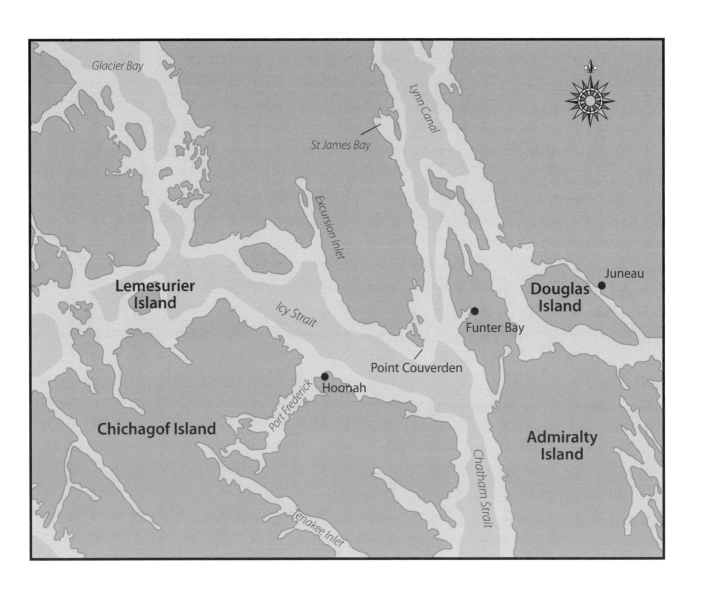

CHAPTER 7

ICY STRAIT

7.1 FUNTER BAY
Aliens in Their Own Country

Our two boats drifted quietly on the calm waters of Sunshine Cove on the east side of Lynn Canal. From *Osprey*'s deck, I watched Gary lean over the side of *Erebus,* and spill a line of ash from an urn. In the dark practical clothes he favored, Gary looked the part of someone performing an official ceremony.

"This is Peggy," Gary said. "She was a good mother to me. We had some good times together. Now she gets to spend more time here in one of her favorite places." Gary's words brought back the memory of the one time I had met his mother. I remembered her friendly smile and her pleasure in seeing her young grandchild, Gary's daughter, but not much else. When Gary had moved to Juneau, we had kept in contact with him but had never seen his mother again. We knew she had joined him many times to sail in these waters, flying north from her home in Grays Harbor, Washington.

There should be more people here, I thought—friends and other family. But she had chosen these Alaskan waters as her final resting place and friends and family were miles to the south. The sheer size of Alaska and its distance from the lower 48 guaranteed isolation.

As Gary finished releasing the ashes, I looked out at a pleasant sand beach curving around the cove and at a rugged little island framing a view of Lynn Canal. Suddenly, the sun came out, lighting up snow-capped mountains.

The two boats drifted apart and Gary went back to *Erebus*'s cockpit to start the engine. "Let's go to St. James Bay for the night," he called. Our plans were for the two boats to sail together for several days in Icy Strait before Gary had to return to work in Juneau. St. James Bay would be a convenient stop on the way to Icy Strait.

As we motored southwest across Lynn Canal, the sun hid behind the clouds and the wind began to ruffle the water. By the time we arrived, the breeze had grown to gusts. We motored around the bay looking for a sheltered spot, but every way we turned the wind followed us. Finally, Gary put down his anchor on the bay's west side, and we tied *Osprey* alongside. The bay protected us from the seas in the canal, but we couldn't escape the

The entrance to St. James Bay is past a gravel bar.

wind that blew up and down the long bay and stirred up an uncomfortable chop. A grand Alaska anchorage, I thought to myself—magnificent to look at, but too large for comfort.

The wind blew into the night and I slept fitfully until the early morning when it finally died down. At 7:00 a.m. the sound of boots clumping on *Erebus*'s deck next door woke me. I stuck my head out of the hatch to see Gary impatiently tying lines and straightening gear.

"Let's get out of here before the wind comes up again," he told me.

Steve and I had gotten into the habit of staying up late reading and writing into the long Alaskan evenings, then sleeping late in the mornings. We'd noticed that it often rains in the morning and clears up in the afternoon, so that's when we preferred to sail. Gary, on the other hand, liked to get underway early.

"We're awake now," said Steve when I returned to *Osprey*'s cabin. "We might as well get going."

Gusts were darkening the water as we motored out of the bay. We raised sail and tacked south down Lynn Canal, heading for Funter Bay on Admiralty Island. An hour later we were motoring on flat water in calm wind when I looked out toward Icy Strait and saw a pod of orcas swimming so close together and so well synchronized they looked

Orcas swimming in Icy Strait appear perfectly synchronized.

like a single creature. "I can see how the Natives at Klemtu thought they saw whales with two dorsal fins," said Steve.

We motored into Funter Bay where we had a choice of two docks: one on the north side in a small cove at the old cannery town of Funter, and a second farther into the bay in Refuge Cove. The Refuge Cove dock isn't connected to the land, a configuration that struck me as odd. Why bother with a dock if it doesn't get you to land? Steve and I wanted to go ashore and walk around, so we headed for Funter. The dock was full, so we put down an anchor and Gary tied *Erebus* alongside.

I looked around at the attractive little cove with its log cabins scattered around the shore and thought how nice it was to see a human-scale cove where we could anchor close to shore. So many of the anchorages that we had visited in Alaska are like St. James Bay—beautiful and grand, but so large that it's hard to find shelter.

I was making lunch when a blast of wind hit us from the east. The boats shuddered and heeled, then straightened up again.

"Williwaws off Robert Baron Mountain," said Gary.

I heard the anchor chain rumbling across the bottom; then Steve said, "that dock sure is close." I looked out to see it getting even closer; our anchor was dragging. Gary started *Erebus*'s engine and motored the two boats to starboard to put a second anchor down. Soon two anchors were dragging. Maybe there's an advantage to those grand Alaskan coves after all, I thought: room to drag without fear of running aground.

Rain had now joined the wind. We separated the two boats, raised anchors and motored across the bay to Refuge Cove where we found plenty of room at the float and quiet water in the lee of the land. A few minutes later, a small black sailboat, the *Shannon Taj*, came up behind us. A man and a woman jumped off. Their tiny stature matched the size of their boat, and the way they moved around the dock made me think they knew what they were doing. When their boat was tied up they introduced themselves as Jon and Susanne of Juneau. With a long evening of bad weather ahead of us, we decided to have a potluck. I made a big pot of Moroccan lentil stew, Gary added chicken, and Susanne and Jon contributed a quiche and brownies.

"I was hoping to tie up at Funter," I told Jon and Susanne over dinner.

"We had a brown bear come on our boat there once," Jon told us. "It sounded just like somebody walking around in boots. We were lucky that he left without tearing the boat apart. Be glad you're here and not there." So now I understood the reason for docks without access to land.

We went to bed that night with the wind howling and the rain drumming on the cabin roof. By morning, however, the wind was down and rain had turned to a light drizzle. Gary set off in *Erebus* toward Icy Strait and we promised to join him later at Excursion Inlet. First we wanted to take that walk we'd planned the day before. We also wanted to see a cemetery at

Jon, a boater from Juneau, prepares his boat to leave Funter Bay.

Aleuts evacuated from the Pribilof Islands during World War II were housed at Funter Bay. Thirty-two of them died in the first two years and were buried in this cemetery.

Funter that Jon and Susanne had told us about.

We motored back to Funter, where there was now room at the dock. On shore, we walked along a boardwalk past neat vacation homes with abandoned cannery machinery serving as planters and garden sculptures. Spotting a group of men filling in a muddy path with crushed rock, we asked directions to the cemetery, and they pointed us toward the beach. Slipping and sliding across a beach of loose slate that looked uncannily like petrified wood, we walked until we came to an orange marker, then took a path into a second-growth forest. Tall hemlock and spruce grew close together, screening out the light and making the forest dark and gloomy. We followed the trail up a small rise to a white wooden archway. Beyond the archway stretched rows of white Russian Orthodox crosses.

We wandered quietly among the graves, reading the Russian names on the few stone markers and marveling at the photographs of Russian Orthodox icons nailed to the second bar of each freshly-painted wooden cross. I wondered who it was that cared for these graves in this isolated settlement.

The graveyard came from a sad chapter in American history. In 1942, when Japanese forces attacked the island of Attu at the end of Alaska's Aleutian Chain, US authorities evacuated 881 Aleuts from nine villages on the Aleutian and Pribilof Islands. Rushed from their homes without time to gather adequate clothing and bedding, they were herded onto cramped transport ships, then delivered to abandoned canneries, salteries, and mine sites in Southeast Alaska. Funter Bay became a refugee camp for Aleuts from St. Paul and St. George, two Pribilof Islands in the Bering Sea, more than a thousand miles away.

Crowded together in drafty buildings without proper heat, sanitation or health care, many of the Aleuts died—32 in two years at Funter Bay alone. When the Aleuts who survived returned to their villages, they found their homes and churches destroyed and their belongings vandalized—not by the Japanese, but by American soldiers. In 1998 congress finally passed a law providing for financial compensation and an apology on behalf of the American people.

As we walked back to the dock, I thought about watching Gary release his mother's ashes. Now, visiting this isolated cemetery only two days later, I groped for a connection between the two events. Gary's mother's death came at the end of a long life and her final resting place was one that was special to her, representing nature and beauty. The Aleuts' deaths were untimely; their final resting place represented isolation. Southeast Alaska had felt remote and wild to me these last few days, with its bears, williwaws and too-large bays. To the Aleuts this land of forests and rainy skies, far from the treeless islands they knew and loved, was even more alien. Forced from their homes, they were strangers in their own country. Only the cemetery remains to remind us of this tragic chapter in American history.

7.2 EXCURSION INLET
Beyond the Guidebook

As we left Funter Bay, I could see whitecaps on the water ahead. Three bodies of water—Lynn Canal, Chatham Strait and Icy Strait—meet here off Admiralty Island. Lynn Canal and Chatham Strait run north and south in a combined distance of 200 miles of open water, while Icy Strait runs northwest toward Cross Sound and the Pacific Ocean. The currents, winds and waves from three bodies of water could give us a rough ride.

We cleared the bay and Steve went forward to raise the jib. I watched the sail start up the forestay, then stall. "It's stuck!" yelled Steve. "Go pull on it."

Osprey's jib halyard often hangs up on the sheaves on a port tack. Freeing it requires a simultaneous downward yank on the jib and upward tug on the halyard.

I went forward to the foredeck as *Osprey*'s bow rose with the waves, only to plummet down a few seconds later. While sheets of icy water poured over me, I muttered to myself angrily, thinking that if we had a roller-furling jib instead of the old-fashioned hank-on jibs that Steve insisted on, we could just pull out the jib with a winch and I could stay warm and dry in the cockpit instead of being cold and wet on the foredeck.

"Pull," yelled Steve.

I gave a tug just as Steve pulled on the halyard, and the jib came free. Then I crawled back to the cockpit on the heaving deck in time to pull in the jib sheet while Steve finished raising the sail itself. Soon we were racing across Lynn Canal on a beam reach, in 20–30 knots of wind.

With the sails set and Steve at the wheel, I went below to towel off my face and wipe the salt from my glasses. My anger was gone, but I couldn't help thinking what a struggle we were enduring to get to a place we knew little about.

Our destination was Excursion Inlet on the north shore of Icy Strait, about 25 miles away. All we knew was that it was the site of a major salmon cannery with some intriguing history. We wanted to do some exploring, to get off the beaten track. Cruising boats, intent on reaching Glacier Bay, rarely go into Excursion Inlet, and our

Mountains in Excursion Inlet dwarf the large cannery complex.

guidebook provided little useful information. We didn't even know if we could stay over-night; the chart didn't show any water shallow enough to anchor, and although the *US Coast Pilot* promised a seasonal float, we had frequently found its facility descriptions to be outdated. But if we wanted to explore beyond the guidebooks, we had to take some risks.

Several hours later we turned north into Excursion Inlet and sailed right out of the wind. As *Osprey* wallowed in the leftover seas, we looked back to see the wind still kick-ing up whitecaps behind us, while to the south a rain squall shrouded the mountains of Chichagof Island. A few minutes later, Gary radioed to say the wind was quiet farther up the inlet and he'd found moorage at the city dock. I thought it was strange to have a city dock where there is no city, but I was glad to hear we would have a safe place to tie up.

We motored up a magnificent fjord where tall mountains streaked with snow disap-peared into a blanket of clouds. Forested shores rising steeply from the water were only occasionally interrupted by an isolated lodge or house. Ahead we could see a tiny row of buildings beneath towering mountains. As we got closer, the complex took shape and became enormous warehouses, wharves and cannery buildings. We tied up behind *Erebus* on a ramshackle string of floats as rain began to fall.

Ashore, we walked past rusty machinery and old building foundations to a complex of dormitories, houses, and other wooden structures. In contrast to the modern factory buildings we had passed on our way to the dock, they looked as if they were from another era. Excursion Inlet is a company town not unlike the many others that once dotted the shores of British Columbia and Alaska.

A sign advised all visitors to check in at the office. We asked some workers, paint-ing a small wooden building in the rain, how to get to the office, and they pointed to-ward the large complex that we had passed on the way in. Four women, wearing brown XTRATUF boots, were walking that way, and we fell in behind them. I listened to the women talking amongst themselves but couldn't recognize the language.

"It's Tagalog," said Steve, referring to a Philippine native language.

Early canneries in Alaska hired Chinese, Japanese and Native workers. Each ethnic group had its own living quarters and often its own boss who shared their ethnicity. In the 1920s, as opposition to Chinese and Japanese workers increased in the States, Alaskan cannery owners turned to Filipino workers. They still employ them today, along with workers from all over the United States.

We passed a row of small clapboard houses with flowers and lilac trees in the yards, then turned onto a dirt road. Next to the road, piles of bicycles, their pedals and wheels tangled in an artistic mess, lay on the grass, while rows of abandoned washing machines, stacks of metal trays and miscellaneous cannery equipment led away from the road. Gary and Steve were so intrigued by this collection of equipment that I feared we might never make it to the office. Finally, we came to a large industrial building where a group of workers in purple aprons were washing piles of screens.

In the office, we told two women behind a counter that we were checking in. They gave us puzzled looks; evidently visitors were not a regular occurrence. One of them left the room and returned with a man in a neatly pressed shirt and slacks. He told us we were welcome to walk anywhere as long as we didn't go in the cannery buildings.

"Be sure to see our small museum while you're here."

I asked him if they were processing fish at the time, and he said there were a couple of boats full of fish just half an hour away. The plant had over 200 workers and was expecting 120 more, he told us.

According to the website of Ocean Beauty Seafoods (the cannery's parent company), the plant processes pink and chum salmon as well as salmon roe, salmon caviar, halibut and sablefish. It's one of the largest plants in Alaska and among the few working canneries, as opposed to fresh and frozen fish-processing plants, left on the coast.

Workers at the cannery in Excursion Inlet clean equipment.

Following a different route on the way back, we came to a straight stretch of road paved in blacktop. It took us a while to realize we were looking at an airport. Next to the runway a shelter of corrugated iron housed a bench where two Filipino women sat waiting. "Excursion Inlet International Airport" announced a sign on the shelter. I walked closer to see notes written in grease pencil and read:

> *928,000 salmon*
> *390 cannery workers*
> *Handful of pilgrims in the bush*
> *The Odd tourist*

If I needed evidence we were off the beaten track, the reference to "the Odd tourist" was it.

Another handwritten sign listed destinations all over the world, including Juneau, Seattle, Fresno, El Paso, Luzon (Philippines) and the Czech Republic.

When visiting small towns, I always like to check out the local store. We found the company store in an old wooden structure in the residential area. Three little Filipina girls were sitting on a bench outside waiting for it to open.

"The store opens at six o'clock," they told us in a chorus, smiling happily.

We wiled away the time by walking back to the dock. In the inlet, two skiffs of sport fishermen floated offshore. Their yellow and orange slickers stood out from the misty background. Every few minutes one of them caught a fish and everybody cheered.

We walked back to what proved to be a typical small-town store with shelves that looked too empty, rows of canned and dry goods, a few jackets and sweatshirts with the company logo, and a sad collection of potatoes, wilted carrots and too-soft tomatoes. Boxes of canned salmon sat on the floor. I bought six cans of red sockeye for $2.50 a can.

The storekeeper pointed out the museum to us—the small wooden building the workers had been painting in the rain.

It was deserted but the door was unlocked, the lights were on and tools were spread on the floor as if someone had been working and just left for the day. We signed the guestbook and wandered around looking at the photographs and memorabilia in the display cases.

A colorful display of can labels hung on the wall along with a list of Excursion Inlet's major events. The first cannery was established on this site in 1908 by the Astoria and Puget Sound Cannery Co., which subsequently sold out to the Columbia River Packers Association. Wards Cove, Bumble Bee Seafoods and finally Ocean Beauty Seafoods all owned the plant at various times.

To this history of company takeovers and expansions was added a strange chapter from World War II. Display cases of yellowed newspapers and military memorabilia told the story. In 1942 the US Army moved in, chopping down trees, laying out roads and constructing buildings for a barge depot for the war in the Aleutians. But before the US Army could use its new facilities, the Aleutian war ended. Not wishing to waste all that good lumber and machinery, the Army imported German prisoners of war to dismantle it. Instead of barbed wire to keep the Germans in their camps, warnings of icebergs and bears sufficed. Alongside photographs of cannery workers were images of German prisoners working and eating.

Among the remnants of this history was the large cannery building, built by the US Army and sold to the cannery in 1951.

As we motored out the inlet the next morning, I looked back to see the thin white line of the cannery dwarfed by the mountains above. It was a good image of Alaskan industry. Even the largest facilities are made small by the immensity of the surrounding scenery.

7.3   HOONAH
Halibut Pizza in Disneyland

The first images we saw as we approached Hoonah, in Port Frederick on the south shore of Icy Strait, were clear-cuts on the hillsides above the harbor. The very next sight was a huge white cruise ship anchored off Point Sophia.

Steve groaned. "What can all those people possibly do in such a small town?" Hoonah is a predominantly Tlingit community of about 800 people of the Huna tribe, who trace their origins to Glacier Bay. It seemed like an unlikely cruise-ship destination.

Then we rounded the point and saw the buildings of Icy Strait Point, a tourist

Cruise ships anchor off Point Sophia and take their passengers ashore in boats to the Icy Strait Point Development.

development. A former cannery complex of warehouses, cannery buildings, houses and docks, it is now painted barn-red and all newly renovated to provide shopping and entertainment for cruise-ship passengers. As we motored by we could see crowds of tourists on the cannery boardwalks.

The redeveloped cannery is part of a trend in the cruise-ship industry toward destinations owned and/or controlled by cruise-ship companies. The big ports of Ketchikan, Juneau and Skagway are getting crowded and cruise-ship companies are looking for alternative destinations.

It was our first trip to Hoonah, in 2006, and we had come to drop off Steve's sister and brother-in-law, Morgan and Bill, at the Alaska State Ferry dock. After a week with us in Glacier Bay, they were returning to Juneau and then home to Virginia. I had been looking forward to exploring the small town and meeting some of its residents. Now there would be something else to explore. And I was curious what impact the cannery development would have on the town.

We motored *Osprey* along the

Hoonah is a busy harbor for both fishing and recreational boats.

waterfront until we spotted the ferry terminal and the marina. Steve called the Hoonah harbormaster, who told us to tie up at the guest dock just inside the breakwater.

A short, energetic black-haired man carrying a VHF radio greeted us at the dock. He was Paul Dybdahl, Hoonah's harbormaster.

Paul pointed to our inflatable dinghy trailing from *Osprey*'s stern. "That dinghy has to go on deck, or I'll charge you extra."

"What if I snug it up tight?" Steve asked. With *Osprey*'s long overhangs, the dinghy could just about hide under the stern.

Paul frowned. "The rules don't allow it. If it's in the water, you have to pay for it."

"I'll pay," agreed Steve.

Morgan asked the harbormaster if he knew when the ferry left for Juneau. One of the ferries had broken down and the schedule had changed, but the recorded announcement was out of date.

"I'll just drive over there and find out," Paul told us.

We watched in amazement as he walked up the dock and got into a pickup truck. Harbormasters that went so far out of their way to help their customers were rare. A few minutes later he returned with the news that the ferry left at 3:30 p.m.

After we thanked him, I asked, "Is there a taxi we can call? They have too much luggage to carry."

"Oh, no. Just be at my office at 3:15 and I'll take them there."

It was just past noon and we had enough time to explore before Morgan and Bill had to leave.

We walked through town, passing a few scattered stores with the traditional Alaskan false-fronts. The chain jewelry stores and T-shirt shops were absent. A sign in the window of the Galley Restaurant and Coffee Shop advertised halibut pizza.

Morgan looked at the sign and laughed. "Halibut pizza! Is that a joke?"

"Sounds fishy to me," quipped Bill.

The restaurant seemed to be doing a vigorous business, with people coming and going and milling around outside.

A row of small houses stretched along the waterfront. More houses perched on a hill above. A few were painted bright colors like orange or turquoise, but most were weather-beaten and bare. Although abandoned cars littered the yards and old stoves and washing machines sat on porches, the weathered wood and uniform-sized houses gave the town an attractive, rustic appearance. A small white church with a Russian Orthodox cross sat on a hillside above the road.

We passed a small grocery store, the Hoonah Trading Center, and came to a bar called The Office. A sign advertised live Dungeness crabs.

A totem pole stands guard over downtown Hoonah.

"I wouldn't mind a beer," said Bill.

Inside we found a typical bar with a wide-screen TV, pool table and a row of bare wooden booths. We took one of the booths that gave us a view of the harbor, and a young woman brought us bottles of Alaskan Amber Ale.

We were admiring the scene out the window when a Native man in an apron came over to us.

"How are you doing?"

"Great," Morgan replied. "We had a good week in Glacier Bay."

The man pointed out the window to a dock. "I've got 350 crabs down there that I have to move into deeper water. There's a minus 3.8 (foot) tide tomorrow. I served 250 crabs today to the cruise-ship passengers."

"Do the cruise ships come every day?" I asked.

He went to the bar and brought back a white laminated schedule, pointing out to us the names of the ships—the MS *Sapphire Princess* today, the MS *Ryndam* the day before. None was scheduled for tomorrow, which meant the cannery complex would be closed.

"The cruise ship is leaving soon," he told us. "In a few minutes the workers from the cannery will be here to party."

As Steve and I motored past the quiet cannery complex the next morning, I told him, "There are two things I'm sorry we missed: the halibut pizza and the cannery."

We returned in 2007, this time with my cousin Carolyn and her boyfriend, Gene, as our guests. Approaching Point Sophia from the east, we noticed what looked like electric transmission lines running down from a mountain to the point. "What do they need so much electricity for?" wondered Steve. Then we saw figures riding the lines in harnesses and realized we were looking at a zip line.

As before, we tied up at the guest dock and Paul, the harbormaster, came down to greet us. "You'll have to move to the other side of the dock," he said. "I've got a 130-footer coming in later this evening."

The Galley Restaurant closes at 6:00 p.m., so we made sure we got there in time to order a halibut pizza.

When the pizza came, it was hot, bubbly and white.

Carolyn, who is always full of enthusiasm, was the first one to sample it.

"Wow! I can't believe how good it is!"

I took a bite and tasted succulent halibut and tangy cheese.

"It's like a halibut casserole on pizza dough," said Steve.

As we got up to leave, a Native woman with long gray hair walked out the door with us. Outside, she turned to us. "I was here when all the houses burned down.

A zip line above the forest provides tourists at the Icy Strait Point development with an exciting ride.

Alaskans don't like to throw anything away. A Hoonah resident has found a practical use for an old stove.

Everyone else was at the Excursion Inlet cannery. No one was here to stop it. It started at one end of the street and traveled to the other."

She was referring to a devastating fire that started on June 14, 1944, underneath a house where two women were smoking salmon. Drums of gasoline were stored beneath many houses and they exploded, destroying not only buildings but valuable art and regalia. Knowing his clan would be held responsible and unable to pay for damages, the leader of the women's clan gathered all his people's regalia and sat in their clan house—sacrificing his life and the treasures to the fire as retribution.

The next day we left Hoonah in the early morning. We had a reservation for Glacier Bay National Park and didn't have time to stay to see the cannery.

In Juneau in 2008, we heard rumors that Hoonah's harbormaster had retired, so when we tied up at the guest dock, we were surprised to see Paul, official VHF in hand. "You can't tie up there. I've got a 130-footer coming in." We remembered last year's 130-footer—it never had arrived—but we moved without comment.

"We heard you retired," I told him.

"Somebody's got to do the work." He looked critically at our yellow inflatable. "That's got to go on deck. I used to charge for them, but now I don't let them stay in the water at all. I can't have dinghies floating around for other boats to bump into."

A cruise ship had been anchored off the point when we arrived, so we knew the cannery would be open. Gary, who had tied *Erebus* behind us, had shopping to do so we made arrangements to meet him later and walked through town past the ferry terminal and the cemetery and around a bend. A large white cruise ship, MS *Serenade of the Seas*,

The museum at the Icy Strait Point Development includes a plastic model of a slime line (where workers cleaned fish) including realistic plastic blood.

came into view. Anchored off the cannery, it loomed over the buildings, a size XXXL in an XL world.

We walked past a stream of passengers heading into town, through a gate with an unmanned gatehouse, and onto the cannery site. A line of tourists waited to get into a brand-new longhouse for a show of Native dancing. Another line waited on the dock to have their IDs checked before boarding boats to return to the ship.

We followed a sign saying "Museum" into a large open room with rough-hewn unpainted rafters and pieces of machinery scattered around. I was immediately reminded of the North Pacific Cannery National Historic Site in Prince Rupert. But where the North Pacific Cannery had been moldy and quiet, this was clean and busy. Professionally made signs explained the history of Hoonah, its cannery, and the fishing industry. Shops and restaurants sold T-shirts, jewelry, art works, and fish and chips. There was even a small bookstore operated by the Hoonah High School. It is amazing what a captive audience of thousands of cruise-ship passengers can do for a museum.

The Hoonah Packing Company built the cannery complex on Point Sophia in 1912. At its peak the cannery employed 92 Hoonah residents and 21 non-residents. After it closed in 1953, Wards Cove Packing used the buildings to store and repair nets and boats. In 1996, Huna Totem, the local corporation authorized by the Alaska Native Claims Settlement Act, purchased the cannery with the idea of developing it as a tourist attraction. Fishing had declined, logging was near its end, and the community was looking for jobs. Huna Totem Corporation partnered with a tourism company in Juneau as the Point Sophia Development Corporation. They named the development Icy Strait Point and entered a contract with cruise-ship companies to bring in the customers.

Huna Totem and the cruise-ship companies envisioned a self-contained Disneyland of canneries. The out-of-town location would keep traffic and crowds away from in-town shops and services and allow cruise ships to focus passenger spending on businesses within the development. Residents and independent travelers like us were to be turned away.

It didn't work as planned. Lee K. Cerveny, who studied the sociocultural effects of tourism in Hoonah for the US Forest Service, told the story in a 2007 report. Hoonah residents were outraged at being kept away from land that was part of their history and owned by their own Native corporation. And on the first day the cannery opened, passengers surprised cruise-ship owners and residents by walking unguided into town. They told Hoonah residents they wanted to see "an authentic Alaskan town." Hoonah businesses thrived. The Office bar cultivated the business of crew members who in turn tipped off the passengers. Cruise ships tried harder to keep passengers on the cannery site by publishing maps with no reference to Hoonah and a clear "guest boundary." They even tried anchoring ships in Icy Strait, out of sight of town. Nothing worked. New local businesses were formed, including tours and fishing charters not owned by the cruise-ship companies.

The passengers and townspeople won the battle. The Icy Strait Point website now welcomes people with the message, "Located down the road from Alaska's largest Tlingit village is Icy Strait Point—the Real Alaskan Experience!" And the gatehouse, which once kept independent travelers like us away, now stands unoccupied.

We met Gary on the boardwalk where we strolled past a row of neat wooden houses until we came to the end of the zip line. The clanging of zip-line chairs and excited screams filled the air. Orange-shirted workers helped customers out of chairs and sent the chairs back up the line. The entire ride took only 92 seconds and cost $92.

"A dollar a second," said Steve. "Some people have too much money."

Returning to the cannery, Steve and Gary went ahead while I stopped to talk to two elderly Hoonah men tending a campfire. When I told them we were on our own boat instead of the cruise ship, one of the men explained that upon arrival at Hoonah the disembarking cruise-ship passengers were given wood chips to toss into the fire for good luck.

"Are you glad the development happened?" I asked him.

"Oh, yes," he smiled. "We went right from logging to this."

"Is this easier?"

"A lot."

As I turned to go, he asked me if I had ridden the zip line.

"No. That's not for me." I asked, "Have you?"

"Oh yes, I can hardly wait until Hoonah Day when I can ride for free!"

We returned to the marina where we discovered the 130-foot megayacht *Miss Sydney* tied across from us. It was just beginning to rain and a crew member stood on the dock handing umbrellas to guests as they disembarked.

As we motored out past Sophia Point the next morning, Steve looked at the cannery and turned to me. "Okay, we've seen it—now we don't have to go back."

Neither of us imagined we would return to Hoonah in just a few days.

7.4 FOURTH OF JULY AT HOONAH

A bear statue serves as a grave marker at a Tlingit cemetery in Hoonah.

I watched the knot meter, which gives our speed through the water, slow from 6 to 5, then 4. The chart plotter revealed even more dismal news: we were moving only 3 knots over ground. We weren't going to make it to Tenakee Springs for the Fourth of July.

"We can go to Hoonah," said Steve. "It has a parade. It's a larger town and there will be more going on. And Bob and Sherry (friends from Seattle traveling in their own boat, *Ponderosa*) will be there." We were off Spasski Island in Icy Strait, less than five miles to the entrance to Hoonah's harbor.

I was disappointed. As a child growing up on the shores of Puget Sound, Fourth of July had been my favorite holiday. I remembered picnics on the beach, bonfires so tall we had to climb on ladders to build them, and fireworks exploding over quiet water. Alaska's small towns are famous for their Fourth of July celebrations and the community potluck that Tenakee Springs is known for appealed to me.

At 11 o'clock the next morning we were standing with Bob and Sherry and a small group of other boaters on Hoonah's main street, waiting for the parade to start. We had arrived the night before in time to hear Sherry's story of their encounter with the harbormaster.

Townspeople wait for the Fourth of July parade.

"I can't believe it," she had fumed, her round, usually smiling face growing red with anger. "He wouldn't assign us a slip until we put our dinghy on deck." This was a new twist to the rule. I suspected it was because *Ponderosa*'s radio had failed and they'd entered the marina without permission, breaking one of the harbormaster's taboos.

In the bright sunlight of a holiday morning, troubles with harbormasters and contrary currents seemed inconsequential. Crowds were gathering along the parade route, milling around a totem pole and sitting on the curb in front of the Galley Restaurant. Young men had perched themselves on rooftops of nearby buildings. Red, white and blue pennants flapped in the breeze.

The parade started with sirens and horns. A police car led the way, followed by a string of tour vans, cars, veterans carrying flags, a pickup truck decorated with paper fish and a US Forest Service truck carrying Smokey the Bear. From each vehicle people threw handfuls of candy into the street. Crowds of children—and some adults—rushed to gather up packages of M&Ms, lollipops and taffy.

"The dentists must be paying for this parade," said a boater standing next to me.

Children riding bicycles, tricycles and skateboards brought up the rear. A little boy on his tricycle was so festooned with red, white and blue balloons we could hardly see him.

A lumberman practises for the log rolling contest, part of Hoonah's Fourth of July celebration.

It was over in a few minutes. The parade turned the corner and headed out of town toward the marina, the crowd behind it. We followed, stopping briefly on the waterfront to watch a logger practising for the log-rolling competition.

The picnic grounds were bustling with activity. The aroma of barbecues wafted across the field where people stood in line at concession stands to buy hamburgers, Indian fry bread, and watermelon. Clouds had crept in during the parade and by the time we reached the picnic area, a fine mist was falling. I feared the rain would stop the festivities, but no one paid it any attention.

The crowd drifted toward a grassy area set up by rows of benches. A man standing on top of a van with a loudspeaker announced a foot race for girls 2–3 years old. Girls toddled into the arms of waiting family members. The little boys raced next and on they went right through to the to 17–21-year-olds.

After the races, a man unloaded a flat of eggs from the van and the announcer called, "Egg toss! Granddaughters and grandmothers."

Middle-aged to elderly women stepped onto the field, facing young women and girls. Each grandmother took an egg and stood a few feet from her granddaughter. On the announcer's "Throw!" the grandmothers tossed their eggs gingerly to granddaughters, who then tossed them back. With each throw, granddaughters and grandmothers stepped farther apart. When someone missed a catch, that pair dropped out.

"Last pair to throw wins!" cried the announcer.

Grandsons and grandfathers came next, followed by mothers and daughters, fathers and sons, mothers and sons, and every possible combination of family relationship, finally ending with husbands and wives. The field became speckled with white and yellow splotches and contestants wiped sticky egg from hands, clothes and even faces. As granddaughters stepped back on the field as daughters, sisters or wives, and as grandsons took their places as sons, brothers or husbands, they got better and better at throwing eggs and the

Sisters pair up against sisters for the egg toss. Last pair with an unbroken egg wins.

inevitable splat became more dramatic. With each contest, the numbers grew as did the laughter. I watched adult brothers and sisters throwing their eggs and laughing good-naturedly. I was amazed. I couldn't imagine this many adult brothers and sisters in one place in Seattle.

After watching the egg toss we stood in line at one of the concession stands to buy Indian tacos, steaming mounds of ground beef and tomato sauce on Indian fry bread, and carried them to a picnic table next to the water. I tried eating mine with my hands and got sauce on my sleeve and more on my nose.

No Fourth of July is complete without fireworks. At 10:00 p.m., the four of us set off through town for the ferry terminal where we settled on benches that looked out over a vacant field.

We were madly shooing off mosquitoes in vain when I noticed a family next to us spraying insect repellent. "Could we borrow your spray?" I asked. The father looked surprised. Clearly, no Alaskan would come out at night without mosquito spray. But he loaned us his bottle.

As the sky darkened, bonfires burned on the field and children lit Roman candles.

The official show started with bursts of red, white and blue stars. Explosions echoed off nearby hills, followed by "oohs" and "ahs" from the crowd. On the field, dark figures were silhouetted against the smoke and fire. The closeness of the fireworks made them seem more intense.

Walking back along the water toward the marina, I smelled the acrid aroma of fireworks and saw wisps of smoke swirling over the harbor, parting to reveal the outline of mountains beyond. I wasn't sure if we were looking at smoke or fog, but it was an eerie and beautiful scene.

"Now aren't you glad we came to Hoonah?" asked Steve. I had to admit Fourth of July here had been fun—almost as good as the Fourths I remembered from my childhood.

A steady stream of humback whales swims by *Osprey* at Lemesurier Island

7.5   LEMESURIER ISLAND
A Perfect Day

We motored west past Point Adolphus toward Glacier Bay National Park, looking for whales in the rain. When Steve and I had passed by here the year before with Morgan and Bill, a herd of humpbacks had entertained us by spouting, breeching and diving. I had hoped to see them again and to show them to this year's guests, Carolyn and Gene. But all we saw were a few distant spouts, barely visible against the gray skies. I worried that Carolyn and Gene, first-timers to Alaska, might be disappointed.

As we approached the dark forested hump of Lemesurier Island, the light westerly that we had been bucking all day died to nothing and the rain stopped. Icy Strait stretched flat and smooth all around us—a shiny undulating gray surface ringed with mountains.

Our Glacier Bay permit didn't allow us to enter the bay until the next morning, so we needed a place to shelter for the night. Off the east side of Lemesurier Island, we found a shallow shelf suitable for anchoring. The island's eastern shore runs straight north and south, making the island a near-perfect barrier to the westerly winds.

I had just set the brake on the anchor chain when I heard a loud whoosh and a splash, then Carolyn's excited cry, "Oh my gosh! There's a whale right here!"

A humpback whale swam calmly past just a few boat lengths away. Behind it came another, then another.

While Carolyn, Gene and I watched the whales, Steve went after smaller creatures with his fishing pole. Jigger sat at Steve's feet and watched the line rise and fall.

"Got one!" yelled Steve, struggling with the pole that now bent nearly double. We all peered over the side to catch the first glimpse of the fish, while Jigger let out excited little meows. A small halibut surfaced, Steve's first.

Gene grabbed the net and leaned over the side, trying to position it behind the fish, which kept swimming back and forth. As soon as he got the fish in the net, it swam back out again. Three times this happened, as Carolyn and I held our breath, and Steve yelled, "Come on, get it!" Finally, Gene gave a mighty yank. Net and halibut came out of the water and into the cockpit.

I took a photograph of Gene holding the fish in the net and Steve standing behind with his pole. "Who's the fisherman here?" I asked.

After Steve had cleaned the fish, we left Jigger gnawing on a chunk of raw halibut and took the dinghy ashore. As I stepped out onto a rocky beach, I turned back to see a humpback swim beside *Osprey*, while closer to the shore, a sea otter played in the kelp.

The beach here resembled a Japanese garden with beach grass fringing the shore and a gnarly tree twining itself around a large rock. A small stream cut through moss and grass to emerge

Who's the real fisherman here? Getting this halibut into the net was as much work as catching it.

clear and sparkling onto the beach. Columbine, sweet peas and trillium had sprouted among the grass, and devil's club grew at the base of some spruce trees. Released from the weight of the massive glaciers that once covered it, the land in this area has been rising at the rate of about one and a half inches a year. Beaches were turning into gardens.

Back on the boat, Carolyn and I went below to bake the halibut and make a salad, while Gene and Steve stayed in the cockpit. Lively notes from Gene's mandolin drifted down the companionway as we worked. Suddenly Steve called, "Come quick!" Carolyn and I ran up the stairs into the cockpit to see a humpback lobtailing less than half a mile away. Again and again it slapped its tail against the water, the sounds echoing off the island's hills.

"Take a bow," said Steve to Gene. "He's applauding you,"

"This has been a perfect day," said Carolyn. "Whales, a halibut, a beautiful beach and now a swimming ovation!"

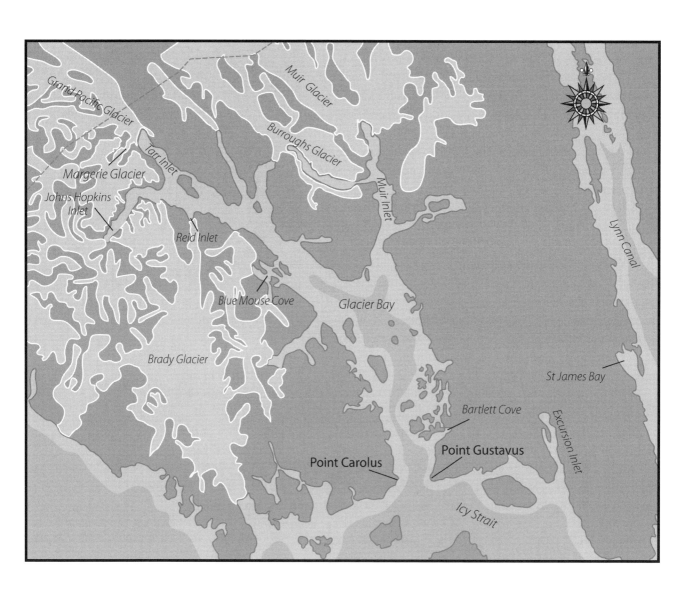

CHAPTER 8

GLACIER BAY

8.1 BARTLETT COVE
More than Glaciers

"Nature trail! We don't have time for a nature trail! We're here to see glaciers!" That was Steve's reaction to my suggestion in 2007 that we take time to walk the Forest Loop nature trail in Bartlett Cove before heading farther into Glacier Bay.

We had just radioed our arrival to the park rangers at Bartlett Cove and were motoring toward it. With the chart in front of us in the cockpit, Steve was discussing our itinerary with Carolyn and Gene. He pointed out Bartlett Cove, only five miles in from Icy Strait, and then the islands and inlets of the upper reaches of the bay, where the glaciers are and where we would be spending most of the next week. They were sixty miles farther, almost two days away.

"If we leave right after we go through orientation, we could get all the way to Blue Mouse Cove (halfway up the bay) by nightfall and see Johns Hopkins Glacier tomorrow," he told them.

"Glacier Bay is not just about seeing glaciers," I said. "It's about geology and biology, and especially plant succession."

I looked at Carolyn and Gene, wondering if they would think me crazy to be interested in something so technical. But Gene nodded. "Of course."

"I think it would be fun to go on a walk," said Carolyn. "I like to look at plants."

"We'll see," said Steve. "Maybe there will be time."

Before our first trip to Glacier Bay, the year before, I had seen so many slide shows of calving tidewater glaciers and icebergs that I too thought glaciers were all there were to see in the park. But traveling up the bay, past shores that had once been under ice, I was awestruck to see evergreen forests give way to alder thickets that in turn gave way to rushes and moss, then to lichens—until finally there was only bare rock. The sight of the changing vegetation brought back lessons from college biology about plant succession: the orderly and gradual supplanting of one plant community by another through ecological processes. I found the changes in the plants as exciting as the glaciers themselves. By taking time to walk the Forest Loop Trail before we visited the glaciers, we would be

The irregular vegetation at Blue Mouse Cove, halfway up the bay, resembles a forest growing back after a clear-cut, but in fact is a new forest emerging on land scoured clean by retreating glaciers.

starting our visit in a mature spruce and hemlock forest, the end of the vegetation cycle, and completing it at the glaciers, the beginning of the cycle.

When Captain George Vancouver sailed this area in 1794, Glacier Bay was only a notch on the shores of Icy Strait, "terminated by compact solid mountains of ice rising perpendicularly from the water's edge . . ." Geologists estimate that this massive glacier was more than 3,000 feet thick. In October 1879, the naturalist John Muir entered the bay, accompanied by Presbyterian minister S. Hall Young and their Tlingit guides. Muir took with him a copy of Vancouver's chart. But the chart, "a faithful guide" elsewhere in Southeast Alaska, failed them altogether in Glacier Bay. Instead of just a notch, they found an entire inlet. Paddling north 30 miles into uncharted territory, Muir and his companions found a bay full of floating ice, freshly glaciated rocks with heavy striations where boulders had ground against them and five huge glaciers whose thunder filled the air. Now, 128 years after Muir, the ice has retreated 30 miles farther. We would be sailing in waters that had been under ice in both Vancouver's and Muir's times.

Muir is the name most commonly associated with Glacier Bay. His lyrical descriptions of glaciers—"jagged spires and pyramids, and flat-topped towers and battlements of many shades of blue . . ."—spurred the beginnings of an Alaskan tourist industry. Nevertheless, it was a biologist from Minnesota, William Cooper, who led the campaign to preserve Glacier Bay from development.

Inspired by the writings of John Muir, Cooper first visited Glacier Bay in 1916. He was searching for a place where the natural vegetation cycle would run its course in a human lifetime. He found it in Glacier Bay. Using geologists' estimates of the length of time retreating glaciers had exposed a particular site, Cooper established permanent one-meter squares of sample vegetation, called quadrats, and returned to them regularly every five years, noting the changes each time. He was testing the hypothesis, then central to the plant-succession theory, that vegetation in any given climatological environment follows a predictable pattern. In doing so he turned Glacier Bay into an outdoor laboratory for studying ecological succession. It was to protect this natural laboratory from human influence that Cooper started the campaign that led to President Coolidge designating Glacier Bay a national monument in 1925 and the US congress designating it a national park in 1980.

We tied up at the dock in Bartlett Cove, noting a sign saying moorage was limited to a maximum of four hours. At 11:00 a.m., we squeezed into a conference room in the ranger station, along with a small crowd of other boaters. A ranger handed out guidebooks and tide tables and welcomed us to Glacier Bay with a discussion of regulations and safety tips, and a video on wildlife.

After the orientation, there was just time for a walk before our four hours of moorage was up. We found the head of the Forest Loop Trail behind the modern glass and wood building of the Glacier Bay Lodge and started south around the loop. The land was level in this area, a result of its location on the former outwash plain of the great glaciers that once occupied all of Glacier Bay. Tall trees shaded the path and devil's club with leaves like umbrellas made up the undergrowth. On the ground, moss turned everything green: covering tree branches, stones and fallen logs.

I pointed out the scaly bark of a spruce tree to Carolyn and Gene.

"They'd make good masts," said Steve, looking up at the straight-trunked trees.

I was surprised at how small the trunks were—only about a foot in diameter. A period of 200 years might be enough to create a "mature forest" but not giant trees. When the first spruce germinate they grow slowly. A 30–40-year-old spruce may stand only knee high with a trunk as thick as a man's ankle. Spruce trees dominate the landscape for a century or two before hemlocks take over. I saw only a few hardy hemlocks among the spruce.

The trail followed the shore of a bog, sprinkled with lily pads. The bog was another indication that we were in land near the end of its vegetation cycle. Bogs develop where the land is level and silty glacial sediments allow little runoff. Over time such places become too wet for trees to continue growing.

Near the bog we came to a tree with the design of an eagle carved into the bark. The eagle, and an octopus on one of the trees near the lodge, had been carved in recent years by Tlingits from Hoonah (the Huna) who consider this their ancestral home.

Huna elders tell the story of how they were pushed from their homes by the glaciers. A young girl named Kasteen, in confinement during her first menstrual period, was eating dried fish when she lifted the cedar curtain of her shack and held the fish out with one hand while calling, "Hey, glacier! Here, here, here . . ." The glacier started moving toward the village, causing the land to shake. The girl had broken a taboo by speaking familiarly to the glacier.

The people gathered their household goods and prepared to flee the advancing ice in their canoes. But Kasteen refused to board a canoe, saying, "What I said will stain my face forever." As her kinsmen drifted in their canoes, they watched the glacier roll Kasteen's house over into the water, drowning her. The people of the village then paddled away, some heading to Excursion Inlet, others to Hoonah.

This oral history is consistent with what geologists tell us of geological history. About 3,000 years ago, the area now called Glacier Bay was a glacial outwash valley with rich salmon streams and grassy meadows. Then, during what is commonly called the little ice age (sometime around 1600 A.D.), the valley's glacier, which had been stable, began advancing—destroying villages, submerging clam beds, disrupting animal migrations and driving the Huna away. Sometime after Vancouver's visit, the glaciers began to retreat. And although the Huna kept their winter homes at the new

The nature trail at Bartlett Cove goes through a mature spruce and hemlock forest, the end of the ecological process.

locations, they returned to Glacier Bay in the spring and summer to hunt seals, gather gull eggs and pick berries.

The Forest Loop Trail led us out of the forest and onto the beach where we paused to admire red and orange Indian paintbrush and black lilies. Then Steve looked at his watch. "Let's get going. If we leave now, we'll catch the tide."

We had seen the end of the vegetation cycle. In two days we would see the beginning.

8.2   BLUE MOUSE COVE
Drama, with Bear

When I read in *Exploring Alaska and British Columbia* by Stephen Hilson that Blue Mouse Cove in Glacier Bay was named for the Blue Mouse Theatre in New York, I was delighted. The idea of Blue Mouse Cove as a place of drama, rather than the home of small timid creatures, fit our experience there in 2006.

We were on our way to see the glaciers in Tarr and Johns Hopkins Inlets when we anchored overnight in Blue Mouse Cove, about 25 miles north of Bartlett Cove. Steve's sister, Morgan, and her husband, Bill, were aboard for a week in Glacier Bay.

After dinner, Morgan and I took our tea out to the cockpit while Steve and Bill washed dishes below. To the east, across Glacier Bay, a giant rock mountain snoozed in the evening light, while in the Cove, the sun's rays picked out the few hardy spruce trees poking above a dense cover of willow and alder. The irregular vegetation reminded me of a forest growing back after a clear-cut, but in fact it was a new forest emerging on land scoured clean by retreating glaciers.

I was admiring the light on snow-capped mountains when Morgan said, "I'm surprised we haven't seen more animals. I expected to see lots—more whales and maybe some bears." I was taken aback by this comment. It was true we hadn't seen much wildlife—only a few humpback whales spouting at a distance. But I didn't expect to see animals continually. To me, seeing wildlife is the icing on the cake, the extra on top of gorgeous scenery and the fun of being on the water. I hoped Morgan wasn't going to be disappointed with the trip.

Morgan picked up a pair of binoculars and started sweeping the shore with them. Immediately inshore of *Osprey* was a large grassy field backed by thick alder. A lone

The National Park Service issues bear-proof canisters to kayakers to protect food from bears.

Bears, like this brown bear, frequent beaches and other foreshore areas where kayakers camp.

orange tent sat in its center. To the left, the field gave way to a fringe of beach grass. Morgan looked at the field, then trained the binoculars on the grass.

"What's that?" Her voice rose in excitement. "It's some kind of animal."

I could see a brown shape walking among the grass. Looking through the binoculars, I studied it more closely. A distinctive hump behind its head told me it was a grizzly bear or brown bear as Alaskans would call it.

At first we were thrilled to see the bear. Steve and Bill came up on deck with more binoculars, and we watched it amble along the beach. As the bear moved closer to the tent, we began to be concerned. We didn't see any sign of the camper. Was he inside the tent, unaware of the bear?

"I wonder what we should do?" asked Steve. "I'm going to call the ranger." A ranger station was just across the cove from us, but calls on the VHF radio to the Blue Mouse Ranger Station received no reply. Steve then called Bartlett's Cove, the main Ranger Station in Glacier Bay, and a voice replied, faint and scratchy from the distance. There was no one at the Blue Mouse Ranger Station, we were told. When Steve explained the situation to the ranger, he advised us "if the bear approaches the tent, inform the camper of the bear."

Steve hung up the microphone and we all looked at the bear that was crossing the open field and working its way toward the tent. How could we "inform the camper"? We certainly weren't going to go ashore and knock on the tent door. Should we blow our horn? Could the horn anger the bear? We had to do something. Steve pressed a button and five short blasts—the signal for danger—echoed in the cove. The bear kept on walking.

We were all holding our breath, eyes glued to the bear, when we saw someone climb out of the tent and start waving their arms back and forth in front of the bear. The bear stood quietly on all fours, looking at the camper who had put on a life jacket and was waving a kayak paddle back and forth. This went on for what seemed like an eternity, but was probably about half an hour, then slowly, deliberately, the bear walked by the tent and into the woods.

We thought the drama was over, but on shore the camper continued to wave the paddle. Steve peered through the binoculars at the woods. "The bear's still there—it's in the woods right behind the tent."

We kept watch from *Osprey*'s cockpit. After awhile the bear circled the campsite and emerged from the woods to stand in front of the camper, who quickly exchanged the kayak paddle for something large and blue. A mattress?

"He's trying to make himself bigger," said Steve. Our park orientation that morning had included training on how to prevent bear attacks. "Speak firmly, don't turn your back, make yourself look as big as possible." But what to do if all of those failed? I thought about how tired the camper must be, standing there as the light faded, waving a mattress. How long could this go on before the bear charged or the camper did something desperate? At least an hour had passed since we first saw the bear.

Finally, Steve said, "Let's get the outboard on the dinghy. I think we should go in. It's getting dark. If we don't go now, we won't be able to see what we're doing."

While Morgan and Bill helped Steve with the outboard, I got out the bear spray and handed it to Steve.

"I don't plan to go ashore, so I hope we don't need that. But I'll take it anyway. We'll ask the camper if he wants to come out here for the night."

"I'd like Bill to come with me in the dinghy," he told me. "I need you to stay here so we have someone on board who can run *Osprey* if necessary."

As the dinghy approached the beach, Morgan and I watched intently through binoculars. The beach was too far away from *Osprey* for us to hear what Steve and the camper were saying, but we could see the camper moving slowly around the tent, gathering gear, always facing the bear. Suddenly, the bear reared up on its hind legs. My heart raced as I watched the scene through binoculars. The bear seemed to tower over the camper, who was slowly walking to the beach, eyes on the bear. When the camper stepped into the dinghy, the bear lowered itself to all fours but stayed where it was.

A few minutes later I reached for the dinghy line, seeing the camper up close for the first time. A slender woman with short gray hair looked up at me. Surprised, I tied up the dinghy and welcomed her aboard.

Over tea and whiskey, we got to know our new shipmate. Joyce Swanson is an elementary-school principal from Whidbey Island, Washington. This was her first night in Glacier Bay; a tour boat had dropped her on the beach near the Blue Mouse Ranger Station that afternoon.

Joyce told us that she had wanted to kayak in Glacier Bay for years, had even bought new gear just for the trip. Then the friends who had planned to accompany her couldn't make it after all. She'd considered joining a commercial tour, then decided against it.

"Maybe that was a mistake," she said.

When Joyce first saw the bear, she hadn't been scared, just concerned she was taking the right approach to alert the bear to her presence. She'd done everything recommended: spoke firmly, didn't back off, but the bear didn't leave as it was supposed to. When it retreated into the alder and remained just a few feet from her tent, she became nervous. The bear looked scrawny, as if it was hungry. She was looking for a way to drag her kayak down to the beach without disturbing the bear when she saw our dinghy coming ashore. "Boy, was I glad to see you!" she said.

"Did you hear our horn?" I asked her.

"Yes, I did. I'd already seen the bear, but it sure was good to know someone else was paying attention."

Joyce slept that night on the settee in the main cabin. In the morning, the bear was gone, the beach empty.

As I was making breakfast, hot cereal and strawberries, Joyce said. "This is a bit more upscale than my kayak."

After breakfast, we all piled in the dinghy and went ashore to inspect the campsite. We beached the dinghy near the tent, and walked through the knee-high grass. An impenetrable tangle of willow and alder surrounded the campsite: a perfect place for a bear to hide. Away from the tent, we found Joyce's two bear-proof food containers, just as she'd left them. Her tent and kayak were also unmolested.

"Maybe the bear was just curious," Joyce said. "He stood there, looked at me and didn't touch any of my things."

As we talked, we had to brush mosquitoes and no-see-ums away from our faces. I looked around at the campsite and out at *Osprey* at anchor and thought about how much more comfortable *Osprey* was than a tent. We had heat, a refrigerator and soft bunks, and we could anchor offshore out of the way of the mosquitoes and the bears—especially the bears. Looking at Joyce's thin nylon tent and folding kayak humbled me. We thought we were adventurous because we traveled in our own small boat instead of a cruise ship, but compared to kayakers we were wimps.

"What will you do?" I asked Joyce.

"I'm not sure."

The tour boat wasn't scheduled to pick her up for another week. If they came in to the cove to drop someone else off, she thought she might be able to go back early. Or she could look for a group of other kayakers and join them. Or simply try to find a safer camping spot.

We left Joyce at her tent, pondering her next step.

After that experience, I didn't hear any more complaints from Morgan about not seeing enough animals. Watching someone else's adventure in the Blue Mouse Cove "theater" was enough of a bear encounter for all of us.

Epilogue

Several months later Joyce and her mother joined Steve and me for dinner at our house in Seattle. Joyce's mother greeted us as the people who had saved her daughter from the bear. Joyce presented us with a bottle of whiskey and homemade raspberry jam in thanks for our hospitality onboard *Osprey*. At that dinner, we learned how Joyce had spent the rest of her week in Glacier Bay. She had packed up her tent and paddled around the Blue Mouse Cove area. Not too far away, she'd found another campsite on a small island free of brush. She walked the beach and the camping area, looking carefully for bear scat and tracks, and had seen none. It felt safe to her so she spent the next week camped there, exploring nearby coves and inlets. She hoped to go back to Glacier Bay again—but next time most definitely with a group.

8.3   REID INLET
A Matter of Perspective

We were prepared for a tourist experience in Reid Inlet, but not for the tricks the inlet would play on us.

In north Glacier Bay, Reid Inlet makes a convenient base from which to explore Johns Hopkins and Tarr Inlets. It also provides two unique opportunities: to anchor in front of a tidewater glacier and to walk to and touch a glacier. Reid Inlet is also one of the few places in Glacier Bay where you can see traces of pre-park history.

We first visited Reid Inlet in 2006 with Morgan and Bill for crew. We arrived in the afternoon after a day of viewing glaciers in Tarr Inlet. The first sight when we entered the inlet was the wrinkled white tongue of Reid Glacier flowing down from the mountains at the head of the inlet.

There were plenty of signs that the inlet had once been completely covered with glacier. The two spits at its mouth were remnants of a terminal moraine. The U-shaped sides of the hills showed the telltale shapes of a glacial fjord. And the sparse cover of low green foliage told us the land was in the early stages of plant succession, with pioneer plants struggling to live among barren rocks.

I hadn't yet learned to appreciate the beauty of Glacier Bay's barren landscape so my first impression of the inlet was that it was desolate, uniform and gray. Only the jagged mountains rising above the glacier gave it any scenic character.

We motored as close to the glacier as we dared. It was low tide, and we could see a mud flat in front of the glacier with a

The sparse cover of low green foliage near Reid Glacier tells us the land is in the early stages of plant succession.

few small bergy bits scattered on its surface. Compared to the growling bear of Margerie Glacier with its cascades of falling ice that we had seen that afternoon, Reid Glacier was a sleeping cub. It looked safe to approach on land, so we decided to come back by dinghy.

We anchored on the west side, close to the larger of the two spits. As we were putting the outboard on the dinghy, Morgan pointed to a small beige tent on the beach off *Osprey's* stern and laughed.

"Look how tiny that tent is!"

"It's probably a one-person tent," I told her.

"No, it's too small for anybody to sleep in."

It was only later that I realized Morgan must not have understood how far we were from shore.

As we headed up inlet in the dinghy, a cold wind started blowing off the glacier and I wished I had worn more layers of clothing. We seemed to be taking forever to get to the glacier. Was something wrong with the outboard? Finally, Steve beached the dinghy next to a pile of rocks.

"This is close enough. We don't want to get stuck on the tide flat. It shouldn't take us long to walk from here."

We tied the dinghy to a rock and walked onto a gray mudflat of fine glacial flour, punctuated by rough-cut rocks. Our boots made a sucking sound with each step, emitting the musty smell of a river rather than the tang of a saltwater tide flat. We climbed up to drier ground and started toward the glacier.

We had been hiking for about 15 minutes when I suspected that we were not as close to the glacier as we had supposed. Like Morgan with the tent, I couldn't judge distances here. Piles of gravel became mounds of rocks. There was nothing at this end of the inlet that our eyes could use to set a scale: no trees, no houses, no man-made machinery; only rocks and ice that could be any size at all, and invariably turned out to be bigger than we first thought.

Finally, we reached the face of the glacier. An irregular wall cut by blue ice caves and white battlements confronted us. Morgan and Steve ran ahead, poking among the caves, while I followed at a slower pace. Bill stayed behind, safely out of reach of any falling ice. I knew that Bill's caution was wise, that even grounded glaciers can calve, burying tourists below in an avalanche of ice, but the opportunity to see a glacier up close was too tempting.

As I approached the glacier, a rush of cold air met me. I touched the blue ice, marveling at its smooth transparency. This ice had started life decades before as snowflakes falling in the mountains above, piling up layer upon layer until the weight of snowflakes combined with time produced this hard blue solid. The glacier represented both the formation of history in its accumulation of ice, and the destruction of history as it moved across the landscape crushing everything in its path.

All around us could be heard the constant drip, drip, drip, crackle and snap of melting ice, as if some glacier-giant were eating mammoth bowls of Rice Krispies. Looking up at the glacier's snout above us, I tried to reconcile its height with the small glacier we had seen from the water. If this small glacier was in reality so huge, how much larger were the

Willows and alder grow over an abandoned prospector's cabin near the mouth of Reid Inlet. When Joe and Muz Ibach lived here in the 1940s the land was almost bare.

Margerie and Grand Pacific glaciers that we had seen that afternoon?

Just then the glacier emitted a sharp crack, a noise so sudden and loud we jumped! We retreated smartly to the beach to watch from a distance, but the glacier remained stationary. The crack had come from somewhere deep in the ice. We turned toward the dinghy and began our long walk back along the beach.

Harry Reid's map of this area from 1892 shows solid ice where the waters of Reid Inlet are today. Photos from the 1940s show the glacier's snout just off the spit—roughly where we had anchored *Osprey*. That something as major as an entire bay could be less than 100 years old struck me as disorienting. Like the distance to the glacier, it forced me to reassess what I was seeing.

Next to Reid Glacier the land is bare, awaiting the first colonizing plants.

Tourist books about Glacier Bay often describe a trip up the bay as "traveling back in time," meaning the closer you are to a retreating glacier, the newer the land is. They're talking not of geological time measured in eons or human time measured in generations, but botanical time measured in species established and plant sizes attained.

As the others walked along the water's edge, I moved inland, still keeping parallel to shore. I picked my way among the piles of rocks, looking for evidence of new plant life. Close to the glacier, the gravel was bare, but as I walked away I saw yellow lichens clinging to rocks, then the first green plants—small pink fireweed scattered in barren glacial soil. Still farther, green mats of Dryas plants spread across the gravel, their size and number increasing with the distance from the glacier. Next to a streambed, I found moss interspersed with rushes.

I was seeing the first stages of the plant succession whose final phase we had witnessed two days before near Bartlett Cove. When a glacier retreats, it leaves barren rock scoured of soil and piles of gravel that lack nutrients. As wind or animals carry in seeds, plants recolonize the land in successive stages, each one preparing habitat for the next. Lichens come first, anchoring themselves on the rocks with root-like structures called rhizomes. As they grow, lichens secrete acid that breaks up the rocks and creates soil for the next settlers: fireweed, Dryas, moss and rush. Willows and alder follow a couple of decades after the glacier retreats. Alders stabilize the soil, pulling nitrogen from the air with the help of special molds in their roots. When alder thickets become so dense their own progeny can't survive, young spruce trees crowd in. We had seen alder and willow near the entrance to the inlet where we had anchored *Osprey*.

When we got back to the dinghy, I looked at the sparse vegetation on the land above it and realized we had about 60 years to travel to get back to *Osprey*.

8.4 JOHNS HOPKINS INLET
Land Reborn

With a great roar, an ice chunk the size of a house tumbled down the glacier's face and into the sea. The force of the splash sent water and ice flying and started waves rolling across the inlet.

We were drifting in *Osprey*, only a third of a mile off the face of the Johns Hopkins Glacier, watching the glacier calve. This was our second trip to Glacier Bay, in 2007, and after our previous expedition and two visits to the glaciers of Tracy Arm, my fear of glaciers had changed to a healthy respect. The sight of the inlet awed me as much as it did Carolyn and Gene, who were seeing it for the first time. White snowfields and craggy mountains topped barren gray cliffs tinged with the green of sparse vegetation. Below the cliffs, a field of small icebergs drifted around the inlet, popping and crackling as they moved. At the inlet's head, the massive Johns Hopkins Glacier swept down the mountainside like a great blue and white river. Simultaneously desolate and beautiful, terrifying and awe-inspiring, Johns Hopkins was not a place I would easily forget. Here was a land so immense and powerful it couldn't be plasticized or trivialized for tourists.

When we think of glaciers, we often think of the phrase, "moving at glacial speed." But behind that slow movement is an inexorable, unstoppable power with the ability to crush everything in its path.

Glaciers may be slow but they never stop; they are always moving, growing or shrinking. They are never silent; they creak, crack, groan and boom. Glaciers form and grow when snow accumulates faster than it melts. The weight of new snow on top of old forces the air out, forming dense ice crystals that look blue because the ice absorbs all colors of light waves except blue. As more snow falls, the glacier builds and gravity moves it downhill, creating a slow river of ice. Friction between land and glacier changes the glacier's shape—forming crevasses, pinnacles and battlements. The glacier's weight scours the land, picking up rocks and soil, and mixing them with the ice to form dark stripes in the white and blue.

If warming temperatures speed the melting or if less snow falls, then the glacier retreats. But even retreating glaciers are still moving; they are like conveyor belts where the ice disappears before it reaches the end.

It would be easy to blame the amazing retreat of glaciers in Glacier Bay, almost 60

With several glaciers, snow-capped mountains and ice-choked waters, Johns Hopkins Inlet is one of Glacier Bay's most scenic inlets.

Tlingit carving of devilfish (octopus) on spruce tree, Bartlett Cove, Glacier Bay.

Alaska is bear country. Photograph taken at Anan Bear Observatory.

Bear print, probably grizzly, Reid Inlet.

Oystercatcher on beach, Reid Inlet.

Fireweed flowers, Reid Inlet.

The Gilman Glacier in Johns Hopkins Inlet dwarfs a tour boat below it.

Steve observes a tidewater glacier up close, Reid Inlet.

XTRATUF boots, Elfin Cove.

Sunset from outer harbor, Elfin Cove.

Another green *Osprey*, a salmon troller, in Port Alexander.

Residents of Pelican are fond of placing amusing signs on their doors.

Tlingit clan membership is passed down from mothers to children. This pole in Angoon represents the killer whale clan crest.

Reflections, Ell Cove.

Halibut fisherman, Kake.

Human figure on totem, Klawock Totem Park.

This pole, showing a whale, will replace an identical pole at the Klawock Totem Park that has deteriorated with age.

Old totem poles lying on the ground outside the Klawock Carving Shed.

nautical miles in 200 years, on global warming. But although scientists attribute the thinning of Alaska's *mountain* glaciers (including the Mendenhall Glacier near Juneau) to climate change, its role in the retreat of *tidewater* glaciers is more complex. Glaciers have a natural cycle and tidewater glaciers dance to its rhythm. As a tidewater glacier advances, it pushes a wall of rock and mud (called a moraine) ahead, gouging out a deep fjord beneath it. But if the glacier reaches a point where the water becomes suddenly significantly deeper, such as in Icy Strait at the outlet of Glacier Bay, it can push its moraine off the edge into deep water. If that happens, water rushes in and begins to erode the face of the glacier, accelerating calving and causing the glacier to retreat. When it retreats, it backs into water made deeper by gouging and so remains without a moraine. Without the barrier of a moraine, the erosion continues and it keeps retreating until it either reaches land or accumulates enough glacial outwash at its face to protect it. It's as if the glacier rushes to the sea, but then finding itself in water over its head, retreats back to the safety of its home base. Once there, it gathers its courage, in the form of outwash sediments, and begins the process again.

Studies of the Columbia Glacier in Prince William Sound complicate this picture. Scientists believe that glacial melt-water from global warming has accelerated the calving process of that glacier by fracturing the ice. However, much of the retreat in Glacier Bay is attributed to the natural cycle.

Rising 250 feet above sea level at its terminus, Johns Hopkins Glacier is currently the only glacier in the bay that is advancing seaward, although others began advancing only to stall later. With an underwater moraine below its face to support it, the glacier flows at the rate of 10–15 feet a day. Its origin, 12.5 miles inland and high in the mountains where snowfall is heavy, ensures a flow of ice.

Our glacier sightseeing had started in Reid Inlet that morning where sunlight had sparkled off Reid Glacier. From there we had motored along a rockbound shore made green by willows and young alder. At the entrance to Johns Hopkins Inlet, we had stopped to admire the small Lamplugh Glacier that stepped down the hillside in white battlements, then we turned to confront what appeared to be an unbroken field of floating ice. But a channel opened up to port and Steve steered *Osprey* through it, pausing every few minutes to find the next opening. Ice crackled and crunched against the hull. Only the memories of hearing this before without damage to *Osprey* kept me from being anxious. As we approached Johns Hopkins Glacier, clouds covered the sun and a cold breeze sent me hunting for gloves and a warmer jacket.

Steve was weaving *Osprey* through an especially tricky channel when I saw dark shapes on ice floes.

"Seals ahead!" I called, warning Steve that we were approaching the quarter-mile limit that the National Park Service recommends we keep between boats and the seals. Johns Hopkins is classified by the Park Service as a critical seal habitat and is closed to all vessels May 1–June 30 and to cruise ships May 1–August 31 to protect seals during pupping. This was July 3, so the inlet had only recently opened to private boats. I felt privileged to be allowed access to this magnificent setting where cruise ships weren't allowed—I didn't want to spoil it by being environmentally insensitive.

Johns Hopkins Inlet is closed to all boats May 1–June 30 and to cruise ships May 1–August 31 for seal pupping season. Seal pups can still be seen in July.

Steve shut down the engine and let *Osprey* drift. The seals watched us warily but stayed on their ice floes.

For the next two hours we drifted in the ice, fascinated by the glacier. Every few minutes the glacier would calve. A section of its face would give way, falling as a sheet, throwing ice and water back into the air and sending swells rolling across the inlet. Determined to capture the sound of calving on video, I was thwarted in my attempts when involuntary "oohs" and "ahs" from Carolyn and Gene drowned out the sound of the glaciers. Their reaction reminded me of the awe expressed by the naturalist John Muir in his descriptions of glaciers.

When John Muir first saw Glacier Bay, he exulted to see the "land reborn" from the ice. From his party's first camp near Geicke Bay, he set off on foot while his companions huddled around the campfire in the rain. He climbed steep slopes and crossed "brown boulder-choked torrents, wading, jumping and wallowing in snow up to [his] shoulders . . ." Reaching a ridge over the camp, he was finally rewarded with a sight of the bay and the faces of five huge glaciers—"a solitude of ice and snow and newborn rocks, dark, dreary, mysterious." When he returned to camp, he learned that his Tlingit guides had been quizzing his companion, the Reverend S. Hall Young, about his motives for climbing mountains when storms were blowing. They didn't understand why Muir insisted on visiting this dangerous place in the wrong season.

Muir believed that glaciers could spark awe in anyone seeing them and that men could be reborn by studying nature. To Muir, Glacier Bay was "Pristine, free of the footprint of lord man." He overlooked the fact that the Huna Tlingits had used this bay for years and were part of its ecosystem. When his guides tried to shoot ducks, he rocked the canoe to spoil their aim.

Huna Tlingits saw the bay from a different perspective. Glacier Bay was their breadbasket and ancestral home: a place to hunt seals, gather gulls' eggs and pick berries. The Huna hunted seals in the spring, camouflaging themselves by wearing white and covering their canoes with white sails, then sneaking up to spear the seals while they lay on the ice.

These two views of Glacier Bay, epitomized by Muir and his Huna guides, persist today. Preservationists and National Park Service strive to keep the bay free of the "footprint of man," while the Huna mourn the loss of seal hunting and egg collecting.

I find myself sympathizing with the Huna. They were here first and a land without its original inhabitants strikes me as unnatural. But I also know Native status doesn't guarantee environmental consciousness—I have seen too many clear-cut forests on Native land to believe that. And with the fierce competition for resources in today's economy, the park needs protection.

Signs of thaw between the National Park Service and Huna have recently appeared. The Park Service recently asked for comments on a proposal to permit limited egg collecting. They have also reached out to the Huna, giving tours to Huna schoolchildren and providing transportation for berry pickers.

The pros and cons of National Park regulations were far from our minds as we watched the glacier calve. The sounds of tumbling ice and cracking glaciers filled the bay. Bergy bits and growlers (smaller icebergs) floated past us, shifting and turning as if in a huge cauldron stirred by a mysterious hidden witch. Like stripes on a sailor's jersey, the color of the water alternated between the blue of seawater and the brown of glacial outwash, adding to the drama of the scenery. Even Jigger was intrigued, sitting on the deck and watching bits of ice swirl by the boat.

Pushed by the currents, *Osprey* had drifted more than a mile across the bay, accompanied by the seals on their ice floes. On the west side of the bay a tour boat, one of the medium-sized passenger vessels that travel daily from Bartlett Cove, was moving freely in what looked like a clear channel. Steve started up the engine and we wove our way through the ice to reach the clear water.

As we motored across the inlet, the cold wind coming off the glacier caused us all to shiver. We had had enough of glaciers for the day. We found the clear channel and followed it out. Leaving the inlet, I turned back for one last look at the craggy mountains, the blue and white glacier, and the small dark dots of seals. We had seen real Alaska wilderness. I hoped it would stay that way.

8.5 TARR INLET
Sharing a Glacier

We motored north up Tarr Inlet in mist and rain, catching only glimpses of the inlet's sweeping glacial plains, sparsely vegetated slopes and barren gray mountains. When we reached the head of the inlet, Margerie Glacier loomed out of the mist, its sheer-faced ramparts glowing white and shades of blue in the soft light.

As Steve brought *Osprey* along the face of the glacier and Carolyn and Gene exclaimed over its beauty, I struggled to keep my camera lens from fogging. Holding the camera up to my face while rain misted my glasses and ran down my sleeves, I was torn between wanting to capture the glacier's beauty and wishing to be somewhere warm and dry.

Kittiwakes, small white gulls, swarmed over the water at the glacier's face feeding on shrimp and fish, emitting a shrill kee, kee, kee. When I went down below to get coffee, I heard what sounded like a pump running on board. After opening up all the

Passengers on the MS *Island Princess* watch Margerie Glacier from their balconies. Only two cruise ships are permitted in Glacier Bay per day making the experience a special one.

compartments in an attempt to identify which pump was running, I finally realized I was hearing the roar of a river running under the ice.

Although Margerie Glacier is the same height and width as the Johns Hopkins Glacier, it is stable rather than advancing, and flows at only half the speed—2,000 feet per year compared to 4,000 feet per year. As a result it produces less ice.

We were drifting in front of the glacier and admiring its subtle blue tones when a large white cruise ship, MS *Island Princess*, emerged from the mist. With less ice in the inlet, there are no seals to protect, hence the Park Service can allow cruise ships to approach the glacier. The Service allows two cruise ships a day to enter Glacier Bay, and all of them go to Tarr Inlet. In 2008, 225 ships entered the bay from May through September, carrying more than 400,000 passengers.

The MS *Island Princess* approached the glacier, coming so close to us that when we looked up at its white hull, it seemed larger than the glacier itself. Crowds of people thronged on the decks while sparks of light from hundreds of flash cameras popped vainly into the mist. In my yellow slicker with rain running down my nose, I looked up at the passengers on the covered decks with envy; some of them weren't even wearing raincoats. And none of them needed to think about cooking lunch.

The MS *Island Princess* is only one of a long line of cruise ships that has frequented this bay. The first ship to bring tourists into Glacier Bay was the side-wheeler *Idaho* in 1883, with travel-writer Eliza Scidmore on board. In her book *Alaska, Its Southern Coast and the Sitkan Archipelago*, Scidmore described icebergs "clinking together musically" as the steamer went by. The *Idaho* crept cautiously forward, using a lead line to sound the bottom, and as it approached the glacier, Scidmore noted that the passengers heard the strange rumblings of subterranean water and the thunder of breaking ice.

Puffins can be seen around South Marble Island in Glacier Bay.

From that first trip to Glacier Bay, Scidmore went on to become an internationally recognized travel writer. Glacier Bay became a major tourist destination with regular steamship excursions to Alaska and Glacier Bay, leaving from Tacoma, Seattle, Port Townsend and Victoria, BC. Pictures from those days show lines of men in suits and women in long dresses streaming across the ice, many carrying new Kodak cameras. John Muir, who witnessed an excursion from the ship *Queen* on his third trip to Glacier Bay in 1890, noted that the 230 tourists, "all seemed happy and enthusiastic, though it was curious to see how promptly all of them ceased gazing when the dinner bell rang . . . "

In 1899 a major earthquake struck Glacier Bay, collapsing the terminus of Muir Glacier and clogging the bay with floating ice. Unable to navigate through this persistent ice field, the Pacific Coast Steamship Company dropped Glacier Bay from its schedule and it was all but forgotten. Then, in 1953, the Canadian Pacific Steamship Company brought the first modern cruise ship into Glacier Bay. The ships have been coming ever since. In 1979, Alaska-bound ships suddenly got significantly larger when an 800-passenger vessel from the TV program *Love Boat* made its first trip here.

Love Boat changed the public's idea of cruising: the ship and the experience passengers have onboard were now as important as the destination. Ships keep growing in size. The original *Love Boat* ships, an earlier *Island Princess* and the *Pacific Princess,* carried 800 passengers but have now been replaced. The newer MS *Island Princess*, which loomed above us, is 964 feet long and carries 1,970 passengers. Ships holding as many as 5,400 passengers are now operating (although not yet in Alaska).

The presence of MS *Island Princess* was almost as diverting as the glacier. For a few minutes we shared the excitement with the cruise-ship passengers, cheering along with them when chunks of glacier slid into the water and sent cascades of ice flying upward. Just as I was thinking it wasn't so bad to share a glacier with a cruise ship, the ship started to move, swinging around *Osprey* to get still closer to the glacier, and blocking our view.

"That jerk!" said Steve. "He didn't need to do that."

To go around the ship would put us closer than a quarter of a mile to the glacier, the distance the Park Service recommends we stay off for safety.

With MS *Island Princess* in front of us, the four of us stood forlornly in *Osprey*'s cockpit, staring at the hull of the cruise ship. The incident left us all disgruntled, as if we had been cut off on the freeway. I was wondering what we should do next when I remembered the second glacier in Tarr Inlet.

"Let's go see the Grand Pacific Glacier," I said.

Steve turned *Osprey* northeast where the dark shape of the Grand Pacific Glacier was just barely visible in the mist. Covered with soil stirred up by the glacier's movement across the land, it was so dark that when I had seen it the year before I had dubbed it the "Darth Vader" glacier.

This dark silent tongue is the remains of one of John Muir's five huge glaciers. The Grand Pacific Glacier, which once stretched across Glacier Bay, obscuring Tarr and Johns Hopkins Inlets completely, is now thinning and receding toward the north at the rate of one to four feet per day. In a few years it will be an all-Canadian Glacier. Its sloping snout is a common feature of a retreating glacier.

We cruised along the glacier's snout, peering through the mist to discern the ice below the layer of dirt and being careful to stay offshore to avoid glacial outwash sediments visible in front of the glacier. At the glacier's east edge a river tumbled down the slope carrying meltwater from the glacier's upper reaches. Hundreds of gulls wheeled above the river, making high-pitched cries as they dove for fish at the river's mouth.

Dark and mysterious though it was, the Grand Pacific didn't hold the same fascination for us as the majestic Margerie Glacier. As we turned to leave, we noticed MS *Island Princess* turning too, and in a few minutes it had disappeared into the mist. We were once again alone with the glaciers. The experience of the MS *Island Princess* passengers in Glacier Bay had been very different from ours. They had been in Tarr Inlet only a short time —and now they were on their way out. We were still there with the glacier.

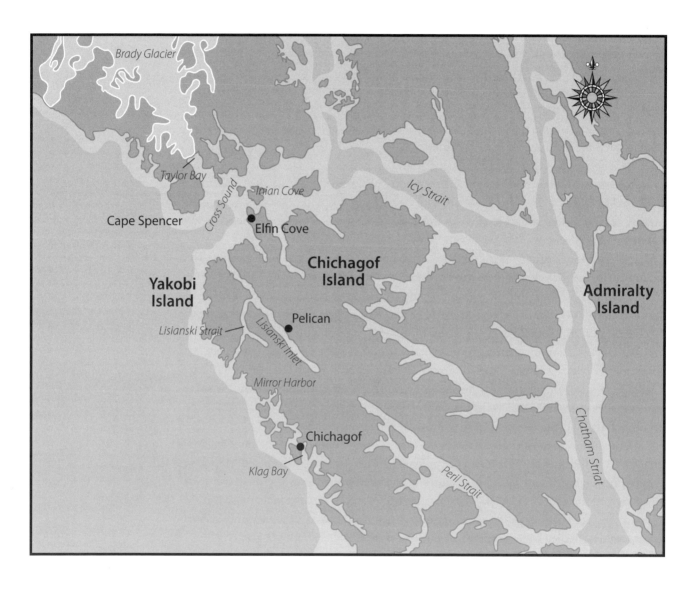

Brady Glacier

Taylor Bay

Cross Sound

Cape Spencer

Inian Cove

Icy Strait

Elfin Cove

Chichagof
Island

Admiralty
Island

Yakobi
Island

Lisianski Strait

Lisianski Inlet

Pelican

Mirror Harbor

Chichagof

Klag Bay

Peril Strait

Chatham Striat

CHAPTER 9

CROSS SOUND TO CHICHAGOF

9.1 INIAN AND ELFIN COVES
"Worth Taking a Look"

Authentic Alaskan fishing villages on a wild and remote coast are what I promised Carolyn and Gene when we left Glacier Bay for Cross Sound and Lisianski Inlet in 2007. We would anchor in Inian Cove the first night, then go around to the village of Elfin Cove the next day before sailing south to Lisianski.

The ebb tide carried *Osprey* out of Glacier Bay and into Icy Strait where the water, a glassy gray sheet, reflected gray skies above. From Carolus Point, the current carried us west, past Lemesurier Island and through North Inian Passage where we turned into Inian Cove. We traveled 20 miles in two hours, a distance that would normally take us three.

We were debating where to anchor when we saw a green and white sailboat anchored in a nook on the north side of the cove.

"It's *Seaquel*," said Steve. "And they're putting out fenders for us."

Steve and I had first seen *Seaquel* and met its owners, Richard and Sandy of Portland, Oregon, earlier that summer in Ketchikan. We had later spent a pleasant evening with them in Wrangell on board their boat, which Richard had finished out himself. Richard's bushy gray beard makes him look like a true mariner while Sandy's smooth brown hair gives her a neat and efficient appearance. We found we had much in common with them. Steve was especially pleased to find another sailor who believes in old-fashioned hank-on jibs instead of modern roller furling.

We tied *Osprey* alongside *Seaquel* and were introducing Carolyn and Gene when the squawk of a loudspeaker coming from shore interrupted us.

"What is this? A sailboat convention?" screeched a woman's voice from behind the trees.

I looked ashore for a house or other signs of habitation but saw only an aluminum salmon troller on the beach. A float stacked with lumber and propane tanks sat offshore.

"She has a house behind the trees," said Richard. "She did this yesterday, too, but stopped when I told her we were leaving today."

Steve shouted to the trees, "We've got 40 more boats coming and we're going to stay four weeks."

The voice erupted in anger, "How would you like it if I parked an RV in front of your house? Alaska is big—find someplace else to anchor. Old rich people, but you never even raise your sails."

I wasn't sure she had really heard Steve—it was a long way to the trees—but I felt uncomfortable about the exchange. I saw no reason to bait her. And, besides, she might have a gun; most rural Alaskans do. There was certainly no point in trying to tell her that our Seattle house was on a public street and RVs could park there, and sometimes do.

We sat down in *Seaquel*'s cockpit, trying to ignore the angry voice. Richard and Sandy told us they had spent several days in Elfin Cove, our next destination, and were now on their way to Hoonah.

"Elfin Cove is a very nice little town," said Richard. "But there's quite a current in the channel and it's shallow so you have to go through at high tide."

This was something we hadn't factored into our schedule and I filed it away for future reference.

An hour later, Richard and Sandy left to catch the flood tide east into Icy Strait and we moved *Osprey* across the cove. As we swung the boat into the wind to put down the anchor, I looked out the entrance of the cove to see the rugged white peaks of the Fairweather Range standing proud above the green hills of Glacier Bay National Park.

"That's what I was hoping to see in Glacier Bay," I told Gene who was helping me with the anchor. We'd spent a whole week in Glacier Bay but had never seen the mountains.

With ice fields feeding 16 tidewater glaciers and Mount Fairweather at 15,300 feet, the range is a significant geographic feature in this area. Given the area's 100 inches of precipitation a year and reputation for bad weather, the name Fairweather, given by Captain Cook in 1778, sounds ironic. But the designation makes some sense. The anthropologist Frederica de Laguna noted that Mount Fairweather's "appearance gives promise of calm seas or warns of storms and it is therefore called 'the paddler's mountain' by the natives." According to de Laguna, white whalers working the offshore Fairweather Grounds in the mid-19th century believed that when they saw the mountain, they could be sure of several days of good weather.

Eating sandwiches in *Osprey*'s cockpit, we discussed our plans. We all agreed we'd had enough of Inian Cove and its angry resident. Richard's information about Elfin Cove made us rethink our itinerary.

"If we wait until tomorrow to go to

The name Fairweather Range, shown with the Brady Glacier below, has been called a misnomer. The range experiences more foul weather than fair.

Elfin Cove, we will have to get up very early or wait for the afternoon tide," I pointed out. "And we'll have to leave early the next morning while the tide is still high"

"Let's just go on to Elfin Cove now," Steve said. "The tide will be rising when we get there."

After lunch we pulled up anchor and motored toward Cross Sound. The sea was still glassy calm and although the sun was out, the air felt chilly. Far ahead we could see Cape Spencer and beyond the cape, the immense unbroken expanse of the Gulf of Alaska. To the north, the white craggy peaks of the Fairweather Range loomed over the landscape. As we motored west across the opening to Taylor Bay, the magnificent Brady Glacier came into view, sweeping down the mountains in sensuous curves. Of all the glaciers I had seen in Alaska, this was one of the most beautiful and impressive.

As Steve turned *Osprey* toward Elfin Cove, I caught my first view of the islands surrounding the village. Tall, steep, and tree-covered with sea caves and arches at the shore, the islands dwarfed the fishing boats at their bases. Even the large blue hull of the mega-yacht *Laurel,* anchored outside the harbor, looked small.

Elfin Cove has an outer harbor protected by a small island and an inner harbor consisting of an almost completely enclosed cove entered through a narrow channel, the entrance Richard had warned us about. When we rounded the island and entered the outer harbor, I was struck by the contrast; the grandeur of the outside waters and coziness inside. *Laurel* was anchored outside because it was too big for the inner cove. We motored along the shore of the outer harbor where we were surprised to find a public dock with room for a couple of boats.

"Let's just tie up here," said Steve. "Then we can leave whenever we want."

At first I was disappointed not to be in the inner harbor, but as we tied *Osprey* to the dock, I looked up to see the Fairweather Range and the Brady Glacier framed in the harbor entrance. Staying in the outer harbor wasn't going to be so bad after all.

On the next dock, sport fishermen were photographing a large halibut while fishing guides prepared to clean it. The number 184, the weight of the fish, was written on its underside. Compared to the 19-pounder we had caught a few days before, it was huge.

Ashore we found a boardwalk that led across a small peninsula to the inner harbor. The hillsides rose steeply around the harbor, leaving little space for buildings; the houses, lodges, and work sheds were crammed so close together they made me feel claustrophobic. Floating docks occupied most of the inner harbor.

I noticed a hand-lettered sign on a post reading, "See Patti in yellow house for smoked salmon." We followed more signs to the yellow house, which was festooned with moose antlers, deer

Large halibut are sought after by sport fishermen.

A street sign, "Skidd Row," in Elfin Cove where there are no streets.

antlers, glass balls and plastic gnomes. A note on the door directed us across the boardwalk to a smaller building. We went in and found Patti, a middle-aged woman with red frizzy hair, sitting at a table surrounded by baskets of vacuum-packed salmon.

"I smoke them for two and a half days," she told us. "I only buy from two fishermen I know, who clean and care for the fish properly. Not all of them do."

As she talked, she reached out her sweatshirt-clad arms and patted a package of salmon with such a proprietary air that I knew it had to be good. We bought a large chunk for making omelets the next morning.

Elfin Cove has been a fishing community since the 1930s when a few salmon fishermen who lived on their boats started spending winters here. The cove's protected harbor and its close proximity to fishing grounds in Cross Sound and the Gulf of Alaska made it a natural for a fishing village. At first it was called Gunk Hole, the East Coast term for a small harbor. Then, in 1935 when a post office was established, the postmistress refused to serve at a town named Gunk Hole ("gunk" refers to the mud commonly found in small harbors). The name was changed to Elfin Cove after her husband's boat, *Elfin*.

The 2000 census gave Elfin Cove's population as 32 people living in 15 households, but those numbers omit the large seasonal population of commercial fishermen, sport fishermen and lodge operators and staff.

Making a circuit of the town on the boardwalk, we passed a bar, a hardware store, a laundromat with shower stalls and then a general store, all catering to fishermen.

The store was one of the best-stocked small outlets on the coast. There were boxes of fishermen's gloves, stacks of XTRATUF boots, racks of brightly colored fishing lures and row upon row of canned goods. In the back we found a cooler packed with fresh fruits and vegetables. With delight I picked out a plastic box of salad greens and a box of strawberries.

As we paid for our purchases, I asked the clerk, a friendly-looking woman with graying hair, about the angry woman in Inian Cove, phrasing my question carefully in case they were friends. The clerk told us the woman's husband is a commercial fisherman and they have lived on Inian Island year-round for many years and raised a son there.

"There's someone like that in every community in Alaska. They are people who want to live totally isolated lives." She went on to say that she had a house in Funter Bay and a neighbor like the woman in Inian Cove. "In the winter I would like to be able to talk to someone over a cup of tea once in a while, but I can't."

That evening we ate salmon pizza at the Coho Bar and Grill. The strong taste of the salmon seemed out of place on pizza dough but was still good. The restaurant, a comfortable and homey place, struck me as more like a coffee shop than a bar with its curtained windows, wooden chairs, and claims to homemade chocolate cake and pizza dough. In the window a bumper sticker proclaimed, "Friends don't let friends eat farmed salmon."

Back at the boat we were playing cribbage when Gene took a break and poked his head out the hatch. "A sunset! This is worth taking a look."

We climbed off the boat to see the Fairweather Range, the Brady Glacier and the sky all a flaming pink. I was standing on the dock admiring the view when I suddenly thought to look back at a small seaplane terminal across from *Osprey*. Two men sat on a small porch, their faces impassive as they gazed out across the water. With long ponytails, dirty canvas pants, sweatshirts and brown boots, they looked like the archetypal Alaskan fishermen.

As the colors deepened, more people came down to look. A small wiry man in fleece pants and jacket lay down on the dock to put a video camera on a short tripod.

"You'd think after 30 years I wouldn't need another picture of this," he told us.

I could well imagine that it would take more than 30 years to get used to sunsets like the one before us.

9.2 PELICAN
A Real Alaskan Fishing Town

Cross Sound stretched around us glassy-smooth, reflecting the broken sky above. Only the most languorous of swells told us the open waters of the Gulf of Alaska were just a few miles away.

We motored along the rocky coast of Chichagof Island toward Lisianski Inlet. Our plans were to sail to the town of Pelican where Carolyn and Gene had seaplane reservations to Juneau the next day.

Rock arches and sea stacks dotted the coast and a fringe of kelp followed the shoreline. Off Graff Rock, groups of sea otters frolicked in the kelp. Mother otters carried youngsters on their stomachs.

As we turned into Lisianski Inlet, a light breeze came up from behind and we raised the jib, drifting alongside snow-speckled mountains. A few raindrops splattered the deck but not enough to warrant foul-weather gear.

Three hours later, the town of Pelican came into view: a row of buildings stretched along the shore between a point of land on the north and a marsh on the south.

Newcomers to Alaska often assume that Pelican was named for a bird. In fact, there are no pelicans in Alaska. The town was named for a fish-packing boat called *Pelican*. During the 1930s FV *Pelican*'s owner, Kalle Raatikainen, bought fish directly from the fishermen on their boats, delivered the fish to Sitka and returned with ice and groceries. Raatikainen became tired of motoring back and forth to Sitka and dreamed of a cold-storage facility closer to the fishing grounds. He chose the site of Pelican for its deep water, protection

Sea stacks and rocks in Cross Sound require careful navigation.

Pelican's only car drives down the boardwalk, the village's main thoroughfare.

from winds, and the nearby lake and river that offered a site for a hydroelectric dam. Construction on the site started in 1938 with a bathhouse, a necessity for the Scandinavian fishermen, and progressed to the cold-storage plant that opened in 1942. Eventually, a cannery opened as well.

The cannery has since closed but the cold-storage plant was still open and boats were hoisting plastic boxes of fish from their holds to the dock as we passed.

"There's supposed to be a famous bar in Pelican," I told the others once *Osprey* was tied up at the town marina. "But I don't remember its name and I don't know where it is."

"Let's go look for it. It can't be hard to find in such a small town," said Gene.

At the top of the ramp we paused to read a bulletin board full of information about the town. Two signs leapt out at me: a "Boil Water Advisory" and a warning that bears had been sighted in town.

Across from the dock was a small hotel, the Highliner Lodge, with freshly painted gray siding and lace curtains in the window. I looked at a menu posted in the window and was surprised to see it was in French—and dismayed to see they offered only fixed-price meals for $60. "Highliner" is the term for the fisherman who catches the most fish in a fleet. The lace curtains and French menu didn't match my image of a rugged highliner.

A wide boardwalk led along the waterfront. Buildings lined both sides of the boardwalk, over water on one side of it and squeezed up against a hill on the other. Many of the houses had signs on their doors, as if their closeness to the boardwalk invited conversation. My favorite was, "One nice person and one old grouch live here." Another sign advertised the law firm of Dewey, Cheetam and Howe.

We walked toward the fish-processing plant, passing fishermen in brown rubber boots, children on bicycles and a small blue electric car driven by an older woman with curly white hair. Ravens clonked from the roofs and eagles cried from the trees above. A faint whiff of seaweed and fish wafted up from the water.

We reached the north end of the boardwalk and were peering into a warehouse full of pallets and miscellaneous boxes when a woman stopped to talk to us. She asked us where we were from and learning Steve and I were from Ballard said, "I used to live there. I'm working here temporarily setting up quality control for the fish-processing plant."

The town of Pelican was named for the fishing boat *Pelican*, not the bird. There are no pelicans in Alaska.

We asked her about the boil-water advisory. "No one bothers," she said. The town population was just large enough to require a special filter, which they didn't have. No standards had been violated. The bear warnings, however, were serious. "Don't walk on the boardwalk alone at night."

While Steve and I were talking, Gene was making inquiries about the bar. He learned it was named Rose's, and apparently there was also another bar in the same vicinity, referred to as the "brown bar," with better food.

We walked the boardwalk to the opposite end of town where we found a plain white building with a banner proclaiming, "World Famous Rose's Bar and Grill."

We walked in the door and into pink chaos: pink booths, pink bar and pink walls. American-flag tablecloths covered the tables and plastic American-flag pennants hung from the ceilings. Christmas lights glowed above the bar. A painting of a nude woman hung on one wall and a bizarre creature consisting of a stuffed fish with deer legs and antlers hung on another. Native-art prints filled the rest of the wall space. Every inch of the ceiling was covered with dollar bills.

The bar stools were occupied as were several of the tables. We took seats at one of the pink booths and a buxom waitress took our orders. When she returned with our beers I asked her why Rose's was famous.

"Ask Rosie, she's right here," she said, pointing to an older woman with short white hair and sunglasses sitting at a table with several Native men. A painting of the same woman, wearing the same sunglasses, hung over the bar.

"For 40 years people have been dancing nude on the bar," Rosie told me. "We were written up in German *Playboy*, *National Geographic* and *Alaskan Geographic*."

None of the customers looked as if they were about to dance in the nude. Men and women had their eyes fixed to a TV showing a Mariners' game.

A pile of eagle feathers on the table in front of Rosie caught my eye and I asked her about them.

Rose's Bar and Grill is famous for its rowdy customers.

"We use them on our regalia in Native dancing. I have 11 children, 29 grandchildren, 28 great-grandchildren and 18 great-great-grandchildren. All do Native dancing."

She pointed to the prints on the wall, "Those were done by my children."

An hour later, we were in "the brown bar" (so called because of the color of paint on its outside walls). Furnished in the style of a basement rec room, it had knotty pine paneling, Formica tables, a jukebox and pinball games.

Steve looked at the menu that consisted almost entirely of fried food and said, "If this is better than Rose's, I'd hate to eat there."

"I couldn't have stood to eat at Rose's anyway," said Carolyn. "Too much pink."

Carolyn and Gene left Pelican the next morning, flying out on a small seaplane in driving rain and wind. As I watched their plane leave, I had mixed feelings about seeing them go. I looked forward to having the boat to ourselves and not tripping over the belongings of two additional people, but their departure also made me feel lonely. Growing up on the opposite coast from all my cousins, I had seen them only occasionally over the years and the last week had been a great opportunity to get to know Carolyn. She and Gene had been good company and good crew.

The rain made it a good day to stay in town, shop for groceries and do our laundry. We donned foul-weather gear, grabbed the grocery cart and headed out.

In the general store, next door to the Pelican Cold Storage buildings, the shelves had the empty look of a small-town grocery store. I looked in the produce section, hoping to find green peppers, zucchini, tomatoes and lettuce but found only oranges, apples, pineapples and watermelon. The store manager, the white-haired woman who had passed us in the electric car the day before, told me she had vegetables coming but produce came in the seaplane and if the plane was full, it got bumped.

We made our purchases and retreated to the Lisianski Inlet Café, a small restaurant on the boardwalk. Customers sat at rough-hewn wooden tables and helped themselves to coffee. Paintings of fishboats and local scenes decorated the walls and a black feathery whale baleen hung over the counter. The restaurant was cozy and warm. There were no vacant tables available, so we sat down across from a burly-looking man and ordered the special, borscht. Our table companion was a fisherman and soon he and Steve were deep in a discussion about boat hydraulics while I enjoyed the pleasure of being in a dry building on dry land (or at least on solid pilings). The soup, when it came, was steaming and savory.

As we got up to leave, I thought how pleasant it would be to hang around town and come back to this restaurant. Then the waitress told us they would be closed the next day. They were going fishing.

At the laundromat two of the four washing machines were broken and the floor needed a good sweep. One look at the showers made me glad we had our own on *Osprey*. As I waited for my wash, a man wearing foul-weather gear walked in with several bags of laundry over his shoulder. He looked at the broken machines and sighed.

"That's the way it's been since last winter. Last year the Highliner had a café upstairs that had good food and they let fishermen use their laundromat. Now everything is for the lodge customers only. It's better to do laundry at Elfin Cove. The woman who runs the general store there manages the laundromat too. Anything breaks, she fixes it right away."

He explained that in 1993 when Pelican Seafoods stopped canning, the Kake Tribal Corporation bought the cold-storage plant but couldn't make it work. For years they just sold ice instead of buying fish. Then the year before, someone new bought the plant. The town was euphoric at first but better times meant more people.

I commented on the grocery store relying on the seaplane to bring in its produce and having the produce bumped by passengers. A system that brings less food when there's more people sounded insane to me.

"That's the way it is in Pelican these days."

Heading back to Osprey in the rain, my laundry safely stowed in plastic bags, I reflected that Pelican might be in flux, with more tourists and fishing lodges, but there was no doubt it was a real Alaskan fishing town—at least for now.

Epilogue

The *Juneau Empire* reported on August 23, 2009, that the fish-processing plant in Pelican—and the general store associated with it—had closed due to impending foreclosure. In its stead, fish-buying boats were operating at the mouth of Lisianski Inlet. The future of the plant and the town remains uncertain.

9.3 MIRROR HARBOR
Through the Kelp

"Steady, steady."

Steve meant "keep steering straight ahead" but that wasn't easy to do with *Osprey* pitching in the waves. My arms ached as every lurch of the boat tried to snatch the wheel from my hands.

We were in the Pacific Ocean, off the west coast of Chichagof Island, on our way south to Mirror Harbor.

The night before, while we rode at anchor in protected Lost Cove inside the west entrance to Lisianski Strait, a storm had moved down the coast. By morning the wind had died, leaving oily-looking seas that heaved and fell in unpredictable patterns like meringue on a pie spread by a drunken cook. Mirror Harbor was only five miles south so we chose to push on, enticed by stories of a tranquil anchorage and a trail to nearby White Sulphur Springs. To escape the seas left over from last night's storm we had opted to take a shortcut, described as a quiet-water passage by Don Douglass and Reanne Hemingway-Douglass in their book *Exploring Southeast Alaska*. They must have taken it in very different conditions than the ones we were encountering. As I looked at foam swirling around rocks, I realized we had been lulled by weeks of motoring through the calm waters of Alaska's Inside Passage into assuming a short trip in the ocean would be safe. Now we were facing real danger.

"Where is that rock?" asked Steve, looking for Three Knob Rock south of Lisianski

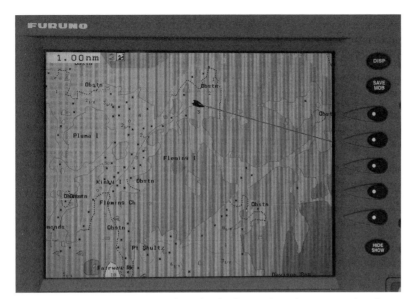

Osprey's chart plotter shows our route through rocky Fleming Channel to Mirror Harbor. The correct route is more easily seen on the water than on the chart.

Strait where we could turn into open water. Although the chart plotter showed our location, there was just enough uncertainty in that plotted position to make it unsafe to turn until we actually saw the rock.

"Is that it?" He pointed to a wave-swept bump off to port. "Darn, they all look alike." Menacing black rocks poked their heads above the waves, then disappeared, engulfed by the next passing wave. The sound of surf crashing on rocks, the tangy smell of kelp tossed by the seas and a dark sky all added to the sense of danger.

Somewhere near here the first European ship to enter Tlingit territory made its landfall. Historians are still debating exactly where. The *St. Paul*, under Captain Aleksei Chirikov, had left Kamchatka along with the *St. Peter*, on June 4, 1741, on an expedition of science and exploration. The two ships separated in the fog, and on July 18 the *St. Paul* sighted land. Chirikov sent the ship's longboat ashore crewed with eleven men and armed with a cannon and flares. Their mission: to look for a safe harbor for the *St. Paul*; to observe the surrounding land, its vegetation and geology; and to collect drinking water. For five long days the *St. Paul* sailed offshore, waiting for the longboat. It never returned. Chirikov sent out a second boat with four men. That too never returned. The next day Natives in two canoes paddled out but refused to approach the ship. As the *St. Paul* tacked back and forth in the night, fires burned on shore and Chirikov concluded that Natives had killed his men.

Chirikov's log placed the position of the *St. Paul* at a latitude of 57 degrees 59 minutes, a location off the mouth of Lisianski Strait, close to where we were struggling to navigate *Osprey* through the rocks. Recent historians have argued alternate locations, citing the inaccuracy of navigation methods of the time. A method to calculate longitude was still 40 years into the future. Even latitude sights were subject to error. Mark Jacobs Jr., a historian of Tlingit ancestry, argues that the men went ashore south of Lisianski, near Sitka, where oral history includes tales of sailors deserting their ship and joining the Tlingits. Other historians have countered that the deserters were more likely Spaniards whose commanding officers were notoriously cruel. Amateur historian Allen Engstrom argues for Surge Bay on Yakobi Island, 10 miles north of Lisianski Strait. He cites a Tlingit story told to English captain Nathanial Portlock in 1787, of a European boat capsizing and its crew drowning in that area. Without a chart to guide him, Chirikov had sent his boats through one of the most dangerous waters on the coast.

Just as I was worrying that *Osprey* would founder and disappear without a trace just like the boats of *St. Paul*, Steve sighted Three Knob Rock. Knowing where we were, we could now turn south out of the passage. *Osprey* entered open water, its bow rising and falling in the more even swells.

"That was a mistake," said Steve. "We should never have gone in there with a sailboat. We would have been better off out to sea."

I was relieved to be safe in open water, then remembered that the worst was still ahead of us. To enter Mirror Harbor we would have to go through the intricate Fleming Channel, shown on the chart as only random rocks with no obvious path through. We would be relying on a sketch in the book by the Douglasses to find our way in.

Our first challenge was to locate a rock called Fairway Rock at the entrance to the channel.

"That must be it," said Steve, as we approached the entrance. Close to shore the seas had turned rough again and I could see surf breaking on rocks all around us, but one rock poked several feet above the water and had what looked like a clear channel beyond it. I put the rock to port as the sketch indicated. A few minutes later, we were in quiet water.

Steve was looking at the chart plotter, the paper chart and then the sketch. "Something's wrong! I don't see the inlet. Go back, now! Turn now!"

I turned *Osprey* around, my heart pounding as I realized we had blundered into a dead end with nothing but islets and rocks in our path. We had mistaken Gull Rock at the entrance to Davison Bay for Fairway Rock.

Back in rough water, Steve pointed to another rock, lower than the first, alternately covering and uncovering in the surf. "That's it."

"Are you sure that's it?" I raised my voice so that Steve could hear me over the sound of surf on rocks. "This is insane! Let's go on and skip Mirror Harbor." The consequences of a mistake seemed dire. I could see little room to maneuver once we passed the rock.

"We'll be fine. This has got to be it. There's nothing else and our direction is right. Leave that rock to port and hug the shore of the island to starboard."

I steered through the surf toward the opening. The waves steepened as the water grew shallow. *Osprey* surged ahead, pushed by the waves. "Keep going," urged Steve. "Steer through the kelp." I gritted my teeth and followed his directions, hearing the swish of kelp brushing against the hull.

"I see the inlet ahead," said Steve.

Suddenly, a clear channel opened up in the center of the kelp and I followed it in, turning to port, then to starboard to avoid rocks. Seconds later we were in smooth water. Rocks were all around us but we were no longer in danger of being swept onto them by waves. A narrow channel between a small tree-covered island on the right and a peninsula on the left stretched ahead of us: a watery path through the forest. I put

A quiet anchorage is the reward for wending through the rocks.

the engine in neutral and we coasted along through the rocks. Steve went up on the bow to guide us through.

"Do you see the channel?" he asked as we maneuvered through a very narrow passage. I looked to starboard and saw a rock next to the boat, then I looked to port and saw a bigger rock.

"No, I can't see it."

"That's because we're in it and it's not much wider than the boat."

We glided past a final rock into a perfectly round bay with pinnacle-shaped mountains beyond.

Later, soaking in the hot springs, I looked out the window of the hot-spring shelter to see a field of rocks. I felt a sense of accomplishment and a kinship with the early explorers who had sailed these waters. We had navigated through some of the most dangerous waters in Southeast Alaska and entered one of its trickiest harbors.

9.4 KLAG BAY
"Hot for Chichagof"

I peered through the rusty bars of an iron gate into the mouth of the old Chichagof Gold Mine. All I could see in the dark shadows was a short timbered passageway ending in a pile of rocks and rubble. Someone had been determined to keep sightseers like us from venturing too far. Just as well, I thought, looking at the rough timbers shoring up the tunnel. They could be rotten.

We had come to Chichagof to see what was left of this once-major gold mine, far removed from the tourist bustle. In Skagway we had learned about placer mining, where prospectors excavated gold in soft sediments with picks and shovels. At Chichagof we hoped to see a hard-rock mine. Hard-rock mining, such as that done in the Juneau area and here at Chichagof, requires capital, heavy equipment and laborers to dig deep shafts into mountainsides.

We had left Mirror Harbor for Chichagof two days before, winding our way south on waters as calm as a lake. The farther we went through the tree-lined passages, the more my confidence that we would see anything of the old mine waned. The idea of a major industry in this pristine wilderness was hard to imagine. We hadn't even seen another boat since leaving Mirror Harbor.

We entered Klag Bay through a passage called the "The Gate," our entrance perfectly timed to avoid swift currents. A light rain stippled the water. Through my mist-covered glasses, I saw a sea lion diving for fish and a bald eagle standing guard on a tall spruce at the bay's entrance.

When we rounded the last island and entered the anchorage at the head of the bay, I could see the broken remains of a wharf, piles of gray slag and a large rusty machine standing on the beach like a long-legged insect. We weren't the only sightseers: one powerboat was anchored off the wharf and another was putting down its anchor.

Historical pictures of the Chichagof Mine show a large dock along with warehouses, factory buildings, houses and a large slag pile. The fact that the buildings were gone in 2007 was not a surprise; abandoned buildings disappear quickly in Alaska—victims of fire, rot and scavengers.

We took the dinghy ashore and walked south along the beach. Steve went ahead but I hesitated. Now that we were here, I worried about collapsing mine shafts, abandoned chemicals, and bears—hazards of a wilderness mine. I wished we had thought to bring the bear spray ashore. Then I heard Steve call.

"I've found a trail. And it's not a bear trail."

I followed him under branches to a wide, slate-covered path leading uphill. To our right, I could see the dim outline of a building through alders and cottonwoods. We came to a narrow-gauge rail bed and followed it to the mine opening.

The story of the Chichagof Gold Mine began in July 1905 when two Tlingit fishermen, Ralph Young and his uncle John Newell, with two other Tlingits, left their fishing grounds in Icy Strait for their home in Sitka. On the way south they stopped to camp at Klag Bay and, the day being hot, sought out a stream for a drink of water. Young and Newell both noticed a shiny rock at the bottom of the stream. Not wanting their companions to see it, they hid the rock in the bush, creeping back in the night to retrieve it. Unknown to them, the other two men each had a similar shiny rock in his pocket.

By 1905 the Klondike Gold Rush was over but dreams of riches lingered on. Three big mines, Treadwell, Perseverance and Alaska-Juneau, operated near Juneau while smaller mines operated at Berners Bay, Eagle River, Port Snettisham, Wyndham Bay and elsewhere.

Young and Newell showed their rock to John Gamble, a teacher at the Sitka mission school, who in turn showed it to Judge Edward DeGroff, a storeowner in Sitka. DeGroff gave Gamble a boat and the equipment they needed to prospect. When Gamble, Newell and Young returned to Klag Bay, they found a vein of gold and their discovery led to a rush of claims. By July of 1906, three mines had been staked: The Hirst-Chichagof Mine, the Golden Gate Mine, and the Chichagof Gold Mine, which had been organized by DeGroff with Gamble, Newell and Young as partners. The *Sitka Alaska* exulted, "We may look forward in the very near future to the sound of the cry 'Hot for Chichagof.'"

An unusual feature of the Chichagof Gold Mine was the high concentration of gold in its ore. The vein was so rich that the company shipped its first ore directly to the smelter in

The Chichagof Gold Mine, a major industrial mine that closed in 1943, is now deserted.

Tacoma without processing. In its early days the mine operated without outside capital—just starter funds from DeGroff and proceeds from the ore.

Local control didn't last. In 1909, James Freeborn, one of the original backers of the large Treadwell Mine in Douglas, purchased the Chichagof Gold Mine. Consolidations with the other Chichagof area mines followed. By 1915, the Chichagof Gold Mine employed 108 men and operated a school and a store to serve the employees and their families. In 1919, the *Douglas Island News* (a Juneau-area paper) reported that DeGroff's widow had earned over $1 million in dividends from the mine. Young and Newell, the two Tlingits who discovered the gold, were each paid $50,000 (about $617,000 in 2008 dollars) for their interests.

The last big years at Chichagof were 1921 and 1922, and then the high-grade ore became difficult to find. The mine closed, sold and reopened repeatedly until it shut for good in 1943. Chichagof had produced more than 500,000 tons of ore, yielding more than 650,000 ounces of gold (about 1,600 gold bars) and 150,000 ounces of silver for a total value of almost $14 million. Mining at the site ultimately reached a depth of 1,800 feet below sea level.

A flurry of new explorations at the mine site followed in the 1980s, several years after the US government allowed the price of gold to float on the world market. Investors drilled new cores and did tests, but when their camp accidentally burned down, they never resumed operations. The US Bureau of Mines estimates there is still ore in the mine, but the concentrations of gold are only 0.1 ounces to 0.4 ounces per ton—far less than the 1 ounce per ton the mine produced at its peak.

Some of the equipment from the 1980s was still visible. Next to the mine shaft we found abandoned tanks and a recent-vintage yellow Caterpillar tractor.

These test cores may be left from an attempt to reopen Chichagof Mine in the 1980s.

"What a waste," said Steve. "I suppose the expense of moving it was too high."

Near the tractor was a small intact railcar and pile of wheels and axels. Outside a shed, we found a mound of corings, cylinders of rock drilled from the earth to test for gold.

It was quiet in the forest and difficult to imagine that in the mine's heyday, rail-cars full of ore rumbled up from the depths of the earth and stamp mills thumped and pounded.

We returned to the beach where an old steam engine rested in the water, its pistons and a boiler still discernible. I picked in the sand looking for artifacts, sifting the dregs of history. An old-fashioned steam radiator poked above the sand. What dreams had people harbored as they warmed themselves in front of it? Were they drawn to the adventure of hunting for gold or were they just looking for jobs?

Before we left the bay, we motored *Osprey* along the shore, looking at the mounds of gray tailings and the odds and ends of machinery that littered the shore. What had once been a major industry was now only a few remains fast disappearing into the forest. In the Old World, ruins serve as cultural mementos, reminders of bygone empires. In Alaska they remind us of past dreams. Ultimately, the earth had defeated the mines— the rich vein petering away to a concentration no longer worth pursuing. The lesson of Chichagof is that even in Alaska, nature's resources have their limit.

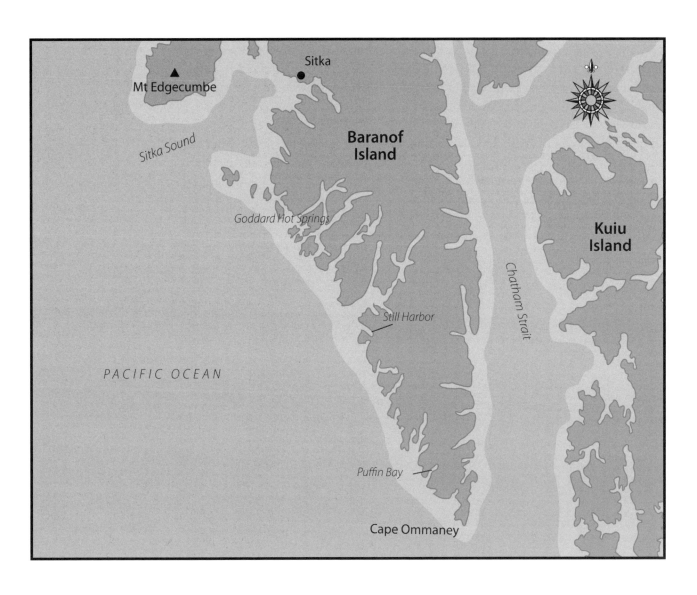

Sitka

Mt Edgecumbe

Sitka Sound

Baranof
Island

Goddard Hot Springs

Kuiu
Island

Chatham Strait

Still Harbor

PACIFIC OCEAN

Puffin Bay

Cape Ommaney

CHAPTER 10

WEST COAST OF BARANOF ISLAND

10.1 SITKA
Russians Among the Tlingit

When I saw the graceful tower and domes of St. Michael's Cathedral soaring above the streets of Sitka, I immediately wanted to go inside. But Steve had other ideas.

"A church?" He had a note of horror in his voice. "I'm sure there are more interesting things to see. Let's walk up Castle Hill and then go to Totem Park."

It was our first visit to Sitka, in 2006, and we were taking a day to go sightseeing. I wanted to discover how the city had been influenced by its history as the former capital of Russian America.

So far I liked what I had seen: an attractive Alaskan town with false-fronted buildings, a bustling waterfront of fish-processing plants and docks, and the impressive red-roofed Pioneer Home, a retirement facility managed by the state of Alaska. The Caribbean jewelry stores so ubiquitous in Skagway, Juneau and Ketchikan were missing, perhaps a result of the fact that Sitka lacks a cruise-ship dock. Cruise ships still come here but they anchor off the Indian River, south of town, and ferry the passengers ashore.

Vowing to visit the church by myself later on, I followed Steve through an alley and then up a path that wound its way to the top of the hill.

Castle Hill, which sits at the edge of Sitka's harbor, is named for the elaborate Russian Governor's mansion that once stood on its apex. Today it is a park with a commanding view of the town and Sitka Sound. Where Russians once looked down

St. Michael's Cathedral dominates downtown Sitka, which includes a bookstore, a pharmacy and other useful stores as well as souvenir shops.

233

Katlian Street is the main route into downtown Sitka from the public marina.

on a frontier outpost, we regarded the stores and houses of modern-day Sitka and the graceful lines of a bridge to Japonski Island.

The first Russian outpost in Alaska was established in 1784 at Three Saints Bay on Kodiak Island. By the 1790s the sea otters that had brought the Russians to America were becoming scarce. Aleksandr Baranov, manager of the Russian American Company, moved his post south in search of new otter territory. He first moved to Archangel Michael, north of present-day Sitka. Then, in 1804, after a battle with the Tlingits, Baranov occupied Sitka where the capital remained until 1867 when the US purchased Alaska from Russia.

By the afternoon, we had toured the city museum and the Russian Bishop's House. My head was reeling from all the names and dates of Sitka's history, but there were two more sights to see. First was the Sheldon Jackson Museum, just beyond the downtown area.

When the US purchased Russia, Sitka remained the de facto capital until the US congress ordered it moved to Juneau in 1900. Protestant missionaries were among the first Americans to move to Sitka. Two of them, Fannie Kellogg and John G. Brady, who later became the fifth Territorial Governor of Alaska, established the Sitka Industrial and Training School for the Tlingit people. It later became the Sheldon Jackson School, and then the Sheldon Jackson College. (The college closed in 2007.)

Dim light filtered through curtained windows high in the octagonal museum building. Glass cases filled with artifacts lined the walls and cabinets with drawers occupied the center of the large room. I opened glass-topped drawers of Tlingit and Haida rattles, all carefully labeled as to date and origin. It was an impressive collection of artifacts from all over Alaska. I looked around the room in awe—until I remembered the motivation for the collection. Reverend Sheldon Jackson, who later became Alaska's first General Agent of Education, collected the artifacts because he believed that Native cultures were doomed to extinction. He was convinced that to survive, Native people needed to abandon their language, culture and art and acculturate to western life. He collected these artifacts so that future generations of Natives would have a place to view their ancestors' art and culture.

From the Sheldon Jackson Museum it was a short walk to the Sitka National Historical Park, locally called Totem Park. We hiked gravel paths through an old-growth forest of hemlock and spruce to admire the 30-some totem poles scattered around the park. Every time we rounded a corner to see one, my heart gave a little jump. Traditionally, Natives had placed their totem poles in rows on the beach in front of their houses rather than in the forest, but in the park the tall poles blended in among the tall trees, highlighting

Membership of St. Michael's Cathedral in downtown Sitka includes descendants of Tlingits who were converted during the time of Russian America.

the beauty of both. I stopped in front of one pole, puzzled by its stylistic designs with overlapping figures.

"That's a Haida pole," I said to Steve. "What's it doing in Tlingit country?"

In fact, none of the poles were from Sitka. I later learned that Governor Brady had collected many of them to display at the world fairs in St. Louis and Portland, Oregon. Most of the poles in the park today are replicas, copied from Brady's collection by modern Native carvers.

The trail came out onto a beach. A cruise ship rode at anchor in the bay, and in the distance the cone-shaped Mount Edgecumbe rose from the sea. It was our first view of the volcano, which had been obscured by clouds on our arrival.

We were standing near the site of the great battle between the Tlingits and the Russians in 1804. When I first read that the park commemorated that battle, I was surprised. Didn't the Tlingits lose the battle and retreat in disgrace? Why commemorate such an occasion? I found the answer to that question in a Sitka art gallery, in a book entitled *Will the Time Ever Come?* (edited by Andrew Hope III and Thomas F. Thornton, Alaska Native Knowledge Network, University of Alaska, 2000). In it, Herb Hope tells the story of the battle from the perspective of the Kiks.adi clan of Sitka Tlingits, a story he had heard from his uncles as a child. His recollection presents a different perspective than the usual one of Native Americans being trampled by Europeans.

In the early days of contact with European fur traders, Tlingits prospered. With a few notable exceptions, such as the American captain Robert Gray, the American and English traders treated Northwest Natives, including Tlingits, with respect, knowing that successful trade depended on good relations. In turn, that trade brought the Tlingits wealth in the form of metal tools, cookware, blankets, western clothes and firearms. The arrival of Russians threatened their new status. Whereas American and British traders bought skins from the Tlingits, the Russians employed their own hunters: Aleuts from the Aleutian Islands and Kodiak. In 1802 the Kiks.adi joined with other Tlingit and Haida villages around Southeast Alaska and drove the Russians and their Aleut serfs out.

Expecting the Russians to return, the Kiks.adi prepared for battle. Near Indian River, where shallow water would keep Russian ships away, they built a strong fort, modeled after the Russian fort.

When the Russians did return, they first tried to negotiate. When that failed, they stormed the Tlingit fort, but were driven back. Next, the Russian ship *Neva* bombarded the fort. Although the Tlingits held firm, they were running short of gunpowder; they had won the battle but were losing the siege. That night they gathered around their campfire to discuss their options. They had lost warriors, old men and women, children and infants in battle. The best plan, they decided, was to abandon their fort and return to fight another day.

According to Hope the Kiks.adi didn't see themselves as retreating, but as marching to survive. Leaving a rearguard near the fort to fool the Russians into believing they were still there, most left under cover of darkness, walking north to what is now called Katlian Cove. From there they crossed the mountains of Baranof Island to Chatham Strait. It was a significant feat for a seagoing people, already exhausted from battle.

From a new village on Admiralty Island, the Kiks.adi Tlingit set up a blockade to stop other Natives from entering Peril Strait to trade with the Russians. Nearby, in a bay now known as Traders Bay, American traders took advantage of the blockade to set up their own trading station.

Each year the Russian American Company's manager, Aleksandr Baranov, sent envoys to plead with the Kiks.adi Tlingit to return but for many years they refused, only journeying to Sitka Sound during the herring season. Then one spring they did come back and built a new village next to the Russian stockade. The sea-otter population had been severely depleted by hunting and the Russians were focusing on inland development. The Kiks.adi announced to the Russians that their clan owned the land behind the fort and that only Kiks.adi could hunt there—which they would do in exchange for Russian trade goods.

The Kiks.adi had returned to their homeland, and on their own terms. According to Hope, the Kiks.adi believe that their determination helped stem the tide of Russian advancement—and changed the course of Russian history in Southeast Alaska.

I had been wondering how the Russians affected Sitka. I should have also asked how the Tlingits affected the Russians.

Late the next day I finally got to visit the cathedral. After laundry, grocery shopping and checking email at the Highliner Café, I stopped by the church where an open door invited visitors in for tours. Inside, I found a large circular room with a few chairs scattered around the perimeter. Ornate gold doors led into an inner sanctuary and on either side of the door hung religious paintings. Gold seemed to be everywhere, on moldings around paintings, on the covers of bibles in a glass case and even on the surface of the paintings, or icons. It seemed alien to me compared to the spare Protestant churches of my childhood.

A tour guide was explaining the history of the church. It was a replica, built after the original burned down in 1967. When the fire started, townspeople rallied, forming a chain of more than 100 people to rescue the icons and other items such as the large chandelier now hanging in the center of the dome.

A fishing boat at the town marina. Fishing and crabbing are some of Sitka's major industries.

The guide explained the church lacked pews because the congregation stood during services. The folding chairs around the edge were for visitors. She went on to tell us that the church had a congregation of 80 to 100 members, mostly Tlingit. That caught my attention; here was a tangible sign of Russian tenure.

Although Russian fur traders treated their Aleut serfs cruelly, Russian Orthodox priests and monks left a legacy

Drawings of a bear and a raven on a house in Sitka's "Indian Village" probably represent the clans of the residents.

Thirty-some totem poles from all over Southeast Alaska are scattered in the forest in Sitka National Totem Park.

of orthodoxy that still flourishes in Alaska. Unlike American missionaries such as Sheldon Jackson, the Orthodox priests didn't demand that Natives give up their culture and languages. Monks and priests learned the Native languages, developed alphabets, translated the bible and taught Native children in bilingual classes. Several of the priests, including Bishop Innocent Veniaminov whose house we had visited the day before, were beloved by their congregations. Veniaminov was canonized a saint in Russia in 1977 for his evangelization of the Native people of Alaska and Siberia.

On my way back to the boat, I walked through an area labeled "Indian Village" on my visitors' guide. The road led through a collection of small-frame houses built close together. A fierce-looking mask with twisted branches for hair glared down at me from under a roof overhang, while sketches of bears, eagles, ravens and devilfish adorned nearby walls. Real ravens squawked from rooftops, watching inquisitively as I walked by. This wasn't a traditional Tlingit village with its longhouses and totem poles but it had enough of a quirky Alaskan flavor to make me realize I was seeing something genuine and not a tourist attraction.

Yes, traces of the Russian history remained at Sitka. And even more important, the Tlingit culture had survived under both the Russian and American rule.

10.2 SITKA TO PUFFIN BAY
Rain Must Fall

"Into each life some rain must fall." These words from a poem by Henry Wadsworth Longfellow, and later turned into a popular song, could have been written for Southeast Alaska. One way to ensure your share of rain is to sail in these waters.

Growing up in Seattle I was accustomed to rain. If it was raining when I left for school in the morning, my mother would make me wear my yellow slicker. At the bus stop, my friends and I would wile away the time waiting for the bus by building elaborate landscapes of rivers and dams in the mud.

During our first trip to Southeast Alaska, in 2006, Steve and I encountered what Alaskans told us was an unusually rainy summer. When day after day brought more rain, there didn't seem much point in waiting for better weather. So, as I had done as a child, I simply donned my foul-weather gear. But our experience on the west coast of Baranof Island taught me that the rain in Alaska is different than those showers in Seattle.

Friends who had visited this coast before us told of jagged rock cliffs, wind-swept trees, and steep-sided coves. On the basis of this description, we decided to head south from Sitka, staying on Baranof Island's exposed west coast, instead of heading east through Peril Strait to more protected waters.

We left Sitka in the rain. The day before, the weather bureau had warned of "unseasonably strong winds" (and rain), cautioning mariners to "monitor the situation closely." As a result we had stayed in Sitka another day, using up one of our precious storm days (extra days in our schedule that we could use to avoid going out in dangerous conditions).

My mood as we left the harbor matched the dark clouds overhead. In the distance we could see waves breaking across rocks, evidence of yesterday's storm and a sign our day might be unpleasant. I looked at the water pocked with raindrops and wished I were just about anywhere else. I consoled myself by looking forward to a hot bath at the end of the day when we would anchor off Goddard Hot Springs.

As we headed southwest across Sitka Sound, seas sent *Osprey* pitching, spilling the wind from the sails and throwing the boom from side to side. Unable to sail, we dropped the sails to continue under power. I went below to stay dry and adjust the radar while Steve took the wheel.

A while later Steve steered to go inside of Persai Island, putting the island between us and the waves.

"Come up here, quickly," he called. "I need you to watch for a rock. Too much is happening at once." On deck, I peered through a sheet of rain, trying to tell the difference between kelp growing on rock and kelp broken free by yesterday's storm. A mistake could put *Osprey* on the rocks. I finally saw a brown fringe of rockweed that was stationary among the waves, and knew there was a rock just below the surface. A few minutes later, I saw the quiet waters of Hot Springs Bay. We were safe.

Goddard Hot Springs

"This almost makes the slog through the rain worth the effort," I told Steve, as we relaxed in a hot tub in a small cabin overlooking the anchorage at the Goddard Hot Springs. Through an open window, I could see *Osprey* and its neighbors, a small yellow sailboat and a fishing boat, floating quietly on calm water. How wonderful, I thought, to have the luxury of a hot bath in the middle of the wilderness.

Goddard Hot Springs are a reminder of the tumultuous geology of this region. Faults in the earth's surface allow water to circulate down to hot volcanic rocks where it is heated, then rises to the surface as hot springs.

Long before either Russians or European-Americans came to this coast, Tlingits soaked in these springs, valuing them for their heat and curative powers. They hollowed out bathing places in the rocks, and sometimes slept in the springs all night to save the work of cutting firewood.

The hot springs have had a procession of owners. In 1805, Urey Lisianski, a Russian doctor, built a hospital near them. He was followed in 1884 by Amos T. Whitford, who ran a dairy farm here. The farm was not successful and Whitford sold the hot springs to Dr. Fred L. Goddard, who hoped to run a mental hospital. When he couldn't get funding, he built a 23-room health resort instead with hot mineral baths in each room. In 1939, after Dr. Goddard had died, his widow sold the hotel to the Alaskan Territory which used it for a retirement home but abandoned it to build the Pioneer Home in Sitka in 1946. Finally, in 1978, the city of Sitka cleared the land and built the two cabins with tubs and plumbing that remain here now.

Still Harbor

The next morning brought a thin mist that washed the colors from trees and rocks. Along this part of the coast a string of islands and headlands juts out from the shore like rocky fingers reaching into the ocean. Our route would lead us through these islands in a complex set of passes and narrows.

We were just pulling up anchor when we saw the fishing boat *Invicta* heading south. "Let's follow him," said Steve. "He's probably been here before."

For the next hour, we followed *Invicta* through the Rakof Islands, into narrow passes and around bends, passing seals hauled out on rocks and eagles perched on tall spruce. As we exited Cameron Passage and approached open water, an undulating mirror of quiet seas stretched out ahead of us. Windswept trees on craggy rocks told us such quiet conditions were unusual. According to the *US Coast Pilot*, from October to March this coast is battered by gales that blow 10 percent of the time and by waves 8 feet or higher 30 percent of the time.

We motored south down the coast. Off North Cape, fog settled in a cottony blanket and the land shrank to dark forms in the mist. We turned into Still Harbor to anchor, passing ragged rocks emerging from the sea like a whale's backbone. Foam swirled around the rocks as swells broke over them and I smelt the salt tang of seaweed. Inside the entrance, a fish-buying boat with its fenders out waited for fishboats. We motored past a small island and anchored in a large bay.

We got into the dinghy and circled this bay, which was fringed with beaches of black rocks. The chart showed a lagoon near the bay's head and we hoped to take the dinghy to explore it. But when we found the outlet, it was impassible in a small boat. Instead of the channel we'd envisioned, it consisted of a spillway with sheets of water coursing across it and a grove of small alders growing on top. We tied to a tree and climbed out, intending to walk across the spillway. Branches pulled at our jackets and we had to step over or duck thick branches. Under our feet the sharp-edged rock threatened to cut our boots. We turned back after catching only a glimpse of a smooth lake beyond.

Waves crash over jagged rocks outside Still Harbor.

We had been bested by the main

geological formation of Baranof Island, a rock called Sitka Graywacke, a metamorphic formation similar to shale. Graywacke breaks easily into its component layers. The moving earth had folded and thrust and even overturned the beds, so that in places sheets of shale stood perpendicular to the beach, presenting sharp edges to unwary hikers.

A fish buyer waits for fish in Still Harbor.

After dinner, I took the kayak out, paddling into the outer harbor. It was dusk and the water was so still I could see the reflection of the floodlight of the fish-buying boat. As I looked out to sea, I saw fog creeping around the rocks and into the harbor. The sight was beautiful—and unsettling; it made me feel vulnerable in my tiny kayak. I paddled back, glad to reach the warmth and light of *Osprey*.

We woke to rain drumming on the cabin roof. It was hard to get enthusiastic about leaving, so we put off going while Steve cooked a breakfast of eggs and blueberry biscuits. By 11:00 a.m., the rain had turned to a mere drizzle and we were ready to move on.

Motoring down the coast through more calm water, shadowy cliffs and islands tantalized us, only to disappear into the mist. A fleet of salmon trollers worked this part of the coast but we could see them only as faint spots in the mist—or green dots on our radar. I began to wonder what the point of being on this coast was if we couldn't see the scenery.

As we passed Sea Lion Rock at the entrance to Puffin Bay, the lazy forms of sea lions lying on the rocks emerged out of the mist, accompanied by their insistent barking and the strong odor of old fish.

Puffin Bay

I could see just enough of the entrance to Puffin Bay to know that in good weather, it would be spectacular with great quartz veins zigzagging across a headland and jagged rocks rearing out of the sea. But even jagged rocks look pale through a filter of mist.

We motored up the bay and anchored in a small cove at its head, as the fog turned to rain. Steep-sided hills rose above us, disappearing into the mist. At the cove's head, a green marsh spread along the shore. From all around us I heard the constant gurgle of creeks tumbling across the beach, the rush of waterfalls pouring down the hills, and the drip of water falling off tree limbs.

The next morning the rain was still falling in a steady drizzle. Steve looked out *Osprey*'s cabin window. "We could take another storm day. We've got enough time. We don't have to go out in this stuff."

Suddenly, the resolve that had pushed me to keep moving since we had left Sitka

Rain obscures the hillsides above Puffin Cove. Southeast Alaska's forests are perhumid rainforests, meaning they are perpetually rather than seasonally rainy.

simply collapsed. I was forced to admit that I didn't really like sailing in the rain; that I would much rather wait for better weather.

We spent the morning down below, reading and relaxing. By afternoon, we were ready to do something, rain or not. Steve got out his fishing gear and headed out in the dinghy while I launched the kayak.

I paddled around the cove, looking at raindrops sending concentric circles across the water. White lion's mane jellyfish hovered just below the water's surface and I watched them pulsing slowly in the current, their long tentacles stretching out several feet in all directions.

Skimming along the shore, I arrived at the cove entrance. The ground rose steeply next to the beach there and I looked up to see massive spruce trees growing up the hillside. I moved in closer to see the base of the trees. Their roots appeared to be growing out of a layer of moss so thin I could see chunks of shale poking out of it. The realization that such large trees relied on only the barest layer of topsoil awed me.

Before we left for Alaska, I had assumed that the Tongass Rainforest, which encompasses most of Southeast Alaska, would be similar to the rainforests of Vancouver Island and the Olympic Peninsula—the amounts of rainfall in both areas are comparable and the temperature in Alaska only slightly colder. In fact, Sitka, at 96 inches of precipitation a year has less than Tofino, BC, at 135 inches. What I didn't understand is that the rainforests I was used to are *seasonal* rainforests, where the driest summer month has less than one-fifth the amount of rain as the wettest winter month, while the Tongass Rainforest in Southeast Alaska is a *perhumid* rainforest, meaning it is perpetually rainy, even in the summer, and little moisture is lost to evaporation.

The perpetual rain, although frustrating to people trying to live or visit here, has its advantages. Topsoil forms quickly here, a usable amount in a few centuries compared to a few millennia in places like New England or Nova Scotia. Where moisture can drain away, such as on porous slopes, trees grow fast and to gigantic proportions—four to six feet in diameter in about 700 years. Hemlock seedlings sprout quickly after clear-cutting, reducing the erosion from logging that plagues lower British Columbia and Washington. And forest fires are almost unheard of.

The rain has other consequences. Trees that grow here have shallow roots, subjecting them to windfall, and where soil is not porous the runoff tends to pool and form peat bogs or muskegs. Large areas of the Tongass are covered with these bogs, where trees are stunted and mosses, ferns, and liverworts grow in mounds.

There was nothing stunted about the trees in Puffin Bay. The steep slopes above the bay kept water running off. And there was plenty of water to run off. After only an hour of paddling, my rain gear was thoroughly soaked. I headed back to the boat and its diesel heater.

On *Osprey* I found Steve cleaning rockfish while Jigger paced the deck waiting for his share. Blackened rockfish would be perfect for dinner, I decided.

Rain still fell in a persistent drizzle the next morning, but we departed as planned. Outside the bay, swells crashed over the rocks and the seas went every which way, a sorry change from the calms of two days ago. The wind blew at about 10 knots, not sufficient for us to sail in the rough seas, but enough to add to our misery.

As we passed Cape Ommaney and crossed Chatham Strait, the waves calmed for no apparent reason and I was able to be more philosophical. A coast where I had expected to see soaring cliffs and rockbound shores had instead given me memories of slate tipped at strange angles and trees rooted into only the thinnest layers of topsoil. No doubt we would see more rain ahead. I didn't look forward to the rain, but was ready for it.

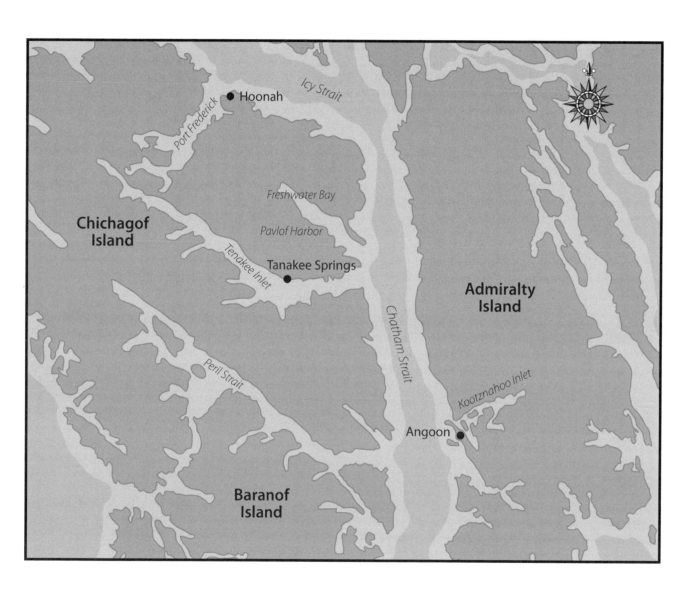

Chichagof
Island

Hoonah

Icy Strait

Port Frederick

Freshwater Bay

Pavlof Harbor

Tenakee Springs

Tenakee Inlet

Admiralty
Island

Chatham Strait

Kootznahoo Inlet

Peril Strait

Angoon

Baranof
Island

CHAPTER 11

NORTH CHATHAM STRAIT

11.1 PAVLOF HARBOR
Looking for Bears

We were looking for a quiet anchorage after a hectic week with Steve's sister and brother-in-law in Glacier Bay when we decided on Pavlof Harbor on the east shore of Chicagof Island in Chatham Strait. An Alaskan couple had recommended it. "It's a great place to watch brown bears," the woman told us. "They come down to the stream to catch fish."

What she didn't mention was the waterfall that tumbled over boulders into the southwest corner of the bay or the white-capped mountains above the cascade. In the afternoon light, the bay was dazzling with spruce and hemlock trees crowning a fringe of bright-green beach grass.

We anchored near the middle of the bay to avoid the submerged reef and the pinnacle rock described in the *US Coast Pilot*.

In the morning when the tide went out, I paddled my kayak among the rocks, admiring red sea anemones, purple starfish, and gnarly sea squirts. Later, equipped with bear bells and bear spray, we took the dinghy ashore, motoring close in to the waterfall as salmon jumped around us. The dank smell of rainforest came out to meet us as we stepped ashore, and the roar of the waterfall drowned out the jingle of our bear bells. We followed a trail through a spruce forest with prickly devil's club in the underbrush. After passing a row of thin stumps gnawed to spikes by beavers, we emerged onto a marsh with grass so tall I had to stand on tiptoe to see the reflection of mountains in a lake as smooth as glass.

A stream tumbles into Pavlof Harbor in the northwest corner. Watch out for bears!

We were walking through the grass when I looked down just in time to avoid stepping on a fresh pile of bear scat.

"Let's get out of here," I said to Steve. "The grass is so tall, we won't see the bears until it's too late."

I was relieved when we got safely back to the dinghy. I wanted to see bears—but at a distance. In going into the marsh, we had broken two rules for preventing dangerous bear encounters. Experts advise hikers to minimize the chances of a surprise encounter by avoiding both brushy areas and salmon streams, exactly where we had gone. Nor were we in a large group. Two people are safer than one, but four is even better.

The next morning on our way out, we motored by another boat to say goodbye.

"Did you see the bear this morning?" one of the men asked us. "It came right down to the beach."

"This place is worth another visit," said Steve, "maybe next time we'll see the bears."

It was better to have not seen the bears, I thought, than to have seen them up close.

11.2   TENAKEE SPRINGS
Who's in Town?

With no cars allowed in town, Tenakee residents walk and ride bikes.

As I opened the door to the hot-springs bathhouse, warm moist air rolled up the stairs, enfolding my bare skin in comforting warmth. I could smell the odor of sulfur and, in the light of a skylight, see steam rising from the pool below.

We had come to Tenakee Springs to enjoy the hot springs, and experience what had been described to us as this town's "funky, laid-back" character. What I'd seen of the town so far was more junky than funky, but I was prepared to let the hot springs make up for it.

Under gray skies on a windless day, we had motored south from Pavlof Harbor and into Tenakee Inlet. As we made the final turn into the marina, we could see the town ahead: a string of houses built on pilings stretched along the shore. We tied *Osprey* up at the marina, then walked the quarter-mile distance into town on an unpaved country lane.

In town, small wooden cottages lined both sides of the lane. Bicycles, handcarts, miscellaneous lumber, tools and firewood littered the small front yards. The most common accessory was a blue tarp. The bathhouse, a small red cottage, was in the middle of town next to the fuel dock. A sign on the door gave hours strictly divided into men's and women's times.

It was 1:00 p.m. and the women's hours ended at 2:00. With towel in hand, I passed through an entryway into a white-painted room with benches around the walls and two stained-glass windows: one showing orcas, the other an eagle. A door from the dressing room led to the bathing room with its hot-springs pool. A sign next to the door announced the rules: no soaps in the pool, wash and rinse before entering the pool, and children of the opposite sex were allowed only with the permission of everyone in the bathhouse.

One other woman was already in the bath, her wet brown hair slicked against her head as she lay back in the pool.

"Where are you from?' she asked when I joined her.

"Seattle. We're on a sailboat. And you?"

"I've been in Tenakee Springs several years now."

"What do you do here?" I asked.

"Mostly build my house."

She didn't look old enough to be retired, so I wondered how she made a living. But she turned away, signaling the conversation was over, and got out of the pool a few minutes later.

I leaned back in the hot water, reveling in the warmth and the quiet of the bathhouse that I had all to myself.

Steve was waiting for me on the dock when I came out.

"Let's get some lunch," he said. "The Blue Moon Café is just around the corner."

The café had a low sagging roof and boards nailed across one of the windows. The sign was so worn I could hardly read it. It was not the kind of restaurant we usually frequented, and when I saw it, I hesitated. Nevertheless the café and its owner, Rosie, have been written up in almost every guidebook and travel article about Tenakee Springs, so I screwed up my courage and followed Steve through the door.

Inside, two bare bulbs lit a low-ceilinged room with dingy white walls and an odor of frying meat. A woman, her dark hair pulled back from her face and wearing a white-flowered sweatshirt and green sweatpants, worked behind a counter. This we surmised was the famous Rosie. A hand-lettered sign on the refrigerator door warned, "No Guns Allowed."

Appalled by the dingy room, I was tempted to flee.

The menu, posted above the counter, was simple: hamburgers.

Two hamburger patties came out of the freezer and onto the grill. As Rosie cooked, she talked. She lives here year-round, she told us, taking one trip "Outside" (an Alaskan term for away from Alaska) every year. Her last trip was to Atlanta.

"Eight days on the ferry and eight days on the train!" she told us, shaking her head in exasperation.

When we left the café, Steve turned to me and said, "My hamburger was undercooked and there was no plumbing in the restroom, just a hole in the floor. Where is the Alaskan health department?"

Steve disappeared into the bathhouse while I took the

It's possible to see how this old log cabin in Tenakee Springs was constructed.

Residents of Tenakee Springs like to hang tools and other paraphernalia outside their doors.

opportunity to explore the town. My first impression improved as I looked more closely at the small homes, noting several old-fashioned log cabins with notched logs. Artfully arranged tools decorated house walls next to many doors: a collection of saws, rusting animal traps and even, in one case, two frying pans hanging by their handles. Were the pans just decorations or a crude doorbell?

On one house, a sign saying "Open at Sunset" and cut in the shape of a crab caught my attention. The door opened and a woman stepped out.

"What's open at sunset?" I asked her.

She shrugged. "Nothing. I just like the sign."

The tools next to the doors made me think of the whimsical prints of the Alaskan artist Rie Muñoz. Her pictures of Alaskans going about their daily lives—cleaning fish, hanging laundry, walking to the bath—make people smile. Among her hundreds of images from all over Alaska are more than thirty from Tenakee Springs. In Muñoz's Alaska, the sky is always blue and the landscape is drawn in uncluttered lines.

That day's skies were gray but the town was bustling with scenes befitting Muñoz's prints: bicyclists careening down the path, dogs trotting at their owners' heels, and eagles swooping overhead.

I returned to the bathhouse to meet Steve. Then we went into the Snyder Mercantile, an old-fashioned two-storey building.

Nostalgia swept over me as I looked around the store. High ceilings, a bare wooden floor, varnished display cabinets and an old-fashioned cash register on a long wooden counter reminded me of an old store in North Haven, Maine, the small community where my grandmother had owned a summer house.

Nostalgia was not an emotion I expected to feel in Alaska where so many things seem raw and new.

I was looking at a black-and-white photograph of a couple in 1890s' clothes when a woman who had been working behind the counter came up to me.

"That's a picture of the Snyders, the original owners of the store."

"This store reminds me of one in my grandmother's town in Maine," I told her.

"Lots of people say it reminds them of other old stores," she answered. "It's a classic building."

According to the website of the Tenakee Springs Business Association, Tenakee Springs was settled by early prospectors and fishermen who came to Tenakee to wait out the winters and take advantage of the hot springs. Today, Tenakee is "enjoyed by both full and part time residents plus visitors looking for some peace and tranquility." Daily seaplane flights and twice-weekly ferries from Juneau make for easy access.

As we walked back to the boat we passed the Party Time Bakery, similar in architecture to Snyder Mercantile. It was closed, but we looked through the window to see tables and chairs.

"We'll have to eat lunch there next time," Steve said.

Next time turned out to be two years later, in 2008. As before, we arrived in early afternoon, but instead of rushing to the bath, I opted for lunch at the bakery. As we walked in the door, the aroma of baking bread greeted us. Music blared from speakers above a counter and a pleasant hum of conversation filled the room. Photographs, watercolors and Rie Muñoz prints covered the walls. T-shirts and sweatshirts hung from racks near the windows.

We found a vacant table and ordered black-bean chili from a harried waitress. This was more like it, I thought, as I tasted the savory dish.

At 6:00 p.m., when the women's bath hours started, I walked back into town. The outer door of the bathhouse was partially ajar but refused to open further when I pushed it. I peered into the entryway to see two German shepherds parked solidly on the floor. I prodded them gently with my foot and they moved a few inches, just enough for me to get by. I wondered if anyone paid attention to the sign on the door asking people to close both doors to keep dogs out.

The scene reminded me of the Rie Muñoz print, *Ladies in the Bath*, showing dogs waiting outside the bathhouse door while women bathe within.

Inside, several women of varying ages were undressing and more were in the pool.

I was just settling into the soothing mineral waters when an older woman came down the stairs carrying a bucket. In a few deft motions, she unloaded shampoo, soap and moisturizer from the bucket, plunked them down on the floor, then turned the bucket upside down, retrieved an empty coffee can from the floor, sat down on the bucket and scooped up some hot water to wash with. I could tell that this was someone who took her bathing seriously and came here often.

The women all seemed to know each other and I sat back in the hot water and listened to them gossip.

"Have you seen (so-and-so)?" one of them asked another.

"No I just got here. Who's in town?"

Snyder Mercantile, Tenakee Springs' general store, retains its old-time appearance.

I remembered that question the next morning as we ate breakfast at the Party Time Bakery. A multi-generational group sat discussing departure plans at the table next to us. Of course, I thought. "Who's in town?" is a question summer people ask each other. Tenakee Springs is a seasonal place, not unlike my grandmother's town in Maine—just a bit funkier.

11.3   ANGOON
A Cultural Difference

Few recreational boats visit Angoon, a small Native village in Chatham Strait on the shores of Admiralty Island. But Steve and I like the adventure of visiting remote villages and Angoon has some claims to fame that intrigued me. In the 1980s, Angoon villagers had taken a stand against logging on Admiralty Island, choosing to preserve their subsistence lifestyle over higher shareholder payments. Another of Angoon's distinctions is that the word "hooch" originated there. During Alaska's early years under American rule alcohol had been strictly prohibited. Angoon villagers had concocted a fiery moonshine using old oil cans and long hollow kelp tubes as stills, called "hootch" after "Hoosenoo," the name of the local Tlingit people (now called Kootznoowoo). Although today it is illegal to even possess liquor within the town limits, the story of "hooch" is still related in almost every guidebook of Alaska.

One reason boaters avoid Angoon is treacherous currents arising from the harbor's location on a peninsula at the entrance to Kootznahoo Inlet, a 10-mile-long channel that winds its way into the heart of the Admiralty Island National Monument and the Kootznoowoo Wilderness. The inlet fills and empties twice a day through Angoon's small inner harbor, creating dangerous currents. The *US Coast Pilot* warns, "The navigation of Kootznahoo Inlet should not be attempted by strangers . . . the inlet should be navigated at slack water, the safest being low water slack." With that warning, I was glad that Ken and Dottie in the powerboat *Dreamweaver* would be behind us.

We timed our departure from Appleton Cove in Peril Strait to ensure we arrived before low-water slack at 12:43 p.m. Favorable currents pushed us along, and we arrived at Danger Point, outside the inlet's entrance, at 12:15. In the inlet we could see small boats drifting on quiet water as their occupants fished for salmon. Wisps of fog trailed across the inlet. The peaceful scene differed so markedly from the description in the *US Coast Pilot* that we decided to enter the inlet early.

We motored into the inlet, weaving between the red beacon of Village Rock and the seaweed-covered Rose Rock, readily visible at low water. A slight current rippled the water around the beacons, but not enough to worry us. To our right we could see the village spread out on the hillside: a church, a store, and houses of various sizes. We passed another red beacon and entered the cove where the town marina lay waiting for us. The entrance had been so easy I almost felt cheated. But then both *Osprey* and *Dreamweaver* had successfully navigated the entrance to Mirror Harbor less than two weeks before. Almost any entrance would seem easy after that.

Our calls to the harbormaster went unanswered, so we took a vacant slip on the outside of the marina, and *Dreamweaver* came alongside.

By now the clouds had moved in and rain fell steadily, that constant patter that's not quite a downpour but still a nuisance. But we were here to see the town and there was no point in waiting; it might rain harder later.

We locked up our boats and picked our way across the dock, skirting piles of fishnets, abandoned batteries and empty oil cans. I had come to expect such scenes in Native marinas and understood I was facing a cultural difference. But I couldn't help thinking, "Why don't they just clean it up?"

Ken carried a white plastic bag of garbage from their boat. When we reached the road, he looked around for a dumpster but there was only an empty parking lot. "I suppose I should have checked to make sure they had a dumpster before I brought it up here. I'll just carry it until we find someplace to dump it."

"Perhaps they can't afford a dumpster," I said. The week before, Steve had pointed out an article in the *Daily Sitka Sentinel* describing Angoon's financial difficulties. The town water department had not paid its electric bills, and the water service had been temporarily cut off. As long ago as 1975, the Bureau of Indian Affairs had noted that Angoon was one of the poorest villages in southeast Alaska. Obstacles to development included the town's remote location, decline of fisheries, and fear of Admiralty Island's ferocious brown bears. Researchers have estimated that between 1,200 and 1,800 brown bears live on Admiralty Island. That's an average density of about 1 per square mile, the highest bear density found anywhere. Brown bears are more aggressive than black bears and therefore more dangerous.

Since the report, the village has acquired regular ferry service, a high school, a sewage-treatment plant, a fishing lodge and a bed and breakfast. The bears, however, are still ferocious.

We set off toward town, walking along a blacktop road, past hedges of thimbleberries and patches of pink flowering foxgloves. We entered a neighborhood of small houses, some freshly painted and neat, others dilapidated. A burly-looking man directed us to a trail that led to the store, a two-storey gray building.

Inside, neat rows of canned goods and coolers of frozen meats greeted us. In the back I found a display of produce. Surprised at the freshness and variety for such a small town, I bought a bag of salad greens and some wasabi peas. Dottie bought a bunch of cilantro for making ceviche.

We walked back outside to find Ken still holding his bag of garbage.

"A store clerk told me she didn't know where I could leave it," he said.

We left the store and continued walking. Minutes later a car pulled over beside us and a woman leaned out a window. "They say there's a bear in town. Be careful."

"Oh great," I said to the others. "Here we are in bear country carrying groceries and garbage."

Despite the warning, we kept walking. There didn't seem to be any point in turning around.

The mountains of Admiralty Island loom over the Tlingit village of Angoon.

We followed along the inner harbor where quaint wooden sheds were built on pilings over the water and skiffs were moored just offshore. Crossing a narrow isthmus, we came to the Chatham Strait waterfront. Rows of rough wooden houses with moss-covered roofs crowded against each other, and a strong scent of woodsmoke filled the air, a scene that brought to mind pictures of early Native towns with their rows of tightly spaced longhouses.

From the waterfront the road circled back uphill to a modern-looking building with a group of totem poles out in front. They were solid-looking wooden poles carved smooth, each topped with a single animal carving. Moss and ferns sprouted from their tops. We were trying to identify the animal figures when a young man stopped to talk to us. Dressed in a light windbreaker and wearing a baseball cap, he seemed unperturbed by the rain. "My father carved those poles," he told us, then explained that the figures represented the clan-crests of Angoon. He pointed out a bear, a shark, a dog salmon, an owl and a beaver. He and his mother were bears, he told us proudly (Tlingit clan membership is matrilineal, passed from mother to children). The building next to the poles had been a museum, but the town did not have the money to keep it open.

Three of the poles had been dedicated in 1982 to mark the 100th anniversary of the disgraceful event that is known as the Angoon Bombardment: the destruction of the original village by the US Navy.

A video produced by the Kooznoowoo Heritage Foundation in 1983 tells that story. In October 1882, a noble-born shaman from Angoon was killed when a harpoon exploded prematurely on a whaling ship that he was working on. As was their custom, the Kootznoowoo demanded 200 blankets in compensation for his death from the Northwest Trading Company, the owner of the ship. To make sure the company paid the compensation, villagers seized two launches from the company headquarters. Rather than paying restitution, the company sent to Sitka (then the Alaska capital) for help. US Naval Commander E.C. Merriman responded with the cutter *Corwin* and the steamer *Favorite*. In what today seems like a nonsensical response, Merriman made a counter demand: that Angoon pay the company 400 blankets. When the Kootznoowoo failed to produce the blankets, Merriman first ordered the village's canoes destroyed, then bombarded the village itself. Six children were killed in the shelling, which also destroyed houses, storehouses of winter food, and priceless ceremonial artwork. Deprived of shelter and food, the villagers suffered a long cold winter. It took them five years to rebuild.

The Navy never apologized, although the US government paid the village $90,000 in restitution in 1973. In a 1982 commemoration ceremony, Alaska Governor Jay Hammon praised the courage shown by Angoon in rebuilding. "The bombardment of this village 100 years ago is the ultimate example of a tragedy which can strike when people no longer listen," Hammond said, referring to Merriman's incomprehensible actions. Hammond hoped all Alaskans learned from such mistakes.

Many white people saw the incident differently than the Tlingits. Some believed that Merriman had put down a Native uprising. That notion is still supported today in at least one Alaska guidebook. Some reports of the incident say the village was evacuated and no one was killed and some versions have the Kootznoowoo seizing two white men rather than two launches. The travel-writer Eliza Scidmore, writing in 1897 in *Appleton's Guide-Book*, claimed the villagers had threatened to murder a white man to compensate for the death of their shaman, an action that would have been consistent with Tlingit customs. Scidmore also claimed that the villagers had not been upset by the bombardment, but had removed their belongings and secured front-row seats across the shore, cheering the neatest shots. Such a story probably tells more about the writer than about the incident itself.

The steady rain had turned our paper grocery bags to sodden tatters, and I was anxious to get back to the boats. We reached the intersection of Kisnahoo Road and Raven Bear Way and looked around at the small neighborhood. We were wondering which way to go next when a stocky man in his sixties sauntered by.

"Where's the town?" Dottie asked him.

He stopped and held out his arms as if to introduce us. "This is the town!"

"No, I mean the town center," said Dottie.

"We're looking for a garbage can," I said. "There was no dumpster at the marina."

"There aren't any garbage cans. First, they wanted us to put our garbage in cans, but the bears got into them. And they couldn't keep the bears away from the dumpster at the marina so they took it away."

Of course, the bears! I knew that brown bears outnumber people on Admiralty Island, and that "Kootznahoo" is Tlingit for "fortress of the bears." But I hadn't connected that fact to the lack of garbage cans. I had assumed their absence was due to poverty, when in fact it was for public safety.

Farther up the hill, behind the town clinic and next to the post office, we finally found a dumpster where Ken could leave his garbage. We walked back to the boats and ate a delicious halibut dinner, thankful we hadn't seen any bears.

Tlingit clan membership is passed down from mothers to children. These poles represent four major clan crests of Angoon residents: owl, beaver, dog salmon and shark.

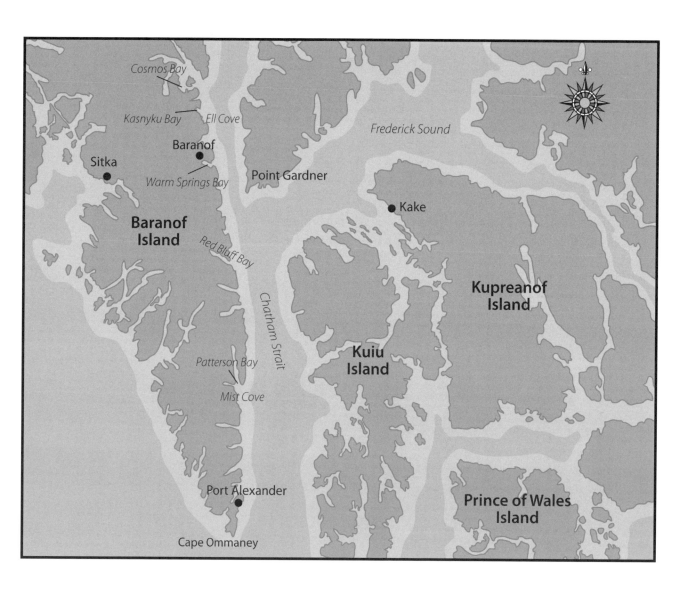

CHAPTER 12

WATERFALL COAST

12.1 ELL COVE
Waiting for an Opening

As we approached the east coast of Baranof Island in 2008, we saw a tall white slash of a waterfall on a green forested slope from a long way off across Chatham Strait. Just one of the many waterfalls that earn this stretch of land the nickname "Waterfall Coast," it is among the very few not hidden inside the many bays and coves.

Near to shore we saw a bustle of activity. Two megayachts hovered at the base of the waterfall. Salmon seiners traveled to and fro, skiffs buzzed back and forth, and fish buyers were anchored in semi-protected coves, their fenders down, ready for customers. An air of expectancy hung in the air as fishermen and buyers awaited a fisheries opening.

We too were waiting for an opening—in our case, of dock space at Warm Springs Bay. Two days earlier, at Tenakee Springs, we had heard rumors the dock at Warm Springs Bay was so crowded with salmon seiners that there wasn't room for even a dinghy. The minute the opening of the fishery was announced, the fishboats would be on their way and there would be space at the dock.

Meanwhile, we headed first to Cosmos Bay near the north end of Baranof Island and dropped anchor there. It was a pleasant spot, with forested shores and eagles feeding in the shallows, but it wasn't spectacular. After a quick lunch, we moved to Ell Cove, a small L-shaped bay a few miles south. There we found steep hillsides cut by a series of small waterfalls and formations of brown- and white-striped rocks on the shore.

Steve said he needed to change *Osprey*'s oil, a signal for me to make myself scarce. I grabbed my camera and launched the

A seiner fishes for salmon in Chatham Strait.

257

Ell Cove is a snug and scenic anchorage.

An eagle works over a salmon carcass outside Ell Cove.

kayak. On our way into the cove, I had noticed a pretty little stream with a flock of eagles perched in nearby trees. I hoped the eagles would still be there.

I paddled out the entrance and around a small point. On the beach, several eagles fought over a fish, their high-pitched cries carrying across the water. As I paddled quietly offshore, one by one they flew away until only a lone eagle remained. Firmly gripping the fish in its talons, the eagle was more intent on his fish than on watching me. I raised my telephoto lens and started taking pictures as the wind pushed the kayak toward shore, closer and closer to the eagle. Through the lens I saw sharp talons and a beak busy tearing up the fish. An image of talons ripping at my inflatable kayak came to me. I back-paddled quickly, leaving the eagle to eat his salmon in peace.

We stayed in Ell Cove for two days, joined on the second day by the sailboat *Kansei* of Everett, Washington. We had met the owners, Sara and Charley, in Tenakee Springs a few days earlier and were glad to have their company. Steve caught three rockfish and a greenling, and the four of us feasted on Cajun-style blackened fish.

The next morning *Kansei* left several hours before we did. We were motoring south down the coast when we heard Sara's voice calling *Osprey* over the radio. When I answered her, she told me they were tied up in Warm Springs.

"The fishermen have left," said Sara. "There's room at the dock."

12.2   WARM SPRINGS BAY, BARANOF ISLAND
Enjoying Alaska As It Is Now

I stood on the dock at the settlement of Baranof in Warm Springs Bay in 2007 and looked with amazement at the broad swath of roiling white water tumbling down the hillside and pouring into the small cove. The roar was so loud I wondered if I'd be able to sleep at night.

From the waterfall a row of summer cottages stretched along the shore toward the

dock. They disappointed me. I had expected more character than was provided by
these modern houses with their aluminum
roofs and dark paint. Photographs from
the town's early days depicted a wooden
bridge across the falls, a "Licker Store"
and picturesque cabins. None of that was
evident. The most interesting aspect of
the current-day cottages was that three of
them had been knocked off their foundations and were sitting catawampus on the
sloping hillside: the result, we learned later,
of the 34 feet of snow the community had
received the winter before.

A kayaker relaxes in the bathhouse at Warm Springs Bay.

We were here for the hot springs, not
the architecture, so we gathered our towels
and bathing suits and headed up the dock.
At the top of the ramp a boardwalk led along the shore toward the forest. A bathhouse
of three small rooms, two with large metal tubs and a third with an elegant wooden tub,
stood next to the boardwalk. Red-striped curtains hung at windows that looked out
across the bay at snow-capped mountains. The tubs, full of steaming hot water, appealed
to me, but Steve was determined to move on to the natural hot springs in the forest next
to the waterfall.

A short distance beyond the bathhouse our steps slowed once again when we heard
the hiss of an espresso machine and smelled the aroma of fresh coffee coming from a
coffee shop on the first floor of one of the houses. Outside the door, several young men
lounged in white plastic chairs sipping coffee. Their neat short hair told us they were crew
members of the Coast Guard cutter *Hickory* anchored in the bay.

"Let's stop for coffee on our way back," said Steve.

We followed the boardwalk into the forest up a hill, past huge skunk cabbages and
ferns growing in the shade of large hemlocks and spruce trees. Trails leading off the
boardwalk into the forest gave glimpses of small wooden houses with cedar-shingled
siding.

When we turned on to the trail to the hot springs, I was glad I had worn boots. We
climbed over tree roots and splashed through thick black mud. Whiffs of sulfur mingled
with the smell of skunk cabbage as we approached the springs, and we heard the roar of
the waterfall. We rounded a corner and looked down upon a steaming pool lined with
rocks and surrounded by trees. From the first pool, hot water cascaded into smaller pools,
finally disappearing into the white roaring froth of the waterfall. Next to the waterfall,
more young men relaxed in another small pool.

A sign directed us to a changing area in a thicket where we donned our swimming
suits. I approached the pool, stuck my toe in, and immediately pulled it out: too hot.

A string of rocks formed a path across the pool. I crossed it carefully, balancing on the rocks, conscious that one slip and I would be cooked. We reached the smaller, cooler pool and the young men moved aside to let us in. I eased in slowly, feeling the cold of an Alaskan summer fade away to the warm bliss of hot water.

Warm Springs Bay has long been a magnet for mariners in Alaska. In the early 1900s, the east coast of Baranof Island was a center for industry. Sawmills, a whaling station, salmon and herring canneries and nearly a dozen herring-reduction plants for converting herring to oil and meal occupied the coast's many bays. Canneries and herring plants attracted large numbers of fishing boats, many of whose crew frequented Warm Springs. Warm Springs Bay itself had a sawmill, grocery stores, liquor stores and commercial bathhouses.

Warm Springs Bay's past is more colorful than that described in history books. In his book, *Alaskan Panhandle Tales or Funny Things Happened up North*, Jack O'Donnell includes a story called, "The Girls of Warm Springs Bay." According to O'Donnell the hill above the town was called Hooker Hill, and its houses sheltered women with names like Petersburg Kate and Halibut Emma. In the 1920s, when O'Donnell was a young boy, he earned an unlimited supply of Hershey bars by watching out for the prohibition boat, the *Valkyrie,* and warning the women when it arrived at the dock.

With the exception of Warm Springs Bay and Port Alexander at Baranof Island's southern tip, the bays and coves of the Waterfall Coast are now empty. Fishermen still come to Warm Springs and they've been joined by tourists, summer residents, and the occasional Coast Guard crew on weekend leave. Residents voluntarily maintain the pools, the bathhouse, and a community picnic area.

When we returned to the dock, we found it full of large salmon-seining boats, rafted two and three deep. At the head of the dock, next to an older powerboat, a man sat carving a wooden mask. More wooden masks decorated a nearby piling.

"Are you sailors?" the man asked us when we stopped to talk to him. "I'll sing you a song." He picked up a guitar that had been leaning against his chair and played a song about a lockmaster and a sailor who saw each other once a year and had an ongoing conversation about which one had a better life, the sailor who saw the world or the lockmaster who loved his family.

We stayed two days at Warm Springs Bay that first year, relaxing in the hot springs and the baths, enjoying the coffee shop and hiking up the hill to a lake above the waterfall. The roar of the falls put us to sleep at night, instead of keeping us awake as I had feared.

On our second morning, we stopped on the dock to talk to a woman on a small powerboat called *Tokeen*. With reddish hair fluffed around her face and her stout figure made roly-poly by a thick fleece jacket, she looked like a resourceful Alaskan. She and her extended family owned a house at Warm Springs, she told us, but she preferred to stay on her boat.

I asked about her experiences of cruising in Southeast Alaska.

"When I was growing up my father owned a powerboat, and our family spent summers exploring the Southeast. People thought we were crazy to go out in a boat for fun." Then she looked up at the shore and said, "When I first started coming back here as an

The wares of a carver who spends summer on his boat in Warm Springs Bay are displayed on the dock.

adult, I was sad. I remembered the time when there were old buildings and a sense of history. Now there is no sense of history, but I have learned to enjoy it as it is."

The next morning as I relaxed in the wooden tub with a view of mountains out the window of the bathhouse, I thought about her words. "Enjoying a place as it is" sounded like good advice for anyone anywhere in Southeast Alaska.

12.3   RED BLUFF BAY
A Change of Scene

When we left Warm Springs Bay heading south in 2007, it had seemed like an ordinary Alaskan day: southwest winds and clouds occasionally interrupted by the rare patch of blue.

We approached Red Bluff Bay where mounds of brick-red rock guarded the entrance. A long narrow bay that winds into the interior of Baranof Island, Red Bluff Bay is protected by a group of islands at its mouth. As we passed the bluffs, the wind died. We took down the jib and motored through the islands into an outer basin. I had seen a picture of a large herring-reduction plant that operated here in the 1920s and '30s, and we motored along the shore looking for the plant—but all we could find of its two large factory buildings were a few pilings and some boilers rusting on the beach.

We rounded a bend and wisps of fog wafted out of the inner bay to meet us. I looked

A series of waterfalls cuts into the sides of Red Bluff Bay.

The view on a good day from Red Bluff Bay is worth waiting for.

behind to see a sailboat and powerboat disappear into the mist. The fog swirled around the bay, alternately hiding and revealing trees, waterfalls and cliffs. I couldn't be sure what I was looking at. Were those mountains at the head of the bay or just a figment of my imagination? All around us I could hear the roar of waterfalls and from the beach the raucous taunts of ravens.

By the time we dropped our anchor in the inner basin, we could only guess where the other two boats were, or if they were even there at all. That night we dined and went to bed still surrounded by thick fog.

In the morning we woke to a clear blue sky. At the head of the bay a broad green delta gave way to a valley and beyond a near-perfect cone-shaped mountain topped with a craggy peak and ringed with a band of snow. I saw no sign of the other two boats.

We ate breakfast, then got in the dinghy and motored toward the broad delta. A brown bear was feeding on sedge grass at the water's edge. I had read somewhere that bears don't feel threatened by anything approaching from the water, so they wouldn't attack a dinghy. We didn't want to test that hypothesis so we gave the bear a wide berth.

A brown bear feeds on sedge grass, a common food in spring and summer.

We wound our way through the marsh, passing a family of merganser ducks out for a paddle. From the marsh we entered a fast-flowing stream, but we made little progress against the current and the water shallowed quickly. Soon the propeller was making horrible grinding noises banging against stones. We turned, letting the current sweep us back to the delta. The bear was still there.

Steve put the outboard on idle and we stayed for some time watching the bear. He seemed indifferent to us, not even twitching an ear in our direction as he ate.

"He looks hungry," said Steve. "I don't want to go close. He might see us as meat."

Bears are opportunistic feeders. Upon emerging from hibernation in the early spring, they will feed on winter-killed deer, dead whales washed up on the beach, or other animal carcasses. In the spring and early summer, when plants are still growing and tender, they move down to deltas like this one in Red Bluff Bay to feed on sedge grass. They also eat skunk cabbages, roots and tubers. Later in the summer they gorge on salmon migrating in streams and rivers. Salmon is the major source of fat in their diet, and critical to their being able to survive a winter of hibernation. After salmon, the bears move on to berries in late summer and fall.

A second bear came down to the water's edge at a good distance from the first. Neither of them looked at each other or at us as they fed.

Overnight this bay had changed from a maelstrom of white mist to a postcard-like picture of scenery and wildlife. I was glad we had taken the time to wait out the fog and see what it had to offer.

12.4 MIST COVE
A Touch of Humor

We anchored in Mist Cove for its waterfall, visible a long way north in Chatham Strait as a white band on the green hillside. Snow-capped mountains above completed the picture.

We were putting down a stern anchor to keep *Osprey* from swinging onto the beach in the narrow cove when two workers from a fish hatchery came by in a skiff to tell us about the trail that leads to the falls and the hatchery on Deer Lake above. "It's steep—400 feet to the falls—but well maintained," one of them told us.

The next morning we found the trailhead on the west side of the cove. "Staircase" was a better term than trail. To make the pathway, workers had leaned logs against the slope and cut notches for steps.

The trail seemed to climb straight up through the forest. I was getting tired from the climb when I looked down and noticed a large "B" carved in one of the steps followed by an "I" on the next step. "BIG BUCK" I read, looking ahead. Farther up we came to "BEAR XING," then "CHICKEN," and "SALAMI," followed by "CHARACTER" and, finally, "CORN."

This carving of a fishing boat sits at an overlook on the trail to the waterfall at Mist Cove.

The falls at Mist Cove are visble a long way out in Chatham Strait.

"They must have been thinking about lunch," said Steve.

Imagining the fun the trail crew had in coming up with these words made the climb easier, but when we reached an overlook with a view of Chatham Strait, I was glad to rest. A plank carved with the outline of a fishing boat marked the spot. Soon we heard the thunder of the falls. We rounded a bend to see the top of the waterfall—a frothing mass of white water hurtling off a cliff into a chasm below. So much mist filled the air that I felt as if I were breathing water. We had to yell to be heard above the roar.

Stone steps snaked up the hillside past the waterfall. As I started up, my foot slipped on the damp stair and when I reached for the wooden banister my hands could barely grasp the slick wood. I turned back. We'd hiked enough for one day. I marveled at the hatchery workers who climbed this trail every day.

Next to the chasm a small wooden bench was positioned on a patio of gray slate. We lingered for a while, watching the water crash down through the gap, and admiring the lush green ferns and moss on the chasm walls. The waterfall makes for spectacular scenery—but for us it was the trail with its touches of art and humor that made Mist Cove so special.

12.5   PORT ALEXANDER
Cheechakoes in Running Shoes

"You should come to Port Alexander," the woman said, leaning toward us in her eagerness to talk about her home. "It's beautiful. I love it. And there are walruses on a rock down the coast."

We were in Ludvig's Bistro in Sitka. No tables had been available at the small crowded restaurant so we ate at the bar where we sat next to a slim woman with flyaway brown hair. Over seafood paella we soon learned that her name was Carol and that she was an artist who owned a house in Port Alexander.

"I'm flying south tomorrow," she told us, "but if you call Steve, my husband, he'll probably cook you a meal."

Carol rummaged in her purse for a card, wrote a number on the back and handed it to Steve. I took the card from him and looked at it, noticing it gave an address of Grants Pass, Oregon. Their Port Alexander house was apparently a summer residence.

I was skeptical about the walruses, which are normally found only in the Arctic. But the idea of going to Port

The narrow and rocky entrance to Port Alexander is marked with buoys and a range.

Alexander with an introduction to a local resident intrigued me. It offered an opportunity to see life in a small town up close. Located on the remote southern tip of Baranof Island, Port Alexander has no road and no ferry. It's about as remote a village as you can find in Southeast Alaska.

Port Alexander had once been a major fishing port where as many as 1,000 fishing boats anchored on summer nights. The fishing fleet first moved to the area in 1913. Fish-buying stations operated there, although most of the fish was transported elsewhere for processing. Grocery stores, bakeries, restaurants, a dance hall and a post office followed the fishermen. The town was incorporated in 1938, but when fishing began to decline and World War II drew workers away, the town went into a tailspin. Although the fishing improved and the town's population partially recovered, the town never regained its former prosperity.

A week after meeting Carol in Sitka, we approached Port Alexander, tacking south down Chatham Strait from Mist Cove against a light southerly. Ahead we could see the horizon where Chatham Strait gave way to the Pacific Ocean. Dark overcast skies, rocks silhouetted against open water and forested mountains streaked with snow on Baranof Island gave the area a wild look. A place where one might even find walruses, I mused.

Port Alexander's boardwalk runs through the forest with houses on either side.

Then I saw the entrance, a narrow channel through kelp and rocks, and I knew this was no place for sissies. With a good sea running, waves would wash right over the rocks.

We motored through the buoys and beacons into the harbor. On the east side of the harbor, a string of houses along the beach retreated into the forest, while to the west, the land rose up as a gentle hill with houses scattered among the trees.

The town dock was on the east side. We tied up *Osprey* between two salmon trollers and walked up the dock. Crossing a vacant lot, we came to a boardwalk that led into the trees parallel to the shore. A public phone, not a pay phone but a regular princess-type household phone, sat in a wooden box nailed to a post.

"Shall we call that woman's husband?" I asked Steve.

"Let's see what else is going on in the town first," he replied. "It seems odd to call a complete stranger out of the blue."

We strolled down the boardwalk, stirring up some chickens that had been pecking at debris. Paths led from the boardwalk to houses on both sides. We were walking through a green tunnel, with tree branches almost touching overhead. Port Alexander had devolved from a bustling port to a quiet village.

We passed a small schoolhouse where jungle gyms and slides fought for the front yard against giant devil's club and salmonberry bushes. Beyond the schoolhouse a bright-blue banner with a smiling sun hung over the boardwalk. On a building next to the banner, the words "Main St General Store" were carved in wood above a small porch.

The store's name, however, must have come from another era. We walked inside to find a craft shop selling knitted scarves, crocheted hats and painted seashells.

We purchased a generic Alaska postcard from a young woman working at a computer and left. As we closed the door behind us, I noticed a sign, "open Mon–Sat, 4–5." We had accidentally hit the only hour of the day the store is open.

"If that's the only store, the town's in trouble," I said to Steve.

We continued our walk north along the boardwalk until we came to the inner harbor, around from the dock we had tied up to. A public float extended out into quiet water now stippled by raindrops. The harbor is no longer dredged, so the boats on the dock were shallow-water skiffs, sport-fishing boats and a shallow-water landing craft.

We turned and headed back, passing a recently built house of natural wood. Rows of identical orange rain jackets and pants hung from hooks on the large front porch.

"Must be a fishing lodge," said Steve.

"I saw a sign for another gift store near the beginning of the boardwalk," I told Steve. "Let's check it out."

We walked back, passing two men in scruffy jeans and jackets, and came to the sign on the water side of the boardwalk. A short trail led from the sign to a house. A man in his fifties or sixties was cleaning a large Chinook salmon outside the house.

"I'll get my wife to open the shop," he said.

He went into the house and returned with a stocky woman with graying hair who led us to a narrow room lined with shelves. At the end of the room, a window overlooked the harbor.

"There used to be a general store on the vacant lot near the dock," she told us. "But it burned down last year. We're trying to fill in as best we can."

"Where do people here buy groceries?" I asked, seeing only T-shirts, fishing gear and other odds and ends.

"They order them from Sitka and they come on the *Eyak*," she said, referring to the mailboat.

Steve was searching through a pile of Port Alexander T-shirts, looking for size XL.

"I think we're out of that size," the woman said. "We ordered lots of XXXL for the fishermen, but they didn't buy many. What they mostly buy is candy, lots of candy." She gestured to boxes of Snickers, Hershey's bars and other common brands.

I noticed a display of jewelry made from colorful rocks and beads.

"My husband makes them in the winter," the woman told me. I picked out a necklace of green stones and orange beads. Steve went back to the boat for a checkbook while I stayed in the store, talking to the owner. I asked her how the town was doing.

Things were changing, she told me. They used to have a fish barge every summer, to buy fish and sell ice to the fishermen, but it hadn't come that year.

"It's a lot quieter without the fish barge," she told me.

All was not completely bleak in the small town, however. The owner of the vacant lot was talking about building a restaurant, and the town was renovating an old building for a museum.

Steve returned with the checkbook, and we paid for the necklace and left. As we approached the public phone, Steve said, "I might as well call that woman's husband."

He got out the card the woman had given him and dialed. A few minutes later we returned to *Osprey* with an invitation to dinner with Steve Preston at a friend's house across the harbor.

Occasional rain had become a steady mist when Steve Preston, a thin man with a receding hairline, brought his aluminum skiff alongside *Osprey*.

"Do we need boots?" I asked him when I saw he was wearing the usual brown XTRATUF boots, jokingly referred to as Alaskan tennies, while we were in ordinary running shoes.

"Probably not," he answered. Then, after we had climbed in the skiff, he said, "The beach over there is reasonably dry." I felt like a *cheechako*, the Alaskan name for newcomer, as I realized we wouldn't be going to a dock. We would be stepping from the boat onto the beach, which almost always results in wet feet. Of course I should have worn boots. Alaskans wouldn't even ask.

We motored across the harbor and landed on a steep slate beach. Only by jumping from the very tip of the bow, did I manage to land without getting my feet wet.

Steve Preston tied up the skiff and led us up a trail to a boardwalk. After a short hike uphill we came to a modern brown house where a man in his forties met us at the door and introduced himself as Ken. We left our shoes in a mudroom just inside the door and entered the living room through a rough-hewn wooden doorway. Inside was the unfinished look of a house being built by its owner, with natural wood beams and vaulted ceilings. Ken pointed out the floor.

"We got these boards from the old cannery in Port Armstrong. I milled most of the rest of the wood myself."

In the kitchen, we met two young women: Ken's wife, Robin Lyn, and their friend Phyllis. Like Ken and Steve Preston, the women were thin and athletic looking. Steve Preston handed Robin Lyn the salad he had brought, and I gave her a wedge of cheese from the Washington State University creamery.

Robin Lyn thanked us and said, "We're having chicken and pizza."

Muted light from overcast skies lit the dining room as we ate. The four Port Alexander residents gossiped about eccentric neighbors who no longer lived there. Feeling left out, I turned to Phyllis and asked her if she lived year-round in Port Alexander.

"Oh, no," she said, shrinking back into her chair. "My husband's a commercial fisherman who fishes here in the summer. We live in Sitka." She went on to tell us about a November she had once spent in Port Alexander. For days the seas were so rough no boats could get in or out of the harbor, and the seaplanes couldn't land.

"Only a few families live here year-round," explained Ken. "Robin Lyn and I live in Fairbanks."

As the evening wore on, the room darkened. While Robin Lyn lit a kerosene lantern, Ken pointed to the unlit chandelier over the table. "I'd rather not turn on the generator."

"Where do you get fuel?" asked Steve.

"On the *Eyak*. Even the propane comes that way. We send empty tanks to town and get full ones back."

I remembered the storekeeper telling us she got groceries on the *Eyak* and was struck by the thought that this remote Alaskan town was almost totally dependent on the US mail service. Hearing them talk, I realized how much I take for granted. Among other things: stores, gas stations, water, electricity and garbage pickup. I was suddenly glad we lived in a city.

"What about garbage?" I asked, gesturing to a chicken bone on my plate.

"There's no garbage collection and no public generator for electricity. The only thing the town provides is water, and only on the east side. But there's a group that collects aluminum cans for recycling, to benefit the school," Steve Preston told us.

"We put food scraps in the bay," said Phyllis. "Everything else, like cans and bottles, we either burn or dump at sea."

I knew it was illegal to dump cans and bottles within 12 miles of land but realized they had few alternatives.

Before we got up to go, I asked Steve Preston, "Carol told us she saw walruses here. Is that true?"

He chuckled, then paused as if trying to find the right way to answer. "That's Carol for you. She probably meant sea lions."

There was only a glimmer of light in the sky when we left the house. Steve Preston lit the way with a flashlight. The boardwalk felt slippery under my feet. Next time someone invited us for dinner, I'd wear boots.

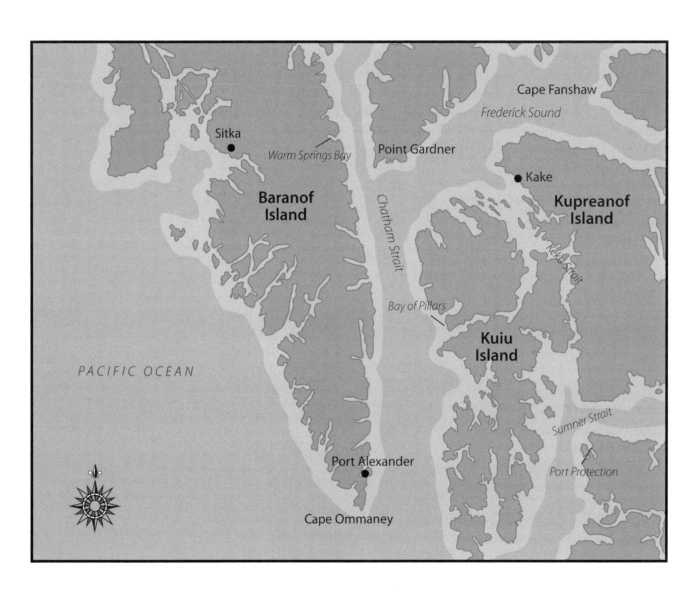

Cape Fanshaw

Frederick Sound

Sitka

Warm Springs Bay

Point Gardner

Kake

**Baranof
Island**

**Kupreanof
Island**

Chatham Strait

Keku Strait

Bay of Pillars

**Kuiu
Island**

Sumner Strait

PACIFIC OCEAN

Port Protection

Port Alexander

Cape Ommaney

CHAPTER 13

KUIU ISLAND AND KEKU STRAIT

13.1 BAY OF PILLARS
Searching for "Alaska Sun"

The rain pattered lightly on *Osprey*'s cabin roof as we ate breakfast in Port Alexander.

Steve had the *US Coast Pilot* open to the climatological tables and was studying them as he ate his granola.

"According to this, it's a lot drier on the east side of Chatham Strait: only 2.3 inches of rain in July in Angoon and 2.6 in Kake compared to 8.2 inches here. Let's get out of here. We can go to the Bay of Pillars today and then around to Kake."

The name "Bay of Pillars" conjured images of sandstone ramparts and weathered stacks that sounded intriguing, but I was skeptical about the weather. We'd been in Angoon a week ago and it had rained all day and into the night.

The rumble of fishboat engines interrupted my thoughts. We went out on the dock to say goodbye to the men we had met the day before. The owner of a green fishboat also named *Osprey*—jokingly referred to as our littermate by the other fishermen—was getting his trolling poles ready.

"My sources tell me it's quieting down out there. But no fish. Don't know why I'm doing this." He shrugged and turned back to his trolling poles.

My reluctance shamed away by the fisherman's perseverance, I too set about getting ready to leave—washing dishes and then filling the water tank. As I dragged a hose down the dock, the rain changed to a fine mist that soon turned my foul-weather jacket shiny and fogged my glasses. Still, it felt good to be out and doing something.

We motored out the narrow channel and into Chatham Strait. Soon *Osprey* was rolling every which way as a southerly swell from the ocean collided with northerly wind waves from the strait. "No fair," I muttered to myself as I huddled under the dodger out of the rain. When we sailed south, the wind blew from the south. Now that we turned north, it blew from the north. Steve, at the wheel, complained that the wind was too light to sail.

As we motored north, the seas smoothed to long swells and the wind dropped even further. To the east we could see the dark mountains of Kuiu Island, while behind us

271

Rows of tanks indicate this abandoned seafood factory was a herring reduction plant.

Baranof Island hid in the mist. Perhaps the climatological tables were right.

The mist scaled up even more as we entered the Bay of Pillars. We could see green-forested hills and a large bay scattered with islands. I looked at the shore, searching for rock pillars, but saw only an unbroken forest of hemlock and spruce. The cluster of islands that, on the chart, seemed a likely spot for pillars looked flat and ordinary from the water—pretty, but not the palisades I expected.

I gave up scanning for pillars and looked at the water instead. All around us I could see the distinctive silhouettes of swimming sea otters: heads and feet above water, bodies submerged. A few mothers carried babies on their stomachs; the babies looking like round humps in profile.

"They should have named this the Bay of Otters, not Pillars," I told Steve.

Motoring farther into the bay, we came to the ruins of a large fish-processing plant. Rows of pilings green with moss marched along the shore. Empty windows in abandoned buildings peeked out of the forest. A tangle of rusting machinery littered the beach and a huge iron vat perched precariously on a bed of rotting pilings. From the vat and two rows of tanks we could tell that the site had been a herring-reduction plant: a factory to turn schools of herring into oil and fertilizer.

Joe Upton, author of *Alaska Blues: A Fisherman's Journal* (1977), described finding the ruins of fish-processing plants in almost every bay he entered in Southeast Alaska. According to Upton, vast schools of herring once swarmed in Chatham Strait, and salmon—kings and silvers—fed on the rich oily herring. Large fleets of trollers caught salmon in abundance. Then herring plants were built on the shore (56 in Southeast Alaska according to one estimate) and big seiners came from California to fish the herring. Herring stocks declined and salmon stocks followed. The reduction plants closed in the '60s but fishermen like Upton still struggled to make a living. Salmon eventually rebounded, but not the great fleets of trollers. Now, thirty years after Upton's book, the herring are being fished for sac roe and fishermen fear the stock may once again be threatened.

We anchored in a small cove on the south side of the bay. It had shallow water for anchoring, shelter on all sides, and a small river with green marshes at its head.

The rain stopped and the sky lightened enough to let brightness and heat through without showing blue sky—a condition I had grown to think of as "Alaska sun." I sat in the cockpit and watched an otter swim in circles around the cove while Steve repaired the dinghy outboard on *Osprey*'s fantail. No breeze penetrated the cove where still waters reflected layers of color: hunter-green trees, bright-green marsh grass and yellow-brown rockweed. On the west shore, a tall spruce with a crown of dead branches supported a massive eagle's nest. On the nest an eaglet waited for its parents.

Suddenly, the kee, kee, kee of gulls broke the silence as a flock flew in to land, their white wings catching the light. As I watched the gulls squabble, I became aware of rings of raindrops spreading on the water. Surprised, I held out my hand. I didn't feel any rain. The drops were so far apart, I only knew they were falling by looking at the water. I stayed in the cockpit, sitting in the rain that wasn't rain. Gradually the number of raindrops increased until I could feel them striking my face and see them darkening my jacket. Drops now stippled the water and the air felt cold. Steve gathered his tools and I followed him below. The "Alaska sun" had been pleasant while it lasted. Better than sitting in the boat all day at Port Alexander.

We left the Bay of Pillars the next day, still mystified by the lack of pillars. Two days later in the town of Kake, we stopped in a Native craft shop. The owner seemed knowledgeable about the area so I asked, "Why are there no pillars in the Bay of Pillars?"

He launched into a story about the fish in the Bay of Pillars, so long and involved I began to wonder if he had understood my question. Then he said, "The Bay was full of fish traps, and in those days they made the traps with posts. 'Pillars' is a bad translation for a Tlingit word. I guess they wanted something grander."

Bay of Pillars definitely sounded grander than Bay of Pilings. It had fooled me.

13.2 KAKE
Helping Each Other

When I first heard the name "Kake," referring to the Tlingit village on Kupreanof Island, I immediately thought of a birthday cake. But the word "Kake" comes from the Tlingit "Keex' Kwaan." Roughly translated it means "the town that never sleeps." And the town of Kake is no sweet confection.

"Kake's a scary place. I'm a big man and I didn't feel safe there," was the report we received from a boater we met in Hoonah in 2008.

The Kake tribe has a history of being frightening. Their bad reputation began in 1857 when Kake tribesmen allegedly beheaded Colonel Isaac Ebey on Whidbey Island in Puget Sound as recompense for the slaying of one of their chiefs at Port Gamble the year before. Ebey was a former customs collector in Port Townsend and therefore of equal standing to their chief. (This slaying has also been attributed to the Haida and the Tongass Tlingit.) Then, in 1869, a Sitka sentry killed a Kake tribesman, and in keeping with their custom, the Kakes demanded compensation in blankets. When the Army refused, the Kakes took matters into their own hands: killing two Sitka fur traders camped on Admiralty Island in what is now called Murder Cove.

In what became known as the Kake War, the USS *Saginaw* pursued the men into Kake villages on Kupreanof and Kuiu Islands. Captain Meade considered it his duty to

Bears really do cross Bear Crossing road in Kake.

teach the Kakes a lesson. To do so he destroyed three villages. It was a classic case of the clash of cultures. White people couldn't understand how Kakes could kill two men who had nothing to do with the death of the tribesman, and Kakes couldn't understand why three villages had been destroyed when the killings involved only one family. Like the Angoon Bombardment later, it was an example of how the US congress mismanaged Alaska in the years shortly after purchasing it: sending the Army and Navy to patrol instead of establishing laws and a system of justice.

Eliza Scidmore described the after-effects of the Kake War in her 1885 book, *Alaska, Its Southern Coast and the Sitkan Archipelago*. Rather than rebuilding their villages, members of the tribe roamed around Southeast Alaska for years after the Kake War, "creating trouble and disturbances wherever they draw up their canoes."

Steve and I had visited the Tlingit village of Kake the year before, and the only time I'd been scared was when two black bears crossed in front of us on a street called Bear Crossing Way. We had arrived in time for the village's annual Dog Salmon Festival. We watched Native children doing the limbo, looked at the world's tallest totem pole (as claimed by Kake) and saw bears feeding on dog salmon below the Gunnuk Creek Hatchery. We had been struck by the friendliness of the people. Walking back from the hatchery to the dock, a red car had pulled up alongside of us and a woman opened her window to say, "Get in—it's going to pour."

Despite our positive experience, we hadn't planned on returning to Kake in 2008, intending instead to sail south down Chatham Strait, one island farther west. But when we got to Warm Springs Bay on the west side of Chatham Strait, we found snow patches still lingering near the water and thimbleberries that were still hard and green. To escape the cold weather we decided to go down Keku Strait and Rocky Pass instead of Chatham Strait. Because it's farther from the ocean, we hoped Keku Strait would be warmer. Kake was on the way so we decided to stop there after all.

We left Warm Springs Bay in a southwest wind, sailing across Chatham Strait, past Kuiu Island and into Keku Strait. As we passed Point Gardner, the wind died, the sun came out and the temperature went up 20 degrees. We motored south along the Kake waterfront, past the abandoned cannery complex and around a stone breakwater into the town marina. Canted concrete floats with missing cleats confronted us. Although the breakwater is new, the marina apparently is not.

We finally found a dock level enough to tie up to, astern of the seiner *Lady Louis* and next to a collection of discarded batteries, used lumber, old nets and miscellaneous cardboard boxes.

Because the marina is more than two miles from town and a mile from the only grocery store, we planned to hitchhike. But as we were tying up *Osprey*, a man with missing front teeth and a New Zealand accent struck up a conversation and offered us a ride.

I had forgotten how dilapidated the town is. Abandoned cars with smashed windows and flat tires sat among shoulder-high weeds next to houses with peeling paint and sagging porches. Like many small Alaska towns, Kake is struggling to survive. The Kake Cannery, which had employed townspeople for years, closed in 1977. Logging had filled the gap, but it too declined. At the time of the 2000 census, the unemployment rate was 25 percent, with almost 50 percent of the adults not in the workforce.

But not all of Kake is derelict. Walking along the waterfront, we came to a small house surrounded by so much garden kitsch we thought it might be a store. Pinwheels and mobiles blew in the wind. Gnomes, princesses, frogs and fairies hid among the flowers. We were staring at these creatures when a man came out and invited us into the garden. He opened a gate and we walked in past a small smokehouse with a wonderful aroma of smoking salmon. "I'm retired now," he told us. "But I still smoke fish. I ask for 50 percent of the fish." He laughed ruefully and said, "Everybody wants theirs done in a different way." As he talked, I took in a breathtaking panorama of islands, reefs and mountains. I found the contrast between the beauty of the scenery and the poverty of the town to be jarring.

Continuing our walk, we noticed a sign on a wall advertising "Eva's Berry Patch, Salmon berries $3.75 a pound." I imagined berries on our cereal in the morning and

A family has created an elaborate garden on their waterfront lot in Kake.

Two young trappers offer marten furs for sale.

suggested we find the store. A woman working in her garden directed us to a building at the end of the street.

"We're buying, not selling," a man behind the counter at the Berry Patch told us. "I just work here, so I can't sell you any."

We noticed a number of Native artifacts around the room and asked if we could look at them. The man got up and took us over to a glass case to show us a collection of carved wooden ladles, masks and woven hats. The room had the look of someone moving out. He told us many of the objects had belonged to his brother, a carver who had died just a month ago.

We left the Berry Patch and wandered through town, passing a neatly painted church, an abandoned café, some burned-out houses and a collection of brightly covered carvings. On a back street by the side of the road I stopped to look at a table spread with brown seaweed. A car stopped next to us and a woman leaned out the window. "We dry it, then grind it, then dry it some more. We eat it like candy."

A few blocks farther, three teenage boys stopped to show us several marten pelts.

"We can sell them to you for $50 apiece, half the usual price."

I was tempted. They were beautiful furs.

"What would we do with them?" asked Steve. "We couldn't even show them to our friends."

"I suppose you're right." We walked away from the young men. Trapping animals for a living, so much a part of the Alaskan culture, would be considered barbaric in Seattle.

It was getting late and we wanted to stop at the store before it closed. We put out our thumbs and a few minutes later a car driven by a young woman with two little girls stopped to give us a lift.

The next morning we were on the road again, hoping to catch a ride to the internet café at the Kake Tribal Center. When no cars went by for 10 minutes I wondered if we were going to have to walk all the way. Finally, a blue pickup towing a boat came around the corner. "Surely he won't stop," said Steve. But he did. A genial Native man invited us to climb in.

I asked him if he'd been fishing and he told us he'd been using his boat to get fish for a culture camp for the children. "We teach our children how to gather and prepare our food in the traditional way," he told us. As he drove, he talked about the importance to the Natives of subsistence fishing and hunting—the taking of natural resources for traditional, personal and family uses as opposed to commercial uses. We rounded a curve and saw a motorboat heading north along the waterfront. We recognized the boat as one whose owner had told us he was planning to go south to Rocky Pass, the winding rock-strewn channel between Keku Strait and Sumner Strait. Steve commented that the boat was going out of the way to get there.

"If I'd known he was going there," the driver told us, "I'd have taken him out there to show him how. We do that here. We help each other."

I remembered this comment on our way back when a small red pickup truck stopped to give us a ride. A light-skinned man wearing paint-spattered overalls moved toolboxes and loose tools off the seat to make room for us.

"What do you do?" I asked him, wondering about the tools.

"Try to grow oysters." He told us about his oyster farm in Keku Strait. He buys spat (baby oysters) from Washington State and puts them on the beach. In Alaska, growers don't have to wait until winter to harvest as they do down south (although they do have to test for paralytic shellfish poisoning).

He took a detour to the old cannery where he dropped off some tools, talking to several people about how to use them.

Although earlier he had told us he wasn't going all the way to the marina, the driver dropped us off there anyway. As we walked down to the boat, I thought about all the people who had given us rides and taken time to talk with us. In urban areas I associate poverty with crime. In Kake I associate it with people doing their very best to help each other.

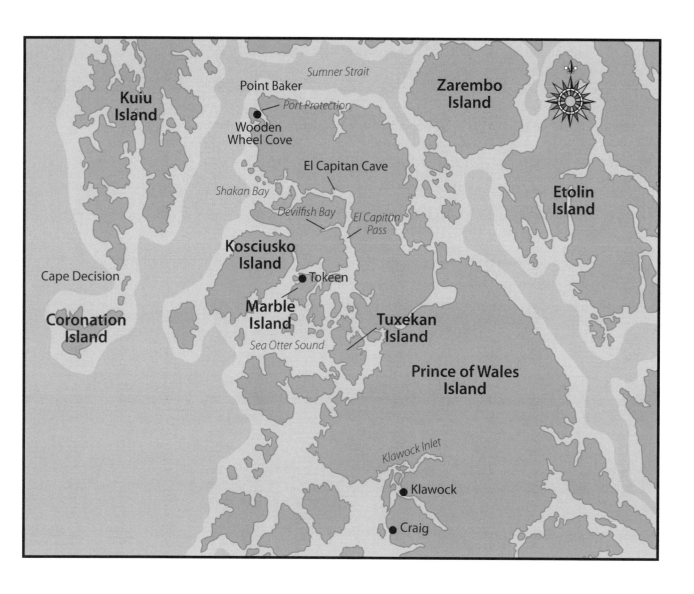

Sumner Strait

Point Baker

Port Protection

Wooden
Wheel Cove

El Capitan Cave

Shakan Bay

Devilfish Bay

*El Capitan
Pass*

**Kuiu
Island**

**Zarembo
Island**

**Etolin
Island**

**Kosciusko
Island**

Cape Decision

●Tokeen

**Marble
Island**

**Tuxekan
Island**

**Coronation
Island**

Sea Otter Sound

**Prince of Wales
Island**

Klawock Inlet

●Klawock

●Craig

CHAPTER 14

WEST COAST OF PRINCE OF WALES ISLAND

14.1 WOODEN WHEEL COVE, PORT PROTECTION
200 Years of Safe Harbor

Sitting in *Osprey*'s cockpit, I looked out across the quiet water of Wooden Wheel Cove in Port Protection and saw a peaceful little fishing community with a fish-buying dock and quaint houses—the type of place where nothing much ever happens. I was looking forward to a whole day here with nothing to do but relax.

My thoughts were interrupted by a voice: "Welcome to Wooden Wheel Cove." I looked up to see the smiling face of a bearded man in a heavy wool jacket. "What kind of boat is this? I've got a sailboat, too." He gestured to an older vessel tied to the float across from us.

We're always happy to talk to another sailor, and soon the man, who introduced himself as Ward Eldridge, was sitting in our cockpit and telling us about Wooden Wheel Cove. While he was from Sitka, he lived here summers, and his children resided here year-round.

"You might wonder why this is called Wooden Wheel Cove." He went on to tell us that a fisherman named Johnson who lived in the cove went out fishing one day and lost his propeller. He beached his boat and whittled a new propeller out of wood. It worked so well, he used it for years. ("Wheel" is fishermen-slang for propeller.)

Ward pointed to his house, a small red

An old cannery at Wooden Wheel Cove now serves as a residence.

A fisherman relaxes on the dock while waiting for a fisheries opening.

building across the cove, and told us it had once been a cannery, vacant for years until they moved in.

"Alaskans don't like things to go to waste," he told us. "If they know something is abandoned, they take it down for lumber and parts. But people knew someone still cared so they left it alone. All we had to do when we moved in was clear out the beer bottles."

This small cove and its residents are described in *The B.S. Counter: Life in Alaska* (Trafford Publishing, 2002) by Marian Glenz, whose father was "Buckshot" Woolery, owner of the Port Protection Trading Post. She notes that people from the "outside," who get their ideas of what makes a "happening" from newspapers and television ask, "What do you do here for excitement?" But to the residents of Wooden Wheel Cove, a happening is something as simple and good as putting out a fire in a neighbor's cabin or pulling a three-year-old sister from the water. She goes on to say that, "a guy on the beach needs to be a mechanic . . . electrician . . . cook, plumber, gardener, logger, fisherman, hunter, trapper, carpenter, painter, shoe repairman, radio technician and every other thing imaginable to make a go of it."

The trading post closed in 1973, but a fish-buying company now provides a store. Although the community has no roads, it boasts three docks: the state float that *Osprey* was tied to (with no land access), a private float that serves the fish-buying dock and the store, and a public float across the cove that serves a residential area.

That afternoon we got in our dinghy and motored over to the fish-buying dock. A group of bearded fishermen, all wearing identical brown XTRATUF boots, sat under a plywood shelter on plastic fish boxes. A collection of rusty chains, hooks and shackles lay at their feet. A burly man with a bushy beard was rigging a trolling pole. "I've been working all day," he told us, as he reached into a box and pulled out a beer. "And months before."

Up the ramp, the fish-buying building provided everything the community and visiting fishermen might need: laundromat, fishing gear, groceries, and XTRATUF boots in every size. In a cooler we saw broccoli, lettuce and tomatoes. This was one of the best-stocked small stores we had seen in Alaska. Port Protection, which includes Wooden Wheel Cove and the equally small community of Point Baker, has an official population of only 56, but in the summer fishermen from boats out of Seattle, Sitka, Juneau and elsewhere swell the population.

We had heard the store had a small café and were looking forward to a cup of coffee and maybe a piece of pie. But the café, in a corner of the store, was quiet, with tools spread on the counter.

A woman stocking shelves stopped to talk to us.

"The cooler isn't working," she told us. "We can't run the café without it. Every time he goes to fix it, he has to send to town for a part."

A fellow boater had told us that blueberries grew in town and I was hoping to pick some. We took the dinghy to the residential dock where a boardwalk led into the forest. Small cedar-shingled houses in various stages of construction peeked through the trees. I was amazed at the number of houses with architectural features like gabled windows and turrets. One house was even hexagonal in shape. In a place with no road access, residents often build their own houses, and such features represent labors of love.

Following the boardwalk, we came to a community center and school with a wooden-decked basketball court in the front yard. A plaque on the wall read:

In honor of Captain George Vancouver
H.M.S. Discovery
discoverer of Port Protection
1793–1973
200 years of safe harbor

On Sunday, September 8, 1793, Captain Vancouver, commander of the HMS *Discovery* and the HMS *Chatham*, was looking for an anchorage. The weather had begun "to wear a very threatening appearance," with wind blowing in heavy squalls from the southwest. Sailing west through Sumner Strait, the two ships passed Point Baker at the north tip of Prince of Wales Island, where they saw an excellent harbor. No sooner had they anchored and furled their sails when the wind shifted to a southeaster, blowing with "increasing violence." The ships spent several peaceful days in the anchorage while the storm blew outside. Grateful for "such an asylum," Vancouver named the anchorage Port Protection.

From the community center we continued up the boardwalk, passing a man carrying a red plastic glass full of beer. He stopped to talk to us and told us he had moved there from Port Alexander. "P.A. is a ghost town now that the last fish scow left. This is much better." He lived on a floathouse on the dock. "I've even got a flush toilet," he said, proudly, "but no door."

Farther along the boardwalk, trees gave way to a field of blueberry bushes—overseen by a wooden statue of a black bear so realistic I hesitated before starting to pick. But black bears are the only type of bear found on Prince of Wales Island and they are less aggressive than brown bears so I felt comfortable browsing among the blueberries. Half an hour later we had enough for a pie.

On our way back, we passed a man with a long bushy beard

A carved wooden bear guards the blueberry patch at Wooden Wheel Cove.

going the other way. He carried a pitcher of strawberries in one hand, rhubarb stalks in another. "I'm going to do some baking," he told us. "Strawberry-rhubarb pie."

As we walked back to the dinghy, Steve told me, "If we lived here, I'd have to let my beard grow longer."

That evening the sun broke through the clouds, setting the houses and water aglow in the setting sun. It was hard to imagine a more peaceful harbor.

We returned a year later. As we entered the cove, we could see three people on the state float: a man moving a skiff aside to make room for *Osprey*, and another man and a woman getting ready to take our lines. I recognized Ward Eldridge from the year before, but although the other two looked familiar I couldn't place them.

"We met you two years ago in Craig," the woman told us when we tied up. "We had a small green and white powerboat. Now we've got a bigger boat." She gestured to a gray powerboat that seemed only slightly bigger. I remembered that even with just a small boat they traveled with a medium-sized dog and a harp.

"What's happening in Wooden Wheel Cove?" I asked Ward, forgetting how the cove's residents felt about outsiders with their questions about "happenings."

But Ward just smiled. "I'm looking at it. A green boat arrives from Seattle; a gray boat from California. Those are happenings in Wooden Wheel Cove."

14.2   DEVILFISH BAY
A Hint of Mystery

We were looking for an overnight anchorage in El Capitan Passage, between Prince of Wales and Kosciusko Islands, when we spotted Devilfish Bay on the chart. Long and narrow with a constricted entrance, it promised shelter from the southerly winds blowing up the passage.

The bay's name comes from a Tlingit legend of a giant devilfish (octopus) rising from the water and washing an entire village away. We pulled out *Exploring Southeast Alaska* by Don Douglass and Reanne Hemingway-Douglass to learn more about the bay and read that in 1975 "a group of "researchers" visited the bay and were so "overcome with supernatural feelings of oppression, depression and alarm that they fled, convinced the area was cursed." Despite these stories, the Douglasses found the bay to be "charming and lovely." Devilfish Bay sounded like an ideal anchorage to us—protected and "lovely," with a hint of mystery.

Even the *US Coast Pilot* warns of dangers in Devilfish Bay. A large rock, awash at high water, is located near the middle of the entrance channel; the *US Coast Pilot* advises that "the channel should not be attempted until seen at low water."

The tide was still ebbing when we arrived outside the bay's entrance. I stood on the bow, ready to warn Steve of underwater dangers. Patches of rockweed at the water's surface revealed the rock's outline and we motored through without incident. Inside, tall rock bluffs surrounded by dark forests rose from the north shore, while a grassy marshland with mountains beyond marked the shore to the south.

We anchored close to the sheltered southwest corner of the bay. That night, rain hammered on our cabin roof and gusts sent *Osprey* dancing on its anchor chain. The wind was still blowing when we left the next morning, and we looked forward to a good sail north to El Capitan Cave.

"Well," said Steve, when we were safely out of the bay, "I certainly didn't sense anything supernatural. Did you?"

I had to admit that I hadn't. And although the weather in the bay had been unpleasant, that wasn't unusual for Southeast Alaska. We raised sail and turned

In one version of the Tlingit devilfish legend, a giant devilfish, killed by two young boys, hung up on this rock at the entrance to the bay.

north, only to have the wind flatten to nothing in less than a mile. I looked astern and saw whitecaps on the water behind us where the wind still blew. If the bay is cursed, I thought, it's because of the rock and local weather patterns, not a devilfish.

But I wanted to know more about the legend of Devilfish Bay. A week later, when we visited the town of Klawock, we stopped at the library to ask the librarian if she had any books about the devilfish legend.

She looked surprised that I would ask, and with a dismissive wave of her hand said, "The devilfish is dead. The nephews killed it." Nevertheless, she directed me to the library's excellent collection of Native lore where I found the story of the monster devilfish in *Tlingit Myths and Texts* by John Swanton (Government Printing Office, 1909).

The story starts with people going to a camp to fish for salmon. They didn't know that a giant devilfish lived under a cliff not too far from the camp. When the devilfish saw the red glow of salmon drying on the beach, it threw its tentacles around the camp and swept everything and everyone into the sea. But three brothers were absent, having left the camp that morning to go hunting. When they returned, they saw pieces of canoes adrift on the bay and their friends gone. The two older brothers told the younger one to climb up and watch them from the top of a hill. Then the older brothers went out in their canoe with rocks and sharp sticks. After a while, the large devilfish came right up under them. They took the sticks and stabbed the devilfish, climbing on top of it and running the sticks into it. As the devilfish died, it sank, carrying the two brothers with it.

Rudy James, aka *Thlau Goo Yalith Thlee* (the First and Oldest Raven), expanded on this basic legend in his 1997 book, *Devilfish Bay, the Giant Devilfish Story: an Alaskan Indian Adventure* (Wolfhouse Publishing). In James' version of the story, the people in the camp know of the devilfish, called Nawk, and consider it to be their "grandchild." The trouble arises from a young boy who challenges Nawk to come out of his house and get some fish. Another young boy, Kaw-goo, watches Nawk destroy the camp from his lookout on the cliffs while his two older brothers are away hunting seals. When the hunters return, they realize it is their duty to destroy the devilfish, knowing they will die in the process. They appoint Kaw-goo to direct them from his lookout—and to tell the story of their loss, honor and sacrifice.

While researching his book, James became convinced that the story was real. He cites oral history, rock carvings of devilfish in the area, recent sightings of large shadowy objects swimming in the bay, and reports of similar large octopus elsewhere in Alaska and in British Columbia. In 1997, James and his family journeyed to Devilfish Bay to perform a peace ceremony, respectfully acknowledging the price the original Nawk paid for his destruction of the camp and presenting a copy of James' manuscript to the current Nawk of the bay by sinking a copy weighted down with a rock.

Perhaps it was that peace ceremony that allowed *Osprey* to anchor in Devilfish Bay without incident.

14.3   EL CAPITAN CAVE
A Limestone Labyrinth

"We're going to be in the dark with each other, so we need to get acquainted. This isn't one of those tourist caves like Carlsbad Cavern with paved pathways and lights." With those words, Moe, a guide for El Capitan Cave, began our tour.

A vast network of limestone caves snakes through the underground on Prince of Wales Island, but only two of the caves are open to the public: Cavern Lake Cave and El Capitan. Of the two, El Capitan is the more extensive, with over two miles of mapped passages. Because it is on Forest Service land, tours of the cave are given by Forest Service guides.

We had arrived at the cave site on El Capitan Passage on the west coast of Prince of Wales Island the evening before, sailing north from Devilfish Bay in pouring rain. It rained all night and into the morning, finally stopping at noon, just in time for our scheduled tour. From the dock we walked a short distance inland to the shack where we met our two guides: Moe, a woman in her sixties with short-cropped gray hair, and Jess, a round-faced young woman with

Water drips from overhead, forming pools in the passageways of El Capitan Cave.

earrings twinkling below her hard hat. Moe was obviously in charge and did most of the talking.

Steve and I were the only two on the tour so introductions didn't take long. We learned that Moe was a retired librarian from Thorne Bay, across Prince of Wales Island, and Jess was a biology student from the University of Illinois. Both wore green Forest Service uniforms, although Jess wore an additional fleece jacket. The Forest Service web page on El Capitan warns that the cave can be cold and I too wore fleece, as well as the recommended boots and rain jacket. Steve and I also carried flashlights.

Moe gave us both hard hats with headlamps and led the way to a wooden staircase, still wet from rain. "The staircase has 300 steps," she cautioned us.

We climbed up a steep hill through a dark forest where the trees grew close together.

"This is young growth," Moe told us, explaining that it had last been logged in the 1960s.

The stairs were steep and I was glad when Moe stopped to give a commentary.

This was an area of karst topography, she explained, defined as limestone laced with sinkholes, caves and underground drainages. Limestone, a sedimentary rock, is made in the ocean. Over years, as animals die and settle to the bottom, trillions of shells and skeletons pile on top of each other so that the top layers push on the lower layers, creating pressure to make limestone. (If you add high heat and even more pressure, the limestone changes into marble, a metamorphic rock.) When limestone fractures, as it would in an earthquake, water flows through cracks, eating it away. The more carbon dioxide in the water, the more acidic it becomes and the faster it dissolves the limestone. The muskeg bogs of Southeast Alaska, with their

The gate protecting the entrance to El Capitan Cave has bars wide enough apart to let bats fly through.

high levels of decaying vegetation and heavy rainfall, create ideal conditions for karst topography. Even so, forming a cave is a slow process taking tens of thousands of years.

As we climbed, Moe pointed out various limestone rocks. In one spot, a root from a red-cedar tree had reached down and enfolded a rock.

Farther up the hill, young trees gave way to majestic old-growth.

"The Forest Service doesn't allow logging on karst topography anymore," Moe told us. "It's too fragile and too precious to risk destroying." (Some environmentalists point out that 80 percent of the karst topography in the Tongass Forest had already been logged before this rule was implemented and that the ban is not always respected.)

We came to the top of the stairs where a gaping round hole framed by ferns led into the side of the mountain. I felt like Alice following the white rabbit as Moe led us forward. Instead of free falling, however, we stumbled over a pile of boulders, then walked down a rocky trail.

Soon we turned a corner to confront a massive iron gate. Moe unlocked it, directing our attention to the large gaps between the bars.

"This is a bat gate." The gaps were wide enough for a bat's wingspan but narrow enough to keep out unauthorized spelunkers. Bats hibernate in the cave in the winter.

"I'm going to lock the gate behind us." Moe swung open the gate and stood aside so we could walk through. "This is where some people have trouble; those with claustrophobia can go bonkers." I had to admit I felt a bit nervous as I imagined being trapped inside the cave.

"This is why we have two tour guides." Moe pocketed the key. "Jess has a key too. If anything were to happen to me, she could unlock the gate."

We continued, descending a long narrow tunnel that just cleared our heads in places. Our headlamps lit uneven sculpted gray rock glistening with moisture. I heard the constant drip of water and smelled a musty wet-basement odor.

Moe went first, followed by Steve, with Jess and I in the rear. Rocks rolled under my boots, threatening to send me falling and I had to fight the urge to brace myself against the side of the cave. Touching the cave sides was discouraged as it could eventually damage the rocks.

When we reached a place where the floor leveled out, Moe stopped. "Find a VCR and sit down." She turned and sat on a flat rock. "'VCR' stands for very comfortable rock."

I found an almost-flat rock and sat down, thinking that "comfortable rock" was surely an oxymoron.

"I want everyone to turn off their lights here," Moe said. She reached up and clicked off her headlamp and we followed suit. For a few seconds, everything looked black, then my eyes adjusted and I could see a dim light coming from the tunnel behind us.

"This part of the cave is called the twilight zone," Moe told us. "We just left the entrance zone and from here we enter the dark zone. We'll turn off the lights here again on our way out."

Our lights back on, we continued on through the almost-level tunnel. In places the ceiling lowered and we had to duck or almost crawl to keep from banging our heads. Showers of water drummed on our hard hats as we waded through ankle-deep puddles.

"The water is coming through the rocks from muskeg above us," Moe explained. "There's more of it today than usual because of the rain last night."

In a small high-ceilinged chamber Moe shone her flashlight up, pointing out geological features: a fault line shown by a crack in the rocks and honeycombed rocks termed "Swiss cheese." Farther on, we came to smooth wavy areas called "flowstones," that formed when water flowed in sheets over rocks.

"This is a young cave, geologically. Few stalactites and stalagmites have formed yet." Moe pointed out some small stalactites—short cream-colored spikes that hung down over our heads. Stalactites and stalagmites form when limestone in water crystallizes as it drips down through cracks in the cave's ceiling.

As we walked and crawled through the tunnels, I was amazed at how far the cave seemed to stretch and was glad we had guides to show us the way back. Moe named the different rooms of the cave as we moved forward: the fault room, the flowstone room, the steam room (which we didn't enter) and, finally, the pool room.

In the dim light of our headlamps I could see an expanse of water stretching ahead under low ceilings.

"This is as far as we go," said Moe.

Looking around the chamber, I saw that from here the cave branched into several small tunnels that would require crawling on hands and knees.

Pointing toward the tunnels, Moe told us that archeologists had found carbon from burnt torches and the fossil bones of bears there.

In the 1990s, researchers exploring a neighboring cave, the On Your Knees Cave on the north end of Prince of Wales Island, found bear bones 35,000 to 40,000 years old. Excited by this find, which might indicate areas that had been ice free during glaciation, the researchers began excavating in earnest and discovered the lower jaws, pelvis and stone tools of a human who lived 10,000 years ago. The finds, supported by DNA research, paint a picture of an early maritime people foraging among the rocks of the seashore and living on a diet rich in seafood. Surprisingly, the bones are not related to the Tlingit, Haida and Tsimshian people who now live in Southeast Alaska, but to coastal populations farther south from California to Chile. These results support a theory that the first people in the Americas came down the coast in boats before going overland, instead of traveling down an ice-free corridor in the center of the continent as previously assumed. Prince of Wales Island would have been at the edge of the giant ice sheets during the Wisconsin Ice Age, and travelers in boats could have passed along this coast.

What must it have been like, I wondered, to explore this cave with only a flaming torch, knowing that outside the cave was ice and inside there might lurk bears? What would happen if the torch burned out? We were about to get a hint of what that was like.

"We're going to turn off our lights for awhile," Moe told us. "Pick a good VCR."

When everyone was settled, we turned off our lights. At first my retina replayed flashes from the lights. Then an absolute blackness reigned. I put my hand in front of my face and couldn't see it at all. I knew the others were there by the sounds of their movements as they shifted on the rocks. The drip, drip, plop of water falling onto rocks and into pools sounded like a discordant symphony. I remembered what Moe had said at the beginning of the tour about getting to know each other because we would be in the dark together. My imagination roamed back to the entrance where the locked gate barred our exit—and presumably the entrance of stray bears and people. What a perfect setup for a murder mystery, I thought, with tunnels and nooks for a murderer to hide in.

The flash of Moe's light banished my fears. With relief I turned my light on too and we started walking back toward the entrance, scanning the walls with our flashlights. Moe pointed to a small side tunnel and asked us if we wanted to crawl through. "It opens up and you can see the river below."

When it was my turn, I ducked down and wriggled into the tunnel, pointing my flashlight toward the floor. A yawning hole opened up. As I leaned over it and looked down, my headlamp flickered dimly on water far below and I heard the rush of a subterranean stream.

"What you saw is the water going into the Rockwell River, which comes out along the shore," Moe told me later.

Returning to the twilight zone, we turned our lights off again. This time I could see the tunnel walls around me where before only a dim light up ahead had been visible. Our eyes had adapted to the dark.

When Jess unlocked the padlock on the gate and swung it open, I felt relieved to no longer be in danger of being trapped. I scrambled over boulders toward the exit, amazed at how bright the light appeared, and felt a surge of joy—the sun must be out! How nice to see it after our two hours deep in the cave. Then we stepped out and I realized my dark-adapted eyes had fooled me: I was looking at the same dull cloud cover we had seen when entering.

14.4 TOKEEN
History in Marble

I looked in awe at marble blocks looming above our heads. Draped in moss and ferns, shaded by branches of trees, and stacked two and three high, the large blocks resembled a long-lost archeological site. Men had schemed and murdered for this marble—and that made it all the more intriguing.

We were at Tokeen, on Marble Island off the west coast of Prince of Wales Island, the site of the largest of the many marble operations that dotted this area in the early 1900s. Tokeen Marble, known for its white background and dark veins, was shipped all over the country and incorporated into courthouses, banks, railroad stations and theaters.

The first thing we saw after rounding the point into Tokeen Cove was a row of modern white houses—not the old factories, dormitories and other industrial buildings I had seen in pictures of old Tokeen. My surprise at this wilderness suburb deepened when I looked through the binoculars and saw that the houses floated on rafts.

Moss-draped marble blocks litter the forest at Tokeen on Marble Island.

Beyond the houses an unbroken forest covered the land. Finding the quarries in these dense trees would not be easy, but perhaps someone in one of the houses would be able to help us.

After anchoring *Osprey*, we motored the dinghy around to the houses. We could see a refrigerator and a couch through one of the windows, but the houses were silent and unoccupied.

I noticed a slender woman in a bright pink shirt standing by a small cabin on shore, a load of firewood in her arms. Steve motored the dinghy closer, and the woman put down her wood and walked to the water's edge. With a friendly smile, she told us her name was Jan and she was visiting

Because of the expense of shipping marble blocks to Tacoma for milling, only the best were selected, leaving many blocks behind.

her friend Richard who was working for the owner of the quarry site. When we asked where the old quarries were, she directed us to go ashore near an old derrick on the beach. From there a road led into the forest and to the quarries.

"Keep in mind that the quarry operations closed in the 1920s," she told us, "and the land was logged in the 1970s. The old buildings just collapsed and everything grew on top of them. Be careful."

We motored the dinghy along the shore past piles of marble chunks stacked like children's building blocks. When we found the derrick, we tied up the dinghy, and scrambled ashore over marble rubble. Piles of gray marble were scattered near the derrick and rows of more marble blocks were lined up right into the trees, like gravestones in a cemetery for giants.

Enthralled, we followed a path that wound around marble blocks into a dense second-growth forest where green moss shrouded every surface including the marble. The old buildings would have been near here, I thought, but with the exception of the occasional nail and stray piece of lumber we saw no sign of them.

Eventually, we returned to the derrick to find the road, overgrown with grass. We followed the road along the base of a shale cliff to a field of thimbleberries. Pushing our way through fuzzy broad leaves and stiff branches, we climbed a small hill into the forest. Suddenly, I stopped. Just a few feet ahead, the land dropped away. Through the trees below I could see water and moss-covered marble walls. Even shrouded in trees, the quarry was unmistakable. If we had gone a few feet farther, we might have gone over the edge.

I was thrilled to realize I was seeing one of the eight quarries that once made up the Vermont Marble Company's operations at Tokeen, an enterprise abandoned almost eighty years ago.

Tokeen's history started in 1895 when a Seattle marble cutter named Robert L. Fox found a piece of prime marble among the curios in a store in Wrangell. Fox learned that a Native had brought the marble from a creek near the village of Shakan on Kosciusko Island, west of Prince of Wales Island. At the time, the west coast of the United States was in the midst of a building boom and the sight of prime marble must have excited Fox like a gold nugget excites a miner. Returning to Alaska the next year for serious prospecting, Fox found good-quality marble at Calder and later at Dry Pass, both on Prince of Wales Island.

Like the hard-rock gold mining that flourished in Alaska during the same period, marble quarries required capital, equipment and laborers, none of which Fox had. To develop his sites, he entered into a series of deals with investors.

In the fall of 1903, after he sold his claims at Calder and Dry Pass, Fox discovered more marble at Tokeen. He traveled to Seattle where he met a man named Robert Ball who with his partners formed a company and named it the Great American Marble Company. They agreed to buy the Tokeen claims for $250,000, however, internal strife rocked the company, with the board stripping Ball of his presidency and no one following up on the assessment work required to maintain their claim. Ball went north to do the assessments and claim the marble for one faction, while another faction sent a man named William Deppe in pursuit, with instructions to jump the claims or run Ball off.

The two men faced off in an isolated cabin at Tokeen. A shot rang out and Deppe fell dead. Ball was tried at Ketchikan in April 1905 in a courtroom packed with curious onlookers. Ball claimed self-defense but during the trial it came out that Ball was really Charles R. Main, a Michigan attorney disbarred for shady dealings and once accused of murdering a witness. Ketchikan jurors convicted Ball—or Main—of manslaughter.

Robert Fox, who had not received his $250,000 payment, eventually won clear title to his claims and sold them to the Vermont Marble Company.

At its peak of production, from roughly 1912 to 1915, approximately 70 employees worked at Tokeen for nine months a year. Photographs from this time show enormous pits with straight rock walls stair-stepping down to a marble floor where workers, enveloped in clouds of steam, operated cutting machines, called channelers.

From the quarries, marble was loaded onto narrow-gauge railcars, rolled to the beach, loaded onto barges and shipped to the Vermont Marble Company mill in Tacoma where it was sawed and polished. Because of the expense of shipping to Tacoma, only the most perfect blocks were selected. Those not absolutely flawless were abandoned, hence the piles of marble along the shore and in the forest. The expense of

Houses waiting to be moved to shore for a new development at Tokeen.

shipping also meant that little of it returned to Alaska. Marble for the Territorial Building in Juneau and the Federal Building in Fairbanks were rare exceptions.

The workers (all men who were not allowed to bring their families) lived in company-owned barracks, ate in a company dining hall and spent their evenings playing cards and reading in the company's well-stocked library.

The Tokeen quarries operated until 1926. They closed due to falling demand; concrete was taking over the market. The quarries opened one last time in 1932 to excavate choice marble for the Fairbanks Federal Building, then closed for good. Today, few of those who visit the many buildings made from Tokeen marble know where it came from.

We left the quarry and returned to *Osprey*. Sometime later as we sat in *Osprey*'s cockpit enjoying the late-afternoon sun, Jan came by in an aluminum skiff driven by Richard, a tall lanky man with dark hair and a beard.

"I wanted to see your boat up close," said Richard.

"Do you like spaghetti?" he asked after he had looked over the boat. "We'd like you to come to dinner."

Jan and Richard returned to their cabin. We gave Jigger his meal, hung our anchor light on the backstay and went ashore.

As Richard opened the cabin door for us, the aroma of spaghetti sauce came wafting out. Inside, the cabin was small with one room and a sleeping loft. Mismatched plastic chairs, a plaid sofa with one of the cushions uncovered and an old wooden table with lions feet served as furnishings.

"The cabin belongs to a friend," said Richard. "But he lets me stay here whenever I work here. Normally we live in Craig."

Congenial people, Jan and Richard made us feel at home and soon we were swapping stories. Richard told us he had a business in Craig and worked in construction but sometimes took on other jobs. The friend, owner of the cabin and the adjacent quarry land, had hired him to help prepare building lots for the houses we had seen floating in the cove. The houses had been barged to Tokeen from various locations.

"Do you know anything about amphibious boats?" asked Richard, when he discovered Steve was an engineer. "I made one to deliver fuel to places like this. It's a pain in the neck to have to transfer fuel on and off a boat."

As Richard and Steve talked boats, I chatted with Jan. I learned she had moved to Alaska only a couple of years before and was enjoying getting to know it. Before she moved here, she'd served as a medic in the air force for 20 years.

"What do you do now?" I asked her.

"Anything but medic work. Right now I work for a radio station."

Steve and I returned to *Osprey*, glad we had come to Tokeen.

Columns of Tokeen Marble frame the entrance to the Alaska Legislative Building.

The quarries were intriguing but the best part of our visit was meeting Jan and Richard. In their resourcefulness and willingness to work at whatever needed doing, they were typical Alaskans.

As we left Tokeen the next morning, I looked back at the houses floating quietly on their rafts, waiting to provide the next chapter in Tokeen's history.

The wharves, bunkhouses and dining hall of the Vermont Marble Company were all gone; only the water-filled quarries and the marble remained. But I had already seen the best evidence of the old marble industry before even coming to Tokeen, having admired the dark-veined marble on the floors and walls of the King County Courthouse in Seattle and the Washington State Capitol in Olympia. I just hadn't known at the time that it was Tokeen Marble.

14.5 KLAWOCK
"Our Big Month"

When the screen on my laptop computer went blank at Warm Springs Bay in 2008 and we learned that the best place to take it for repairs was Klawock, I was dismayed. We'd visited Klawock the year before, and hadn't planned to go back. I didn't know what we would do in this small town of 800 people if we had to wait several days for a repair.

Our 2007 trip to Klawock had been by land, driving across Prince of Wales Island in a rented truck from Thorne Bay where we had gone to wait out a storm. We toured the totem park in the center of town, walked along the waterfront with its fish-processing plant and then, after less than two hours, left to drive south to the more populous town of Craig. Klawock was a nice little town, but I didn't think it warranted another visit.

Klawock as seen from the water.

What we were about to find out was the difference that interacting with people at work could make to our enjoyment of a town.

As we approached Klawock from the water in 2008, we saw first the red-roofed fish-processing plant on the shore with houses spread out on the hills above it. Then we turned into the mouth of the Klawock River and the town marina came into view, tucked behind a small island. When the harbormaster failed to answer our radio call, we motored into the marina anyway and pulled into a vacant slip.

We had just finished tying up *Osprey* when a man on another dock called out,

"That's my uncle's spot." Steve walked up to the harbormaster's office to check on this, but returned a few minutes later with the news that it was closed until the next morning.

"I don't see any 'reserved' signs. Let's stay where we are."

We called the computer-repair company and left a message, then decided to take a walk. From the top of the dock, we followed a path next to a modern school until we came to a small white building labeled "Library." We have learned that a library can be a rich source of information about a town, so when we saw the door was open, we walked in. Inside, we found a small room with the usual shelves of books, a large loom in one corner, and a desk with

Subsistence hunters bring home a deer. Federal law assures rural residents the right to hunt, fish and pick berries for personal use on federal lands.

a middle-aged Native woman working behind it. The woman smiled at us. "Welcome to the Klawock Library." She introduced herself as Susie and invited us to look around.

I was browsing through an extensive collection of books about Alaskan Natives when I noticed a room full of computers around the corner.

"Do you have internet access?" I asked Susie.

"We're supposed to; it's not working. But there's hope." She reached into a desk

Subsistence fishing for sockeye salmon at the mouth of the Klawock River.

A Klawock fisherman.

drawer and pulled out a brochure from the Bill & Melinda Gates Foundation. "We've got a grant. There are some good people left, even if they are rich.

"The grant will buy computers and send me to school to learn about them. I'm a fiber artist, not a librarian. Nobody else wanted the job and I didn't think the library should close, so I took it. My daughter used to tell me I should learn about email and I'd tell her I'd just ask the librarian if I needed it. Now I *am* the librarian."

"What kind of artist did you say you are?" I asked, thinking I had misheard. The term "fiber artist" was new to me.

"Fiber artist. I weave." She gestured to the loom in the corner. "I'm making curtains for the library now."

She walked over to the loom and sat down, her feet working the treadles as her hand drew the shuttle through layers of thread.

"Here, you try it," she said to me. Under her tutelage, I was soon weaving a black-and red-patterned cloth. A call on my cell phone from the computer-repair company ended my weaving experience. We walked back to the marina and met Karen Cleary, the company owner. Dressed in neat slacks and a sweater, she looked as if she could be at home in an office in Seattle. She took my computer, promising to return it the next evening, fixed or not. As she left the boat, I asked for a recommendation on a place to eat.

"The Fireweed Lodge is really the only place; just follow the main road out of town."

The road out of town led over a bridge, across a creek and alongside a large green marsh with a view of mountains beyond. Fireweed Lodge sat at the edge of the marsh, next to a dock with a fleet of sport-fishing boats. A sign advertised meals and lodging. We walked into the restaurant to see a scene of white tablecloths and gleaming china. I smelled grilled salmon and heard hearty laughter from a group of men in jeans and sweatshirts gathered around a fireplace.

"We'd like dinner for two," said Steve to the young woman at the door.

She looked at a pad of paper. "The earliest we could help you would be next Thursday." The restaurant was fully booked with lodge customers, she explained.

Disappointed and disgruntled, we headed back to the boat for a meal of lentil stew. We were approaching the marina when an elderly Native man hailed us. "Did the mayor send the chief of police after you for being in his parking spot?"

"We don't have a car," said Steve, "so we can't be in his parking spot."

We walked on as I puzzled over the strange question. Then I remembered the man who had told us we were in his uncle's boat slip.

"Oh, no!" I said. "I bet we're in the mayor's slip!"

The next morning we were preparing breakfast when Steve looked out the window and said, "A deer!"

I looked out, expecting to see a deer grazing on the nearby shore, but instead saw an aluminum skiff with a dead deer in the bow, its head strapped to the boat like a bowsprit and its tongue hanging out. Two young men and a woman were in the boat. I grabbed my camera and rushed out into the cockpit. The driver turned and brought the skiff close to us.

"There were four deer where we shot this one," the woman said. "We left three behind, including one with big antlers."

When the hunters had left, I looked out toward the river mouth and saw several pairs of skiffs with seine nets out. Two or three people were in every skiff, and in each one someone herded fish into nets with what looked like giant plungers while others pulled in the net.

"I want to catch this," I told Steve and headed down the dock with my camera.

We were standing on the end of the dock watching the seiners when a man in a fishing troller tied alongside the dock spoke up: "This is our big month. We pick berries, shoot deer and seine fish. Then we're through." He gestured toward one of the boats. "My business partner's out there." He raised his voice and called, "We've got to get to work." The boat came up to the dock. "Why don't you give these people a fish for their dinner?"

One of the fishermen, dressed in oilskins and a black hat with "Native" stitched on its front, reached into the boat, pulled out a small sockeye and tossed it to Steve.

"That's the way I like to catch fish," said Steve.

We were witnessing subsistence fishing and hunting, the taking of natural resources for traditional, personal and family uses including food, clothing, and ceremonial. The Alaska Native Claims Settlement Act extinguished all Native claims to special hunting and fishing rights in exchange for money and land, but congress recognized the importance of subsistence hunting and fishing activities to the Natives. To ensure Natives could maintain those activities, they mandated that rural residents be given a preference for subsistence hunting and fishing on federal public lands when they passed the Alaska National Interest Lands Conservation Act (ANILCA) in 1980. Because so much of Alaska is federal land and many Natives live in small rural towns like Klawock, the right of Alaska's Natives to hunt and fish is assured.

We took our fish back to *Osprey* where Steve cleaned it and put it in the icebox before walking up the dock to the harbormaster's office.

"We *are* in the mayor's slip," Steve told me when he returned. "But the harbormaster said not to worry. The mayor found another spot on the other dock."

The morning had turned into one of the most beautiful days we had ever experienced in Alaska: blue skies and (almost) warm sun. We walked out of town, following the main road, until we reached a Native longhouse and carving shed. Old totem poles with cracked, rotting wood and peeling paint lay on the ground next to the shed: a junkyard for totem poles.

The poles were identical to those in the totem park. As the poles in the park aged, carvers replaced them with replicas. Seeing the number of old poles that had been replaced made me realize what a commitment it was for a community to maintain a totem park.

Inside the shed, a hefty-looking Native in a vest and a red baseball cap sat in front of a collection of carving knives, talking to a group of tourists. Nearby a young man worked on one of several new replica poles under construction.

When the group of tourists left, the carver, Jon Rowan, took up a carving knife and began chipping away at a thunderbird on a pole. As he worked, he told us that in addition to poles he carves halibut hooks and other small intricate pieces. He also teaches the art to students at the high school in Klawock; the youth working with him was one of his students.

Later that afternoon Karen Cleary returned my computer. She hadn't been able to fix it but had connected it to an external monitor and downloaded all my files to my external hard drive so I could access them on Steve's computer.

When I asked what we owed her, she shook her head. "Nothing. I wouldn't want you to remember Klawock as the place that couldn't fix your computer but charged you for it anyway."

There was little chance of that. In Klawock, we'd witnessed subsistence fishing, seen the results of subsistence hunting, and met people, like the librarian, who cared enough about the town to change their lives for its well-being. The real Klawock had been here all the time; we'd just needed to take the time to get to know it.

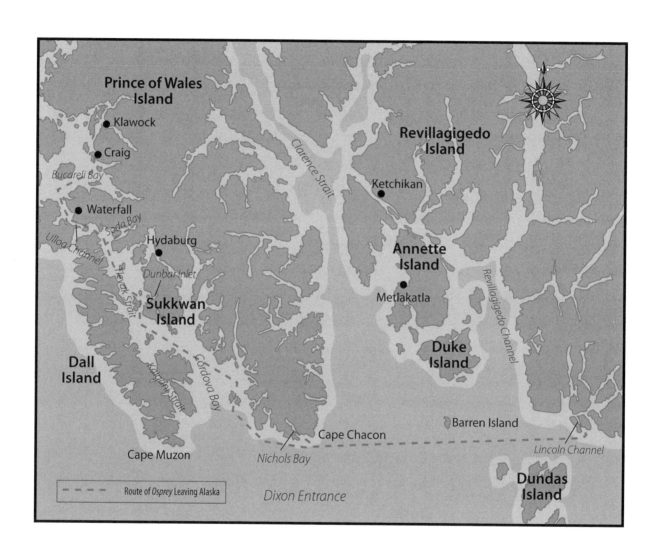

Prince of Wales
Island

● Klawock

● Craig

Bucareli Bay

● Waterfall

Ulloa Channel

Soda Bay

Hydaburg ●

Dunbar Inlet

Sukkwan
Island

Tlevak Strait

Dall
Island

Kaigani Strait

Cordova Bay

Cape Muzon

Nichols Bay

Cape Chacon

Clarence Strait

Revillagigedo
Island

Ketchikan ●

Annette
Island

Metlakatla ●

Duke
Island

Revillagigedo Channel

Barren Island ●

Lincoln Channel

Dundas
Island

Dixon Entrance

– – – – – Route of *Osprey* Leaving Alaska

CHAPTER 15

LEAVING ALASKA

"Wait for good weather to cross Dixon Entrance!" This was our mantra when planning our southbound trip in 2008. By choosing to end the Alaskan leg of our journey on the west coast of Prince of Wales Island, we were exposing ourselves to the most treacherous part of Dixon Entrance.

We knew the challenge only too well. Two years before, we had made the same crossing, leaving from the Barrier Islands on the southwest corner of Prince of Wales Island, towing our dinghy as we usually do. Southeast winds, predicted to be only 15–25 knots, rose to 40-knot gales. The dinghy became airborne, flipped, and nosedived upside down into the waves. We watched helplessly as wind and waves tore the rings that held the painter (the rope tying the dinghy to the boat) out of the dinghy's bow, sending it sailing back toward Prince of Wales Island.

As darkness fell, we limped into an anchorage at Dundas Island, BC, wet and tired from the 65-mile sail. Then, the next day, Canadian Customs chastised us for not continuing on another 25 miles to Prince Rupert to clear customs that night. Only the fact that the Canadian Coast Guard heard our call on the VHF radio to the US Coast Guard, alerting them to the lost dinghy and incidentally documenting the bad weather, saved us from fines.

This year we planned to do things differently. We would wait for good weather and, rather than leave from the Barrier Islands, would depart from Nichols Bay on the southeast corner of Prince of Wales Island—cutting 15 miles off our passage. Once across Dixon Entrance, we'd anchor near Tongass, Alaska, before crossing to British Columbia the next day.

But as we waited out a storm in the town of Craig, on the west coast of Prince of Wales Island, the dubiousness of waiting for good weather came home to me. We had planned to stay in Craig for only a couple nights, but a 994-mb low was headed our way. The weather radio first predicted a gale, then upgraded the gale to a storm. We stayed another night, then another, as rain hammered on our cabin roof. How long could we wait for good weather? A week? Two weeks? Just to get to the south tip of Prince of Wales Island and the beginning of Dixon Entrance, we would have to sail another 65 miles south through Tlevak Narrows and Tlevak Strait, a challenge in itself.

We had struggled to get to Alaska at the beginning of the summer, with one equipment breakage after another. Were we now going to have to struggle to leave?

South to Tlevak Strait

The morning we finally left Craig, the barometer was up to 1,000 mb and rising, the sun was making sporadic appearances and the wind was blowing only lightly in the harbor. The worst of the storm was over, or so we thought. We left the marina and motored into Bucareli Bay—right into 35-knot winds. We raised our smallest jib and sailed toward Ulloa Channel, thinking the wind would moderate in the confined channel. Instead, winds of 40-plus knots came roaring off the hills, churning the water into white foam. Gusts blew every which way, but mostly out of the narrow channel where we were headed. We lowered sail and motored. I looked at the knot meter and saw we were only making 3.5 knots. The wind must be really slowing us down, I thought. Then I looked back to see our dinghy—a sturdier replacement for the one lost in Dixon Entrance two years ago—upside down and looking like a yellow and black whale. We stopped the engine and with difficulty dragged the dinghy alongside and turned it over. Miraculously, the oars were still in the oarlocks. Even more important, the rubber patches holding the rings where we tied the painter were still intact.

That day we got no farther than Soda Bay in north Tlevak Strait. The next day found us tacking south against 30-knot winds and driving rain. To the west, dark clouds streamed toward us across Dall Island from the Pacific Ocean. To the east, mist shrouded Prince of Wales Island. Rain fell relentlessly, seeping into my foul-weather gear and

A sailboat waits out a storm at Dunbar Inlet on Sukkwan Island.

making me shiver. I was tired of the rain, tired of the wind, and tired of the cold. Even Steve complained, "I've had about enough of bashing to weather."

We were aiming for Rose Inlet on Dall Island, but in late afternoon, with almost 10 miles to go, our determination failed. We turned and sailed through a group of small islands toward Dunbar Inlet on Sukkwan Island. As the wind died to nothing and the rain gave way to sun, we drifted, enjoying the quiet. Finally, we started the engine and motored into the inlet. Near its head, I let the anchor go and Steve turned off the engine. In the sudden peace, I heard the rush of a creek coming down the hillside and the croak of a raven in the forest. A fringe of bright-green marsh grass lined the shore, accented by round black mounds of conglomerate rock. In the anchorage the sun glistened off the white hull of a sailboat, *Sequoia* of Portland, which stood in relief against a backdrop of dark hills. We had gone from cold, wet misery to this magical scene. Just when we'd had enough of Alaskan weather, Alaska handed us this gift of beauty.

Crossing Dixon Entrance

Two days later we left Nichols Bay at the south end of Prince of Wales Island to cross Dixon Entrance. As we motored away from the island, I looked back at the twin cones of Cape Chacon standing serenely in the morning sun and couldn't believe our luck. Just when it mattered most, we had perfect weather. We motored across a calm sea, the engine comfortably chugging along.

At 2:00 p.m. wind came up from the north and we raised sail. As we approached Kanaguni Island, south of Tongass, we saw a small white sport-fishing boat bobbing all alone near shore. "Calling the green sailboat," said a voice over the VHF. When Steve answered, we heard, "This is Bud. There's no one else out here, so I thought I should call and say hello." We talked for awhile about fish and fishing, then signed off. How like Alaska, I thought, for a stranger to call us. We could sail all day in Puget Sound surrounded by other boats and never talk to anyone, certainly not to anyone in a boat so different from ours.

We rounded the south end of Kanaguni Island and tacked into Lincoln Channel. There we found a bight on the east side of the island with water shallow enough to anchor. I let the anchor out and listened to it grating across the rocks below. I let more scope out and it grabbed abruptly, swinging *Osprey* into the wind.

Lincoln Channel

That evening I took the dinghy out for a row, past a sandy beach washed by a low surf, then along a rock face. I saw some very large barnacles clinging to the rock and rowed closer to investigate. Among the barnacles was a large brown snail, about four inches long. Its considerable size surprised me. While the dinghy surged back and forth, I reached out with an oar and dislodged the snail. I rowed away, then stopped to look at my find, picking it up. Fine brown tufts prickled my hand and with the prickles came a memory. The snail was an Oregon triton. When I was in my early teens, my hobby was shell collecting. My friend Frances had found an Oregon hairy triton, and I remembered holding the empty shell in my hand and feeling the same prickles. Wanting a triton

Osprey anchored in Lincoln Channel. Our last anchorage in Alaska.

A row along the shores of Lincoln Channel reveals sea creatures like these plume worms.

for myself, I had searched the beaches in Puget Sound, but to no avail. It had taken me 50 years, but I had finally found one. I marveled at how the feel of the snail shell in my hand had brought back the sense of wonder from my childhood.

I put the snail on the seat of the dinghy and continued rowing. Green starfish shared the rocks with clusters of tube worms. Reddish-brown patches glistened in the late-evening light. I wondered about the patches but couldn't find any close enough to examine. Could they be garnet, a gem occasionally found in Alaska?

I turned to row back, then remembered the snail. It was still on the dinghy seat but now the animal was reaching its foot out of the shell, trying to crawl away. I picked it up again and studied it. A tiny pink starfish clung to the top and a calcareous worm wound around a whorl. The snail was its own ecological community. I rowed back to the rocks and returned the snail to a ledge.

As a teenage shell collector, I would have had no compunction about killing the snail to remove the animal and keep the shell. But as an adult, I collect memories, not things. And Alaska had given me many memories. We had drifted among icebergs in front of calving glaciers, observed brown bears feeding on sedge grass, braved treacherous rocks to enter still harbors, and watched Native artists carve totem poles. And now I had held a live Oregon triton in my hand.

Had we found the real Southeast Alaska? Earlier that summer, in Ketchikan, I had been intrigued by the suggestion that the tourist business portrays an Alaska that isn't real. Certainly we had seen artifice in the tourist centers. In Ketchikan, Juneau and Skagway, we walked by renovated buildings that had once stocked tools and dry goods but now sold jewelry and were owned and operated by corporations based outside Alaska. In Skagway we had ridden a train that remains in business only to give rides to tourists. Outside Ketchikan we had visited a fishing lodge that creates a world of luxury for their guests, serving teriyaki salmon when real Alaskans eat salmon loaf.

Like the cruise-ship passengers who had walked out the gate of the cannery development to discover the authentic town of Hoonah, we had left the tourist centers in search of the real Alaska. There we had found a different world. If it wasn't exactly the mythical Alaska where hardy and independent souls conquer the wilderness, it wasn't like life in Seattle either. In Meyers Chuck, residents horde old Coleman lanterns in case they need them for spare parts. In Port Alexander groceries come by mailboat and if the weather's bad, there are none. In Wooden Wheel Cove, pony-tailed fishermen in scruffy clothes gather on the dock enjoying beer and a sense of camaraderie as they swap tales of fishing and adventure on the sea. And almost everywhere in Southeast Alaska, life takes place with a background of breathtaking scenery complete with snow-capped mountains, calving glaciers and teeming wildlife. No tourist hype can top that.

Most importantly, I realized in our search that the real Alaska is much more than what is portrayed by the tourist offices. In the Tsimshian town of Metlakatla, we learned that the myth of acculturated "Indians" hides a vibrant Native culture. In Hoonah, a Fourth of July egg toss revealed family and community ties that run generations deep. In Kake, we discovered that people with a reputation for being fearsome believe in helping each other. And in Skagway, where workers have turned the tourist industry into a new gold rush, we saw that tourism sometimes *is* the real Alaska, and that too shows real Alaska spirit.

SOURCES

Introduction

Garfield, Viola E. *The Seattle Totem Pole.* University of Washington Press, Seattle, 1980.

Chapter 1. The Voyage North

Carey, Betty Lowman. *Bijaboji: North to Alaska by Oar.* Harbour Publishing, Madeira Park, BC, 2004.

Department of Commerce, National Oceanic and Atmospheric Administration. *United States Coast Pilot 8: Alaska: Dixon Entrance to Cape Spencer.* 2007.

Hale, Robert. *Waggoner Cruising Guide.* Weatherly Press, 2010.

Lawrence, Ian. *Far Away Places: Fifty Anchorages on the Northwest Coast.* Orca Book Publishers, 1995.

Minister of Fisheries and Oceans Canada. *Sailing Directions: British Columbia Coast (South Portion) Vol. 1 Sixteenth Edition.* 1999.

Moore, Bill. "The town that vanished." *British Columbia Lumberman*, July, 1974. http://www.wdmoore.ca/articles/047%20July%2074.htm.

Newell, Dianne. *The Development of the Pacific Salmon-Canning Industry: A Grown Man's Game.* McGill-Queen's University Press, Montreal and Kingston, London, Buffalo,1989.

Scott, Andrew. *The Encyclopedia of Raincoast Place Names: A Complete Reference to Coastal British Columbia.* Harbour Publishing, Madeira Park, BC, 2009.

Butedale, British Columbia. http://en.wikipedia.org/wiki/Butedale,_British_Columbia.

Great Bear Rainforest. http://www.britishcolumbia.com/regions/towns/?townID=4120.

Namu, Discovery Coast, BC. http://www.britishcolumbia.com/regions/towns/?townID=3716.

The Path to Sustainability: A Brief History of Conservation in the Great Bear Rainforest. http://www.nature.org/wherewework/northamerica/canada/work/art26147.html.

Prince Rupert, British Columbia. http://en.wikipedia.org/wiki/Prince_Rupert,_British_Columbia.

Chapter 2. Ketchikan Area

Allen, June. "Fish Pirates and Fish Traps: Ketchikan's Real Melodrama!." *Sitnews—Stories in the News*. Ketchican, Alaska, August 30, 2002.

Allen, June and Patricia Charles. *Spirit! Historic Ketchikan, Alaska*. Historic Ketchikan, Inc., 1992.

Askren, Mique'l Icesis. *From Negative to Positive: B.A. Haldane, Nineteenth-Century Tsimshian Photographer*. Master's thesis, University of British Columbia, October, 2006.

Douglass, Don and Reanne Hemingway-Douglass. *Exploring Southeast Alaska: Dixon Entrance to Skagway*. Fine Edge Productions, 2000.

Dunning, Mike. "Tourism in Ketchikan and Southeast Alaska." *Alaska History*, Vol 15. No. 2, 2000.

Murray, Peter. *The Devil and Mr. Duncan: A History of the Two Metlakatlas*. Sino Nis Press, 1985.

Raban, Jonathan. *Passage to Juneau: A Sea and Its Meaning*. Pantheon Books, New York and Random House, Ontario, 1999.

Roppell, Patricia, *Misty Fiords National Monument Wilderness, Alaska*. Farwest Research, Wrangell, Alaska, 2000.

Roppel, Patricia. *Alaska Salmon Hatcheries, 1891–1959*. Alaska Historical Commission, 1982.

Sisk, John. *The Southeastern Alaska Salmon Industry: Historical Overview and Current Status*. Southeast Alaska Conservation Assessment—Chapter 9.5. http://www.conserveonline.org/workspaces/akcfm/pdfs/9.5_SalmonIndustry.pdf.

Stowell, Harold H. *Geology of Southeast Alaska: Rock and Ice in Motion*. University of Alaska Press, Fairbanks, Alaska, 2006.

Vancouver, George. *A voyage of discovery to the North Pacific Ocean and round the world, 1791–1795 : with an introduction and appendices*. Edited by W. Kaye Lamb. Hakluyt Society, London, 1984.

Chapter 3. In the Land of Kaigani Haida

Alaska Geographic Society. "Southeast: Alaska's Panhandle." *Alaska Geographic*, Vol 5, No. 2, 1978.

Dombrowski, Kirk. *Against Culture: Development, Politics, and Religion in Indian Alaska*. University of Nebraska Press, Lincoln and London, 2001.

Eastman, Carol M. and Elizabeth A. Edwards. *Gyaehlingaay: Traditions, Tales, and Images of the Kaigani Haida. Traditional tales told by Lillian Pettviel and other Haida elders*. Burke Museum Publications, Seattle, 1991.

Kramer, Pat. *Alaska's Totem Poles*. Alaska Northwest Books, 2004.

MacDonald, George F. *Haida Art*. University of Washington Press, Seattle, 1996.

Reid, William with photos by Adelaide de Menil. *Out of the Silence*. Outerbridge & Dienstfrey, New York, 1971.

Scidmore, Eliza Ruhamah. *Alaska, Its Southern Coast and Sitka Archipelago*. Lothrop, Boston, 1885.

Strankman, Anna Marie. *Re-capturing a legacy: in search of the poles of Old Kasaan*. Master's thesis, University of Washington, 2003.

Wilson Duff (editor), Jane Wallen and Joe Clark. *Totem pole survey of southeastern Alaska*. Alaska State Museum, 1969.

Chapter 4. Clarence Strait to Petersburg

Alaska Community Database Community Information Summaries. Meyers Chuck. http://www.commerce.state.ak.us/dca/commdb/CIS.cfm.

Allen, June. "Meyers Chuck AK 99903: Ever Been There?" *Sitnews*. Ketchikan, Alaska, November 2, 2002. http://www.sitnews.org/JuneAllen/110202_meyers_chuck.html.

Bell, F. Heward. *The Pacific Halibut: The Resources and the Fishery.* Alaska Northwest Publishing, 1981.

Department of Commerce, National Oceanic and Atmospheric Administration. *United States Coast Pilot 8. Alaska: Dixon Entrance to Cape Spencer.* 2007.

Ellis, Pat. *From Fish Camps to Cold Storages: A Brief History of the Petersburg Area to 1927.* Clausen Memorial Museum, Petersburg, Alaska, 1998.

Glenz, Marian. *Meyers Chuck!* 1994.

John Sabella and Associates, Inc. [video recording]. *Petersburg: the town that fish built.* Produced by Clausen Memorial Museum, 1998.

Haycox, Stephen. *Alaska: An American Colony.* University of Washington Press, Seattle, 2002.

Keithahn, E.L. *The Authentic History of Shakes Island and Clan.* Wrangell Historical Society, 1981

Muir, John. *Travels in Alaska.* Houghton Mifflin, 1915.

Petersburg Alaska Chamber of Commerce. http://www.petersburg.org/.

Wharton, David. *They Don't Speak Russian in Sitka: A New Look at the History of Southern Alaska.* Margraf Publications Group, Menlo Park, California, 1991.

Foods for Trade. Company Profile—Icicle Seafoods, Inc. http://www.foodsfortrade.com/manufacturers/profile.php/id/297.

Chapter 5. Frederick Sound to Gastineau Channel

Alaska Division of Community and Regional Affairs. Alaska Community Database Community Information Summaries (CIS) http://www.commerce.state.ak.us/dca/commdb/CIS.cfm.

Bailey, Edgar P. 1993. *Introduction of Foxes to Alaskan Islands—History, Effects on Avifauna, and Eradication.* U.S. Department of the Interior. Fish and Wildlife Service, Resource Publication 193, Washington DC, 1993.

Balcom, Mary Gilmore. *Ghost Towns of Alaska.* Balcom Books, Chicago, 1965

Baker, Marcus. *Geographic Dictionary of Alaska*, 2nd edition. Government Printing Office, Washington, 1906.

Borneman, Walter R. *Alaska: Saga of a Bold Land.* Harper Collins, 2003.

Catton, Theodore. *Inhabited Wilderness: Indians, Eskimos and National Parks in Alaska.* University of New Mexico Press, Albuquerque, 1997.

Colp, Harry D. *The Strangest Story Ever Told.* Exposition Press, New York, 1953.

Hassler, Robert. *Traveler's Guide Southeastern Alaska.* 1973.

Hilson, Stephen E. *Evergreen Pacific: Exploring Alaska and British Columbia, Skagway to Barkley Sound.* 1997, reprinted 2002.

Isto, Sarah Crawford, Earl F. Graves and Jule B. Loftus. "Territorial Veterinarians for the Fur Farms." *Alaska History*, Vol. 23, Spring/Fall 2008. pp. 1–17.

Kelly, Brendan P., Thomas Ainsworth, Douglas A. Boyce Jr., Eran Hood, Peggy Murphy and Jim Powell. *Climate Change: Predicted Impacts on Juneau*. Report to Mayor Bruce Botelho and the City and Borough of Juneau Assembly, April 2007.

Kelly, Sheila. *Treadwell Gold: An Alaska Saga of Riches and Ruin*. University of Alaska Press, 2010.

King, Mary Lou and Laurie Ferguson Craig. *Treadwell Mine Historic Trail*. Taku Conservation Society.

Muir, John. *Travels in Alaska*. Houghton Mifflin, 1915.

Lewis, Linda. *Inside Passage Blog. Discovering Fords Terror*. August 3, 2007. http://www.fineedge.com/ARTICLES/inside_passage_blog/blog_27.html.

O'Donnell, Jack. *Alaska Panhandle Tales or Funny Things Happened Up North*. Frontier Publishing, Seaside, Oregon, 1996.

Olson, Wallace M. *A History of Fort Durham, Hudson's Bay Company Trading Post Located in Taku Harbor, 1840–1843, Within the boundaries of present day Juneau, Alaska*. Heritage Research, Juneau, Alaska, 1994.

Petite, Irving. *Meander to Alaska*. Seattle Book Company, Seattle, 1970.

Redman, Earl. *History of the Mines and Miners in the Juneau Gold Belt: A Collection of Stories about the Mines, the Miners and Their Dreams*. 1988.

Scidmore, Eliza Ruhamah. *Appleton's guide-book to Alaska and the northwest coast: including the shores of Washington, British Columbia, southeaster Alaska, the Aleutian Islands, the Bering and the Arctic coasts*. D. Appleton, New York, 1897.

Stowell, Harold H. *Geology of Southeast Alaska: Rock and Ice in Motion*. University of Alaska Press, Fairbanks, 2006.

Chapter 6. Skagway

Berton, Pierre. *Klondike, The Last Great Gold Rush 1896–1899*. Anchor Canada paperback edition, 2001.

Borneman, Walter R. *Alaska: Saga of a Bold Land*. Perennial (Harper Collins Publishers), New York, New York, 2004.

McCune, Don. *Trail to the Klondike*. Washington State University Press, Pullman, Washington, 1997.

Klondike International Historic Park. Interpretive exhibits at the Skagway and Seattle Units.

Morse, Kathryn. *The Nature of Gold: An Environmental History of the Klondike Gold Rush*. University of Washington Press, Seattle and London, 2003.

Pullen, Mrs. Harriet S. *Soapy Smith, Bandit of Skagway*. Sourdough Press, Seattle, 1910, reprinted 1973.

White Pass and Yukon Route. *All Aboard! The Complimentary Onboard Magazine of the White Pass & Yukon Route Railroad*. Summer 2006.

Chapter 7. Icy Strait

Alaska Division of Community and Regional Affairs. Alaska Community Database Community Information Summaries (CIS) http://www.commerce.state.ak.us/dca/commdb/CIS.cfm.

Aleutian World War II: Evacuation and Internment. http://www.nps.gov/aleu/historyculture/unangan-internment.htm.

Cerveny, Lee K. *Sociocultural Effects of Tourism in Hoonah, Alaska.* United States Department of Agriculture. Forest Service. Pacific Northwest Research Station. General Technical Report PNW-GTR-734. 2007.

Cueva, Christopher. "The Aleutian Evacuation: A Grave Injustice." *Alaska History and Cultural Studies.* http://www.akhistorycourse.org/articles/article.php?artID=215.

Guimary, Donald L. *Marumina Trabaho "Dirty Work": A History of Labor in Alaska's Salmon Canning Industry.* iUniverse, Inc., New York, Lincoln, Shanghai, 2006.

O'Clair, Rita M., Robert H. Armstrong and Richard Carstensen. *The Nature of Southeast Alaska.* Alaska Northwest Books, 2003.

Chapter 8. Glacier Bay.

Arendt, Anthony A., Keith A. Echelmeyer, William D. Harrison, Craig S. Lingle, Virginia B. Valentine. "Rapid Wastage of Alaska Glaciers and Their Contribution to Rising Sea Level." *Science,* 19 July 2002:Vol. 297. no. 5580, pp. 382–386.

Catton, Theodore. *Inhabited Wilderness: Indians, Eskimos and National Parks in Alaska.* University of New Mexico Press, Albuquerque, 1997.

Cruikshank, Julie. *Do Glaciers Listen? Local Knowledge, Colonial Encounters, and Social Imagination.* Vancouver, UBC Press, 2005.

Dauenhauer, Nora and Richard (editors). *Haa Shuká, Our Ancestors: Tlingit Oral Narratives.* University of Washington Press, Seattle, Sealaska Heritage Foundation, Juneau, 1987.

Glacier Bay National Park and Preserve. *The Fairweather Visitors Guide.* 2010.

Muir, John. *Travels in Alaska.* Houghton Mifflin, 1915.

National Park Service. US Department of Interior. Division of Publications. *Glacier Bay: A Guide to Glacier Bay National Park and Preserve, Alaska.* Washington DC, 1983

National Park Service, US Department of the Interior. *Glacier Bay National Park, Vessel Management Plan Regulations; Final Rule.* 36 CFR Part 13. Federal Register, Thursday November 30, 2006. http://www.nps.gov/glba/parkmgmt/upload/Fed%20Register%20volume%2071%20%2036%20CFR%20Part%2013%20New.pdf.

Scidmore, Eliza Ruhamah. *Alaska, Its Southern Coast and the Sitkan Archipelago.* Lothrop, Boston, 1885.

Stowell, Harlold H. *Geology of Southeast Alaska: Rock and Ice in Motion.* University of Alaska Press, Fairbanks, 2006.

Island Princess (ship). http://www.nationmaster.com/encyclopedia/Island-Princess

Pacific (ship). http://en.wikipedia.org/wiki/Pacific_(ship)

Love Boat (ship). http://en.wikipedia.org/wiki/The_Love_Boat

Chapter 9. Cross Sound to Chichagof

Berg, Henry C. and Donald J. Grybeck. USGS Alaska Resource Data File. Sitka Quadrangle. Open File Report 2005-1376.

Carson, Norm. *A glimpse of Pelican's beginning.* January, 2009. http://www.pelican.net/history.html.

De Laguna, Frederica. *Under Mount Saint Elias: The History and Culture of the Yakutat Tlingit.* Smithsonian Institution Press, Washington DC, 1972.

Douglass, Don and Reanne Hemingway-Douglass. *Exploring Southeast Alaska: Dixon Entrance to Skagway.* Fine Edge Productions, Anacortes, Washington, 2000.

Engstrom, Allen. "Yakobi Island, the Lost Village of Apolosovo and the fate of the Chirikov Expedition." Juneau, Alaska, 2007. In, Dauenhauer, Nora Marks, Richard Dauenhauer and Lydia T. Black, editors. *Anóooshi Lingít Aaní Ká: Russians in Tlingit America. The Battles of Sitka, 1802 and 1804.* University of Washington Press and Sealaska Heritage Institute, 2008.

Forgey, Pat. "Pelican Fears Loss of Fish Plant." *Juneau Empire*, August 23, 2009.

Jacobs, Mark Jr. "Early Encounters Between the Tlingit and the Russians, Part One." In, Dauenhauer, Nora Marks, Richard Dauenhauer and Lydia T. Black, editors. *Anóooshi Lingít Aaní Ká: Russians in Tlingit America. The Battles of Sitka, 1802 and 1804.* University of Washington Press and Sealaska Heritage Institute, 2008.

Redman, Earl. *History of the Mines and Miners in the Juneau Gold Belt: A Collection of Stories About the Mines, the Miners, and Their Dreams.* Earl Redman. Box 34801, Juneau, AK 99803, 1988.

Speidell, Mary. *The Front Porch is the Post Office: An Oral History of Elfin Cove, Alaska.* (no date or publisher).

Chapter 10. West Coast of Baranof Island.

Adrienne. Goddard Hot Springs. Pacific High Goddard Project. http://www.ssd.k12.ak.us/phs/web2001/KARAS/KGODDARD.html.

Alaback, Paul. "The Tongass Rainforest—An Elusive Sense of Place and Time." *The Book of the Tongass.* Edited by Carolyn Servid and Donald Snow. Milkweed Editions, 1999.

Borneman, Walter R. *Alaska: Saga of a Bold Land.* Harper Collins, 2003

Emmons, George Thornton. Edited with additions by Frederica de Laguna and a biography by Jean Low. *The Tlingit Indians.* Papers of the Anthropological Papers of the Museum of Natural History, No. 70, 1991.

Haycox, Stephen. *Alaskan: An American Colony.* University of Washington Press. Seattle. 2002.

Hope, Andrew III and Thomas F. Thornton. *Will the Time Ever Come? A Tlingit Source Book.* University of Alaska, Fairbanks, 2000.

Knapp, Marilyn R. with Mary P. Myer. *Carved History: The Totem Poles and House Poles of Sitka National Park.* Published in cooperation with National Park Service, U.S. Dept. of the Interior [by Alaska Natural History Association], Anchorage, Alaska, c1980.

Reifenstuhl, R.R. *Geology of the Goddard Hot Springs Area, Baranof Island, Southeastern Alaska.* Alaska Division of Geological and Geophysical Surveys, 1983.

Chapter 11. North Chatham Strait

Alaska Geographic Society. "Southeast: Alaska's Panhandle." *Alaska Geographic,* Vol. 5, Num. 2, 1978.

Bureau of Indian Affairs, Department of the Interior. *Angoon, its history, population, and economy.* Billings, Montana, 1975

Durwood Zaelke, Sierra Club. *New York Times.* Letter to the editor, May 6, 1984.

Friends of Admiralty Island. *Brown Bears of Admiralty Island.*

New York Times. "The Indians of Alaska. A glance at a people who are little known." November 23, 1884.

Scidmore, Eliza Ruhamah. *Appleton's guide-book to Alaska and the northwest coast: including the shores of Washington, British Columbia, southeastern Alaska, the Aleutian Islands, the Bering and the Arctic coasts*. D. Appleton, New York, 1897.

Tenakee Business Association. http://www.tenakeespringsak.com/.

U.S. Department of Agriculture, Forest Service, Tongass National Forest. *Angoon Hydroelectric Project*. Draft Environmental Impact Statement. April, 2007.

Rie Muñoz: A Unique Style. http://www.riemunoz.com/unique.htm.

Chapter 12. Waterfall Coast

Alaska Division of Community and Regional Affairs. Alaska Community Database Community Information Summaries (CIS) Port Alexander. http://www.commerce.state.ak.us/dca/commdb/CIS.cfm.

DeArmond, Robert N. and Patricia Roppel. *Baranof Island's Eastern Shore: "The Waterfall Coast."* Arrowhead Press, Sitka, Alaska, 1998.

Friends of Admiralty Island. *Brown Bears of Admiralty Island*.

O'Donnell, Jack. *Alaska Panhandle Tales or Funny Things Happened Up North*. Frontier Publishing, Seaside, Oregon, 1996.

Chapter 13. Kuiu Island and Keku Strait

DeArmond, Robert N. *The USS* Saginaw *in Alaska Waters 1867–1868*. The Limestone Press, Kingston, Ontario and Fairbanks, Alaska, 1997.

Emmons, George Thornton. Edited with additions by Frederica de Laguna and a biography by Jean Low. *The Tlingit Indians*. Papers of the Anthropological Papers of the Museum of Natural History, No. 70, 1991.

Rauwolf, Andy. An Expose on the History and Controversy Surrounding Commercial Herring Management in Southeast Alaskan Fisheries (excluding Sitka Sound). *Sitnews*, Ketchikan, Alaska, January 17, 2006. http://www.sitnews.us/0106Viewpoints/011706_andy_rauwolf.html.

Scidmore, Eliza Ruhamah. *Alaska, Its Southern Coast and Sitka Archipelago*. Lothrop, Boston, 1885.

Upton, Joe. *Alaska Blues, A Fisherman's Journal*. Alaska Northwest Publishing Company, Anchorage, 1877.

Pacific herring. http://www.adfg.state.ak.us/pubs/notebook/fish/herring.php

Chapter 14. West Coast Prince of Wales Island

Alaska Division of Community and Regional Affairs. Alaska Community Database Community Information Summaries (CIS). Klawock. http://www.commerce.state.ak.us/dca/commdb/CIS.cfm.

Borneman, Walter R. *Alaska: Saga of a Bold Land*. Harper Collins, 2003.

Bryson, George. "DNA tracks descendants of Tlingit, Haida and Tsimshian in Southeast Alaska." 2009. http://indiancountrynews.net/index2.php?option=com_content&do_pdf=1&id=5389.

Burchard, Ernest F. *Marble Resources of Southeastern Alaska*. Department of the Interior, United States Geologic Survey, Washington Government Printing Office, 1920.

Douglass, Don and Reanne Hemingway-Douglass. *Exploring Southeast Alaska: Dixon Entrance to Skagway*. Fine Edge Productions, Anacortes, Washington, 2000.

Glenz, Marian. *The B.S. Counter: Life in Alaska.* Trafford Publishing, 2002.

James, Rudy (aka Thlau Goo Yalith Thlee). *Devilfish Bay, the Giant Devilfish Bay Story: an Alaskan Indian Adventure.* Wolfhouse Publishing, 1997.

Roppel, Patricia. *Fortunes from the Earth: An History of the Base and Industrial Minerals of Southeast Alaska.* Sunflower University Press, Manhattan, Kansas, 1991.

Rozell, Ned. "Southeast Cave Reveals Clues to Ancient Alaska." *Alaska Science Forum,* Article #1520, December 7, 2000. http://www.gi.alaska.edu/ScienceForum/ ASF15/1520.html.

Swanton, John. *Tlingit Myths and Texts.* Government Printing Office, 1909

U.S. Forest Service. Tongass National Forest. Prince of Wales Island. *El Capitan Cave Interpretive Site.* http://www.fs.fed.us/r10/tongass/districts/pow/recreation/rogs/elcap. shtml.

Vancouver, George. *A voyage of discovery to the North Pacific Ocean and round the world, 1791-1795 : with an introduction and appendices*; edited by W. Kaye Lamb. Hakluyt Society, London, 1984.

Alaska History and Cultural Studies. Southeast Alaska 1922–1942 Between Two Wars. http:// www.akhistorycourse.org/articles/article.php?artID=79.

Athena Review, Vol. 4, No. 2. "Oldest Human DNA in the Americas: Teeth from an Alaskan Cave Provide Clues to Ancient Migration Patterns." http://www.athenapub. com/oldestDNA.htm.

INDEX